JUDY BLUME STILL ROCKS!

"Funny, poignant, honest, and reverential, these stories will resonate strongly with the legions of readers who, like the authors, are grateful and lifelong Blume devotees."

—Booklist

"From bittersweet to laugh-out-loud hilarious, the essays in this collection all sparkle with charm, style, and wit. No doubt about it, if you grew up reading Judy Blume, you will love this book."

—Sarah Mlynowski, author of *Spells & Sleeping Bags* and *Me vs. Me*

"Writing in the spirit of Blume, these women present their experiences as a series of personal truths: 'girl moments. Woman moments. Human moments.'"

—Publishers Weekly

"Judy Blume's adolescent books have left such an indelible mark that two dozen of today's female writers of young adult fiction wrote essays about the impression her novels left on them. . . . This is the gift we Judy Blume–raised mothers can give our daughters now: the voice that told us everything we were feeling was normal."

—The Record (Bergen County, NJ)

"By turns funny and poignant, this essay collection captures the essence of Judy Blume's appeal."

—Library Journal

"These stories are intensely personal recollections that offer an insight into the influence that Judy Blume's works have had on everyone who reads them."

—Teens Read Too

This title is also available as an eBook.

Everything
I Needed to Know
About Being a Girl
I Learned from

Judy Blume

Edited by
Jennifer O'Connell

Pocket Books

NEW YORK LONDON TORONTO SYDNEY

POCKET BOOKS
A Division of Simon & Schuster, Inc.
1230 Avenue of the Americas
New York, NY 10020

Contents

Everything I Needed to Know About Being a Girl I Learned from

Judy Blume

THEN. NOW. FOREVER . . .

| Megan McCafferty |

You can't blame Mrs. Henderson for giving her daughter a copy of *Forever* on her eleventh birthday. Like all of us in Girl Scout Troop 196, Kim was a die-hard Judy Blume fan. Of course, I prided myself on being the most avid admirer of all, the only one in our troop to have read every Judy Blume book available in the Bayville Elementary School library, from *Are You There God? It's Me, Margaret* to *Then Again, Maybe I Won't*. So as I watched Kim tear open the Smurf wrapping paper to reveal a previously unheard-of novel by my favorite author—one that promised a timeless teenage love story on its cover—I became instantly and insanely jealous.

And that was before I learned that *Forever* was The Sex Book.

This discovery didn't take long, as I had taken it upon myself to "hold on" to the book as Kim opened up other gifts. I feigned interest in her new Duran Duran cassette, the assortment of rainbow ribbon barrettes, even the Cabbage Patch doll named Annalisa Marie. My fascination with the book and disinterest in the birthday loot deepened, until I was finally able to usher Kim and the rest of the guests upstairs to her bedroom.

"Listen to *this*," I whispered as I went on to read the book's notorious first sentence, about a girl genius named Sybil who had "been laid by at least six different guys." *Been laid! In the first sentence!* Could this be the same Judy Blume I knew and loved? I wondered what was more stunning: The sex or its source? It was a far cry from the bust enhancement exercises in *Margaret* or even the wet dreams in . . . *Maybe I Won't.*

With the provocative opening as incentive, Kim, the other girls, and I bounced up and down on the frilly pink canopy bed, each taking turns skimming through the book, trying to outdo each other with the discovery of another dirty passage. Page 20: Michael tried to unhook Katherine's bra. Page 25: Michael felt her up under her sweater, then fumbled on the snap of her jeans. Page 40: Katherine's eleven-year-old sister accused her of "fucking" Michael in her bedroom!

Our fingers flew over page after page, only stopping when we hit a word such as "sex," "sexy," "moans," "penis," "sex," or "sex." Not surprisingly, we gave ourselves away. Mrs. Henderson—alerted by our eardrum-cracking shrieks—came through Kim's door, demanding to know the source of our hysterics. Mrs. Henderson was a divorcée, the neighborhood Avon lady, and our acting troop leader. She favored pearly pink lipstick, acid-washed jeans, and brassy hair teased to Jersey perfection—a combination of artistry and products that I admired and never mastered. We *all* loved Mrs.

Henderson and copped to the book's carnal content just as quickly as she removed it from Kim's clutches. She must have known that Troop 196 viewed her as being more hip and progressive than the other moms, so rather than merely banning *Forever* from our fourth-grade social circle, Mrs. Henderson told all our mothers that she would be *happy* to lend it to anyone in the troop, if they gave written parental permission.

My mother, of course, flatly refused. Though she didn't seem that different from Mrs. Henderson on the outside—she, too, wore jeans and rarely left the house without applying mascara or "hot rollering" her highlighted blonde hair—she was, at heart, the result of sixteen years of Catholic education.

"Mooooooooom," I whined as she prepared that night's dinner, something involving red meat and a few token vegetables in a crock pot. "Why can't I read it?"

"It's not appropriate for a ten-year-old," she replied without looking away from the flesh on the cutting board.

"I'm almost eleven!" My birthday was, in fact, a week after Kim's.

"It's not appropriate for an eleven-year-old!" she said, slicing down the blade. "I'm not sure it's appropriate for anyone at all!"

"Mooooooooom."

"Megan Beth, if you want to know about . . ." She hesitated here, waving her knife in the air. "*That sort of thing* . . . you should ask me."

This was a horrifying and altogether impossible proposition. Who wanted to talk to her mom about *that sort of thing*? But my mother had invoked my middle name, so I knew better than to continue my fight. Fortunately, all my years as a precocious book lover had paid off. Reading comprehension was my strong suit, so even though I'd only skimmed the book, I got the gist of the whole plot: Katherine and Michael were seniors in high school. They met. They fell in love. *And they had sex.*

Some crucial details I committed to memory and could still recall twenty-one years later:

1. Michael named his penis Ralph (page 73).
2. Michael "came" too soon, before they got a chance to do it (page 100. I had only the vaguest idea what that meant. Something *came* out of him? Like pee? And why would that stop them from doing it?)
3. Michael devirginized Katherine on a multicolored rug because her blood could have stained the bedsheets (page 101).

After Kim's sleepover, *Forever* turned into a game I played alone in my bedroom. Katherine (my Brooke Shields doll) made love with Michael (Ken) in an empty tissue-box bed. Pre-*Forever*, making love had meant sleeping in a bed naked with someone. Very little effort involved. Post-*Forever*, I pretended that Ralph was hidden inside Brooke-as-Katherine. Of course, Ken-as-Michael didn't have a penis, and his anatomical incorrectness suited my fantasies just fine. I still wasn't sure what a penis looked like, having only glimpsed at my baby brother's teeny unit as my mother changed his diaper, but I was simultaneously enthralled and repelled by the idea of seeing one. My nascent pangs of lust left me confused and queasy, similar to the nausea I felt whenever I tried to read a book in the backseat of a moving car.

Later that spring, Troop 196 earned points toward community

service badges by cleaning up a local beach. After a heated argument in Mrs. Henderson's minivan over one pop star's supremacy (Cyndi Lauper vs. Madonna was a popular debate at the time, and I was always in the minority opinion), the other girls piled out of the van together singing "Girls Just Wanna Have Fun" louder than necessary as I stomped off to a more secluded area to work by myself. I stuffed my trash bag in defiance, silently mouthing the lyrics to my favorite song. *Like a virgin. (Hee!) Touched for the very first time . . .*

It was almost time to head back when I discovered a tattered copy of *Playgirl* hidden among the bottle caps and cigarette butts in the dune grass. The centerfold was miraculously intact. The model was in full-on hair-band mode, wearing a black leather studded jacket and nothing else. He was posed in front of a microphone, head thrown back, eyes shut tight as if he were belting out a power ballad . . . or on the verge of splooging all over the stage. His ginormous penis was obviously impressed with the performance, as it was in the throes of a standing ovation.

Even at eleven years old, this whole setup struck me as absurd. I mean, what would possess this guy to perform in a leather jacket and no pants? Duh. It made me wonder how Katherine could possibly look at Ralph-the-Penis without cracking up. How could she get hot and bothered by the idea of that . . . that . . . *thing* poking around inside her? It made no sense.

As unsexy as it was, I had no doubt that my fellow Scouts would take a prurient interest in the centerfold. My find could catapult me into popularity, if only for the rest of the afternoon. But I also knew if Mrs. Henderson found out and told my mom, the possession of pornographic materials would surely lead to a major grounding. My parents would be appalled, but my peers would be impressed. It was the virgin/whore, Cyndi/Madonna conundrum, and in this case, the good girl in me won out. I stuffed the *Playgirl* pages deep in my trash bag and didn't say another word about them.

Not long after that mystifying first introduction to the male genitalia, my mom took it upon herself to educate me in *that sort of thing*. She brought me across the street to my best friend Adrienne's house, which to this day remains the most orderly and pristine place I have ever visited. If Adrienne or her mom ever wore jeans, they were of the starched-stiff, high-waisted variety that could be subcategorized as slacks within the taxonomy of denim. We sat on the plump couch. Me, slumped and skeptical. Adrienne, respectful and ramrod straight like the ballet dancer she was. Together, in their darkened, dust-free family room, we watched a very special filmstrip borrowed from the middle school health class I would take two years later.

The mere mention of the word "filmstrip" hopelessly dates me, I know. As a brief primer for those who have come of age in the digital era, a filmstrip entertained and informed one boring picture at a time, with a breathy narrator on a cassette tape going on at length about the subject represented by each still frame. When the anonymous speaker finished her oration, the cassette would signal the need to manually forward the reel to the next boring picture with a mechanical-sounding *BOOOOOP!*

A diagram of the female reproductive system. *BOOOOOP!* A bottle of douche with a red slash warning that it is *not* a valid method of birth control. *BOOOOOP!* A grinning girl running rapturously through a field of wildflowers feeling so free and April fresh . . . ummm . . . because she has just used the douche for non-birth-control purposes? *BOOOOOP!* This last image was particularly striking. I had just branched out of the Blume canon to read *Go Ask Alice,* and it seemed more likely to me that this girl was having some sort of acid freak-out and was not, as the voice-over implied, simply carried away by the joys of reproductive maturation.

It was this primitive form of audiovisual infotainment that taught me all about the 3 P's: Puberty, Periods, and Pregnancy. I'd go through Puberty, get my Period, and—if I wasn't careful—I'd get Pregnant *and ruin the rest of my life.* One P conspicuously deemphasized was Penis, which was discussed in the most clinical manner and only in regard to how it could be used to get me P for Pregnant and (repeat it with me) *ruin the rest of my life.* I remember thinking how much more interesting the lesson would have been if the filmstrip had been an actual movie starring Brooke Shields with a soundtrack by Michael Jackson. Yet it had the desired effect on my best friend. Adrienne had six years of Catholic school education behind her and couldn't wait to make a vow of lifelong chastity.

"I'm *never* going to have sex," she proudly declared to her mom.

And I thought, *That's because you didn't read the good parts in* Forever.

Over time, *Forever* lost its hold on me as the dominant inspiration behind my sweatiest daydreams. As I left my (secular) elementary school behind, The Sex Book was replaced by more visual and visceral stimuli including (1) the T&A teen flick *Private School,* in which a rich red-haired temptress taunts Matthew Modine with a bouncy topless horseback ride; (2) the "Take My Breath Away" *Top Gun* tongue bath between Tom Cruise and Kelly McGillis; (3) any River Phoenix movie. At twelve, thirteen, and fourteen years old, these were the images that aroused confusing pit-of-my-belly long-ings for . . . for what exactly?

I figured I'd finally find out at fifteen, when I got my first seri-ous boyfriend. B. was the first boy to kiss me. It took place in our school's parking lot right before the buses were about to pull away. A meaty proboscis pried open my puckered lips and proceeded to probe the rest of my face. His wet tongue roamed around, more outside my mouth than in, perhaps so that it could be easily viewed at a distance, thus putting an end to the hassling the basketball team was giving him to "French" me already. This inauspicious start might have served as a warning of letdowns to come.

Back then, I never could have imagined that those disappoint-ments would serve me well and I would be lucky enough to make my living just as Judy Blume made hers, telling fictional stories about teenage girls struggling with the choices before them. And though I imagine our story is more common than not, when B. asked me out at fifteen, he had no idea that I would turn out to be a professional writer. Or perhaps he did. Either way, despite count-less battles and breakups and get-back-togethers, B. turned out to be my only serious boyfriend in high school. Together, we fumbled through that first kiss and the other firsts that followed.

And none of it was his fault.

Now

Not too long ago, I spotted a paperback copy of *Forever* at my local library. I hadn't picked it up since squealing over the good parts at Kim's sleepover two decades earlier. I couldn't help but notice that it hadn't been checked out in more than a year. No surprise there. In a discussion about influential authors, I'd once asked an audience of about a hundred high school students if they had read *Forever,* and only about a half-dozen hands went up. And these girls had read it only because they had been encouraged by their *moms,* for whom it had been an unforgettable rite of passage.

Yes, what my mom had once forbidden was now a source of mother/daughter bonding. When I shared this irony with my audience, they were dumbfounded. "What was so scandalous?" asked a particularly blunt sophomore. "Katherine didn't even give him a blow job." They were even more surprised when I told them that *Forever* remains one of the most banned books by parents and educators. Of course, these conflicting attitudes regarding teen sexuality are reinforced in the media, which depicts our nation's youth as being equally torn between public purity pledges and private rainbow parties.

I'm on the more liberal side of the ideological divide, so I picked up *Forever* that day in the library thinking it would be nothing more than a nostalgic hoot. A quaint throwback to the era of fondue parties, "queers," and VD. And yes, as I read it for the first time in its entirety, I chuckled at the seventies-style Public Service Announcements I had originally skipped over in favor of more salacious material. Like when Katherine's grandmother—her grandmother!—sent pamphlets from Planned Parenthood and encouraged her to go on the pill. Or when her mother wanted to have a heart-to-heart talk about a newspaper survey on the subject of sexual liberation. And when Katherine's acquaintance, Sybil— the nympho genius from the infamous first sentence—got pregnant because she made the most heinous error of all: sex without love.

And yet despite the infrequent lapses into corniness, Judy Blume's perspectives on teen sex were indeed more progressive than I had expected. Here was a seventeen-year-old female narrator who knew her desires were natural and didn't deny them to herself or her boyfriend. In an era when even pro-sex advocates focus more on *Girls Gone Wild*–style provocation than actual pleasure, Katherine's candor and unapologetic lust struck me as revolutionary. Specifically, here's what I had missed about *Forever:*

1. Katherine described losing her virginity as a "letdown."
2. Katherine "came." Without foreplay, from intercourse alone. Multiple times.
3. Katherine checked out Ralph-the-Penis not because Michael pressured her to but because *she* wanted to.

Now, all these years later, I realized getting up close and personal with the contents of my first boyfriend's tightie-whities had been totally out of the question. I know this sounds bizarre—and it is—but in three years of dating, I never so much as sneaked a peek, let alone studied B.'s penis with scientific interest. And yes, this means that I never performed that certain sexual act that the oh-so-jaded millennial sophomore took for granted. Never. Not before, during, or even after we did *it.* Which we did, after more than two years of dating, a few weeks after both of our seventeenth birthdays, on an overnight retreat for peer leaders at a religious campground. (Sorry, Mom and Dad.) While the actual act turned out to be less than what I'd hoped for, at least my devirginization at a faith-based gathering was steeped in irony.

I can identify with Katherine's anticlimactic deflowering. And yet while she was honest about how it was more of a relief to have it over and done with than anything else, I lied to myself (and one or two confidantes) by turning my first time into an exquisite body-and-soul transforming experience that it never was and wouldn't be until years later with the man I married.

It wasn't because I was inhibited by the classic virgin/whore dilemma or the threat of a bad reputation. And despite my filmstrip indoctrination, I wasn't worried about pregnancy (or STDs for that matter) because I was vigilant about protection. Nor was I still haunted by that first hilarious glimpse at Mr. Rock-n-Cock in *Playgirl*. No, it wasn't even the capital P for Penis that made me so uneasy about sex and my first love.

Forever . . .

Katherine and Michael believed in the first-and-only vows of ever-lasting love. When the newspaper survey asked a question about how the relationship would end, Katherine was deeply offended by the query. B. would have been, too.

He told me many times that I was his female equal, and he was wrong. B. was far more popular than I was, and I took some comfort in my elevated status by association. He was good-natured and charismatic. He was as adept at being the sensitive guy who listened to girls' troubles as he was at engaging in grossed-out guy humor. I was moody, quick to judge, and used sarcasm to shield typical teenage insecurities. His body was amazing, with the carved-in-stone musculature of a natural athlete, and he had no shortage of girls who would have been more than happy to do anything for him in and out of bed. As for me, if any other guys in high school thought I was hot, I certainly never knew about it. These disparities might have been why we weren't considered for Class Couple in our high school yearbook. I wouldn't have even voted for us.

But I guess we were well matched in the sense that we were considered the male and female Most Likely to Succeed. We were both ambitious straight-A students, three-sport varsity athletes who rounded out our college applications with a long list of extracurriculars. Maybe this was enough for B. He was so convinced that I was The One that he repeatedly reminded me in furtive late-night phone confessions and in tightly folded notes he left for me in the pocket of his varsity jacket—the one that he said I didn't wear often enough. But usually he'd gasp promises in my ear during frenzied sessions of making out (and more): *We're meant to be together forever.* Less often—but often enough—he told me if I ever broke up with him, he would kill himself. The vein in his forehead bulged, and my bicep turned white in his grip.

Before asking Michael to drop his pants so that she could examine Ralph-the-Penis, Katherine confessed, "I want to see everything . . . I want to know you inside out." The truth is, I didn't want to know B. inside out. In a way, the less I knew, the better. This emotional detachment was indistinguishable from my physical detachment when we were intimate, an odd not-really-there feeling that I needed in order to cope with this intense relationship for which I was not at all prepared yet couldn't bring myself to get out of. Unlike Katherine, I thought about how our relationship would end all the time. And it never went well.

So what makes *Forever* still relevant for me isn't the genius nymphomaniac, the famously personified penis, or any other dirty detail. It's what the novel says about love—especially first love—and how it dies.

Katherine bravely ended her first relationship because she wanted to experience physical and emotional passion with someone else. She was no doubt emboldened by the knowledge that someone else was already waiting for her in the form of Theo, the hunky tennis instructor she met during her summer away from Michael. "I thought of pretending," Katherine said after she reunited with her boyfriend and realized she wanted out. "I'm no good at pretending. And anyway, pretending isn't fair." I knew that, too. And yet the good girl in me pretended.

After six months with B., I pretended that I wasn't curious to kiss the cocky actor I met at a summer arts camp. After a year, I pretended that I wasn't intoxicated by the class lothario, a poet/addict who went out of his way to flirt with me in front of B. After two years, I pretended that I wasn't completely taken by a shy, smart sophomore who once dated B's younger sister. For nearly three years, I pretended that I saw a future for us because I was afraid of what would happen in the aftermath of our breakup. But I wasn't very good at faking it, either, and I spent the greater portion of my high school years acting like a bitch, blaming every frustrated attraction on too much PMS or not enough sleep. Why B. put up with this, especially with so many other options available, I'll never understand. Perhaps he was driven by the same fears of what would happen if he stopped.

I'm not sure when or how we broke up, and I would be making it up if I said otherwise. I remember a protracted series of dramatic fights and exhausting crying fits, of jealous flirtations and violent empty threats, and a failed attempt (his) at one last boozy fling for old time's sake. I went to my senior prom with B.'s best friend, an arrangement that indicates we split well before graduation. I cannot recall the final break, and this monumental event is mysteriously absent from the pages of my journal. But I don't think I've blocked out the details as a defense mechanism. I prefer to believe that I've let go of the most bitter memories because I didn't need to hang onto them.

Not too long after high school, I fell in love again. I had my heart broken. I later regretted not sleeping with someone I cared about deeply and then got involved with someone else who should have never been more than just a friend. I withheld empty promises of tomorrow. And finally, I made the only lifelong vow worth believing in.

I moved on. And B. did, too.

I still can't help but wish my mom had let me read *Forever* from start to finish instead of showing me that lame filmstrip. By the last chapter, it's clear that Katherine and Michael got over each other. Their lost love wasn't a tragedy. It was inevitable. And if I had read more than just the good parts, maybe I would've mustered the courage to break up with B. sooner, sparing us both many tears and much pain in the process.

Then again, maybe not.

Probably not.

We were fifteen, sixteen, seventeen years old and had no clue what we were doing. We were each other's trial and error, as all first loves are. And I'm not convinced Judy Blume's wisdom would have helped one bit back then.

I was at the library to return the book—my husband browsing down the shelves, our three-year-old son grabbing my hand—when

I realized that I'd never noticed the ellipses in the title: *For-ever* . . . Only after a few decades of living, of loving and being loved in return, can you comprehend that *Forever* . . . means something very different than *Forever.* Only then can you understand that any vow uttered by an adoring adolescent is accompanied by invisible ellipses. "Forever . . . Then. Now."

————

Megan McCafferty is the author of Sloppy Firsts, Second Helpings, *and* Charmed Thirds. *She is currently working on the fourth Jessica Darling novel. Megan also contributed an essay to* It's a Wonderful Lie: The Truth About Life in Your Twenties, *but she prefers hiding behind fiction, especially when the topic is sex. Until she wrote for this anthology, her parents had no idea how or when she lost her virginity.*

WE INTERRUPT OUR
REGULARLY SCHEDULED PROGRAMMING
FOR A JUDY BLUME MOMENT

| *Jennifer O'Connell* |

Someone else's birthday isn't exactly a milestone that's supposed to remain ingrained in your memory forever. Your first day of kindergarten, the day you got your braces off, senior prom—those were the significant moments that got counted down and circled on the Ziggy calendar hanging inside our closet doors.

But I remember one party better than I remember my own. It wasn't just any ordinary seventh-grade birthday. It was Christine McCall's, and Christine was going out with Robbie—an eighth grader. Christine's wasn't any ordinary birthday party. It was a boy–girl party complete with AC/DC's "Back in Black" on the boom box and contraband Jack Daniels snuck inside the jean jackets worn by Robbie and his eighth-grade friends.

I can still describe in detail how Robbie's friend Doug Keener nonchalantly asked me if I wanted to go out to the garage with

Robbie and the birthday girl. I can tell you how I followed him out the family room door into the dark two-car garage and how we climbed into the backseat of Mr. McCall's Buick sedan (Christine and Robbie got the front seat, although in hindsight it does seem like a less desirable choice). And I can, though I won't, explain exactly what I was thinking when I let Doug Keener, a boy who hadn't said two words to me up until that invitation to join him in the Buick, slip his hand up my sweater and get to second base.

No, it wasn't my birthday. It wasn't my first kiss. It wasn't even that I'd finally gotten the attention of a popular guy who I'd had a crush on (while Doug was indeed one of the more popular guys, he was way too short to be on my five-foot-six radar). So why, to this day, can I remember exactly what I was wearing (turquoise blue knit sweater constructed of synthetic material that left red scratchy imprints on my skin and made me swear off sweaters for good); how can I remember the color of the backseat's upholstery (navy blue velour with light blue pinpoint design on the cushions); and why haven't I forgotten that the following Monday, when I passed Doug in the hall, he acted like he'd never seen me before in his life?

Very simply, it was a Judy Blume moment.

Fifteen minutes after entering the garage, I walked back into Christine's family room, arranging my sweater so that nobody was the wiser, and watched Doug rejoin his friends by the table of Doritos and Sprite as if nothing had happened—as if a few misguided attempts to undo the clasp to my bra were less noteworthy than the empty basket of Pringles he seemed to be lamenting. And as I watched Doug lick the orange Dorito dust from his fingers—the very fingers that had been groping my white cotton bra not ten minutes ago—it hit me. The friend's birthday party; the cute guy's invitation to make out in a dark place; the knowledge that said cute guy would try get to second base; and the fear of what would happen if I said no. There was another girl I knew of who'd gone through the exact same thing, and her name was Deenie.

I thought about how Deenie had debated whether to wear her back brace to her friend's party, how she was sure the cute guy was going to want to feel her up and she didn't want to disappoint him. Only Deenie had her brace to protect her, and I just had an irritating sweater that, quite frankly, made the idea of a soft hand against my skin seem way more enjoyable than poorly knit nylon. Even though Deenie and I made different choices when faced with a five-fingered assault on our training bras, we both had something very much in common. And that something is what I've come to call a *Judy Blume moment.*

Sally sat on the Murphy bed and watched as Mom put some more rouge on her cheeks, went over her lips a second time and dabbed a drop of perfume behind each ear. "You smell good," Sally said. "Like Lillies of the Valley."

"It's called White Shoulders," Mom said. "It's my favorite . . . here, I'll put some behind your ears too."

"Ummm . . . I like that," Sally said, wondering if Latin lovers would be attracted to it. Maybe she'd try it out on Peter Horton.

—Starring Sally J. Freedman As Herself

My parents went out on Saturday nights. I know now that they couldn't possibly have gone out every single Saturday night, every single week of the year, but that's the way I remember it. And I didn't mind. We had nice babysitters who let us stay up past our bedtime, watch the *Love Boat*, and build forts with the sofa cushions. Besides, my parents would let us get whatever we wanted for dinner (McDonald's for my brother, Hardy's for me), so their Saturday night plans were hardly something to complain about.

I couldn't tell you where they went on those nights—out to dinner or over to a friend's house or just to catch a movie. But I can recall with total clarity how my mother stood in front of her bathroom mirror while I sat on the edge of the toilet lid (complete with shaggy rug cover) and watched her get ready for a night on the town. I scrutinized her selection of eye shadow, dipped my fingers in pots of brilliant pink blush, and sat mesmerized by the wondrous transformation taking place before me—a person turning from my mom into a woman who seemed beautiful and sophisticated and so, well, *unmotherly*.

I can tell you the name of the lipstick my mother wore and describe the slim gold fluted tube that I loved so much I carry my own in my purse today (Estee Lauder Starlit Pink). I can't walk by a bottle of Charlie at my local drugstore and resist the temptation to take one short sniff of the glass bottle with the familiar man's name etched in script across the front. And when I inhale, it's not the old perfume commercials I see, with the sassy models flipping their blonde Farrah hair as they cross the street and a man sings about how *they call her Charlie*. No, I see my mom staring into the mirror, her image illuminated by the brilliant lightbulbs dotting her reflection, like a movie star preparing to walk on stage.

Judy Blume moments are the ones that keep you going to the Estee Lauder counter long after you're sure no one else is wearing

Starlit Pink, simply because it reminds you of your mom and the possibility of a Saturday night.

> *We looked through a pile of nighties before we found one made of two layers of the softest nylon. The top layer was pink and the underneath was purple so when you moved it around it had a sort of lavender look to it.*
> *"It's perfect!" Janet said, holding it up to me.*
> *"What do you think Deenie?" Midge asked.*
> *"It's beautiful!" I said.*
>
> —Deenie

My nightgown was blue. Baby blue, to be exact. Paler than a robin's egg but darker than the light blue eye shadow I hoped to some day wear on my lids like Olivia Newton-John in *Grease*. And, like Deenie, my nightgown was purchased for a special event. My first slumber party.

I couldn't tell you what it felt like to wear the yellow tea-length dress I selected for my junior prom; nor could I tell you that I felt anything special when donning a white cap and gown for my high school graduation. But I can instantly describe how I felt dressed in that cotton floor-length nightgown with matching robe, can recall every detail. The small embroidered roses around the neckline, the kind that curl around the edges when they come out of the wash and never seem to flatten out again. My nightie was sleeveless, and the robe had loose ruffles that skimmed my shoulders, like pale blue fairy wings. It buttoned up the back, small white spheres like pearls.

A nightgown. Not my first slumber party or who attended or

the games we played. (I'm sure *light as a feather, stiff as a board* must have been attempted at least once that night.) What stays with me is a pale blue cotton nightgown with matching robe that probably ended up in a Hefty bag headed for Goodwill when it no longer fit me.

A Judy Blume moment makes a girl feel like a princess in a blue cotton nightgown long after the slumber party ends and the Ouija board is put away.

Sally couldn't fall asleep. She tossed and turned trying out different positions. Legs outside the bed sheet, arms at her sides; arms outside the sheet, legs inside. One leg out, one arm out; curled in a ball; spread eagled on her stomach. Nothing worked. I need a story, she thought.
— *Starring Sally J. Freedman As Herself*

I can't sleep. And when I can't sleep, I lie awake in the darkness and listen to sounds (which certainly doesn't help my efforts to fall asleep). In my mind, the creaks and rappings and rattlings begin to sound like doors opening, the wires of our alarm system being snipped with scissors, and windows sliding up their tracks until the opening is just wide enough for a body to slip through. The body is always clad in black. And it's big.

Do I get out of bed and investigate? No way. Instead, I construct my own elaborate story—the one in which I save my husband and two children from the perilous hands of that large stranger hiding in the bushes outside our family room. Much like Sally J. Freedman envisioned herself standing up to Adolph Hitler and, as a ten-year-old girl, single-handedly ending World War II, I will rescue my family from danger. And knowing that I have a story, that I've already worked out all the details to the plan in my head, helps me feel a little better as I close my eyes and fall asleep listening for footsteps.

Apparently a Judy Blume moment can occur at 3 A.M. and involves the use a retractable fire escape ladder as pictured on page 87 of *SkyMall*.

> *Caitlin held her at arm's length for a minute. "God, Vix . . ."* *she said, "you look so . . . grownup!" They both laughed, then Caitlin hugged her. She smelled of seawater, suntan lotion, and something else. Vix closed her eyes, breathing in the familiar scent, and it was as if they'd never been apart.*
> —*Summer Sisters*

We rented a house on Martha's Vineyard for a week in August. Vicki and Vangie, my two best friends from college, and our families. Our families! We had husbands! And children! Somebody was entrusting their home to us for seven days (although their trust was backed up by a healthy $1,000 security deposit). The fact that we were staying in a four-bedroom house instead of the nylon Target-purchased tent Vicki and I shacked up in during a postcollege cross-country trip made it very clear: we were grown-ups.

We lit the barbecue at night, drank beers, and laughed. During the day, we hit the sand and surf. And when I ran out of magazines, I explored the bookshelf in the living room, desperate for some beach reading.

The first book I picked out had a familiar name on the cover and a photo of an Adirondack chair. It was a story about childhood friends who reunite every summer on Martha's Vineyard. (I was on Martha's Vineyard!) The novel followed the girls through high school, college, and adulthood. (I was with my best girlfriends from college and now we were adults!) It chronicled their changing lives, and more importantly, their changing friendship as they grew up and grew apart.

I remember reading that book surrounded by two friends who'd known me since I was an eighteen-year-old girl, a college freshman for all of four hours. And I remember looking around me, watching our young children and husbands, and wondering if our friendship would change as our lives continued to be separated by miles and marriage and careers and the noise of everyday life. And I remember being wistful and sad and nostalgic, but most of all I remember being hopeful. And now, so many years later, our children have grown, our marriages have changed and in some cases dissolved, but we're still hopeful. And this year we'll be on Martha's Vineyard in August, and we'll light the barbecue, drink some beers, and laugh.

A Judy Blume moment is realizing that even as we get older, even as our lives and the people around us are changing—even as *we're* changing—we'll always be the girls who play in the waves and giggle with our friends.

There are the experiences we know we're supposed to commit to memory, the days we're taught to believe are pivotal—our first kiss, our sweet sixteen, the first time we thought we were in love, and the inevitable first time our heart breaks in two. So why is it that the seemingly mundane experiences are the ones we can recall with such vividness that they seem to have happened only yesterday? A baby blue nightgown. The smell of Charlie. An eighth grader copping a feel under a natty turquoise blue sweater.

Most experiences don't earn the recognition of a Hallmark card or an announcement in the newspaper or a notation on a calendar. They're moments that last maybe minutes and yet remain for a lifetime in our memories, turning an experience that could be summed up in a footnote and stretching it to mythical proportions (much like I remembered the party scene from *Deenie* as taking up the majority of the book, only to discover recently that it was less than a single page at the end of the story).

So why do these seemingly insignificant experiences take on such significance? Judy Blume knew the answer. They're significant because we're significant. They help define who we are and contribute to who we will become. They're moments that matter because they matter to us.

They're not the July fourth fireworks display that you're expected to *ooh* and *ahh* over with the other three hundred people gathered by the parks and recreation building. They aren't choreographed to symphonic music and accompanied by parades. Instead, they're the sparklers we remember holding between our fingers, mesmerized by the sparks spitting from the burning wire stick and how they leave a trail of light as we wave them in figure eights above our head.

They're girl moments. Woman moments. Human moments. And all these years later, it's what continues to make them Judy Blume moments as well.

Jennifer O'Connell still wears Estee Lauder Starlit Pink lipstick and has been known to light up a sparkler or two, but she no longer wears scratchy blue nylon sweaters or night-gowns with embroidered rosebuds. The author of four novels, including Insider Dating, Off the Record, Dress Rehearsal, and Bachelorette #1, *Jennifer continues to live out Judy Blume moments in her teen books, including* Plan B *and* The Book of Luke. *You can find Jennifer at www.jenniferconnell.com and www.jennyoconnell.com.*

THE ONE THAT GOT AWAY

| Stephanie Lessing |

The first thing I learned from Judy Blume was that God is the wrong one to ask for bigger breasts. If I had written *Are You There God? It's Me, Margaret,* I would have included a scene where Margaret finally visits a decent plastic surgeon. Not only for Margaret's sake but because I had a certain body part of my own that needed a little fixing.

The second thing I learned from Judy Blume was that I wasn't normal. I had nothing in common with Margaret or Gretchen or Nancy or any of the other girls in her books. They were the kinds of girls I hung out with in school. They were girls I pretended to like, pretended to be friends with, and pretended to be, but I was nothing like them. I was always watching them, trying to figure them out, trying on their personas, and trying not to get caught. Judy Blume was a master at getting inside normal girls' heads, and I was grateful for the blueprints. Without Judy Blume, I never would have been able to pull it off. Because of Judy Blume, I fooled everyone.

I never felt like a regular girl. I had too much to hide.

I remember all those sleepover parties where the main activity was making a list of all the boys we liked. When we handed over our little folded-up pieces of paper, all the other girls always had the same two or three names written down. They must have been surprised to see that I had written down the name of our home-room teacher, Mr. Nettles. When they looked up at me for an explanation, I pretended I was joking even though I honestly believed he and I were both patiently waiting for me to finish middle school so that we could finally settle down. I was constantly doing the math in my diary. "When I turn thirteen, he'll only be forty-three!" I crooned. "That's still mobile!"

In my fantasies, we were always riding side by side in an MG convertible. For some reason, I was always wearing a white cotton pique dress with a kerchief tied under my chin and incessantly opening and closing my purse. I'm not sure why I chose to dress up as an old woman for these imaginary wild rides through the countryside.

My taste in men wasn't the only reason I didn't exactly fit in with any of my friends. There was also the issue of trying to cover up what was going on in my house and the fact that I sprouted hips when I was eleven. They weren't sexy hips and they didn't come with premature womanly breasts. They were just hips that showed up out of nowhere—unruly appendages that made no sense whatsoever in relation to my height, my age, or even my personality or background. Why I had hips that started two inches above my waist, I'll never know. I was always pulling my sweaters all the way down and was forced to bend slightly forward to hide them, which threw off my gait and made it appear as though I had a backache.

As time went on, the constant bending did, in fact, give me a back-ache. I was certainly the only twelve-year-old I knew who needed to hold on to something in order to get up. "Damn these stairs," I used to say while the other kids were sliding down the railings and flipping over the balconies.

When I got a little older, I noticed that Cher had the same elon-gated hip problem I did. I noticed it because someone called it to my attention.

"Hey, you have the exact same hips as Sonny!" my best friend announced at one of our late-night soirees.

"You mean, Cher?" I asked

"Yeah, whichever one's the girl," she said, chewing her hair, not a care in the world. "If you measured her hips—top to bottom—they'd probably be two feet long. Maybe you'll grow up to look like her," she said encouragingly.

I looked over at my best friend, sitting in the lotus position, with her long, lanky legs that screamed *this is how you're supposed to look,* wondering why God felt it was necessary to give someone legs that shot right up to her neck, and me, the hips of an aging belly dancer.

I also couldn't help wondering if I'd gone to a different school, where I wasn't best friends with the tallest, skinniest, most popular girl in our class, if my status would have plummeted to that of, say, Blubber. The possibility loomed large, but the truth is, I wasn't blubbery at all. At least not in the Linda Fischer sense of the word. I was actually quite muscular. It occurred to me, sitting there watching Cher flick her hair around, in her backless, second-skin evening gown, that my biggest problem was that I didn't know how to dress properly for my body type. Jeans are all wrong for girls

with long hips. And I must have been wearing the wrong underwear, too, because Cher had no visible panty lines whatsoever.

I thought about writing Cher a letter asking her what type of
underpants she wore and where she shopped for gowns, but I
didn't want to take the chance that she'd read my letter on TV or
something.

Because of the uniqueness of my figure, I much preferred so-
cializing with my mom's friends. They, too, had figure problems!
When they confided in one another that everything they ate went
right to their thighs, I totally understood. There I'd be, slapping my
hips, yelling, "Ain't it the truth, ladies!" But I just couldn't muster
any sort of real enthusiasm when my own friends told me secrets
about their bodies. Every time one of them announced she'd gotten her period, I'd hold her hands in mine, jump up and down a
few times, and force myself to do a creaky old cartwheel, all the
while wondering if the blood rushing to my head was my first hot
flash.

It wasn't only the cushy familiarity of my mom's friends' figures
that intrigued me; it was the stuff they talked about. For instance:
Mrs. Feinberg was cheating on her husband with the pool boy—
two, sometimes even three times a week. Mrs. Diamond caught her
housekeeper stealing right out of her wallet, and Mrs. Denberg
wore falsies. These were things I wanted to know! Especially the
part about the pool boy. My mom was interested in that little tidbit,
too. We were both trying to figure out what Mrs. Feinberg saw in
him. We weren't nosy or anything. We were doing detective work.
If we could figure out why Mrs. Feinberg no longer loved her husband, we could apply that information to what was happening in
our own house, something neither of us understood.

I used to love to lounge around with my mom's friends, quietly nodding and yawning, pretending to smoke, drinking water out of a coffee cup. There was a rhythm in the way they wove in and out of conversation with their long, languid pauses and a certain beauty in the way they didn't run around the house or climb on the furniture to get to the phone. I had no desire to do anything that involved sudden movements, since they made me feel arthritic. When given the choice, I always opted for a nice quiet game of canasta over a raucous sleepover. I hated jumping on the bed. I was always afraid I'd fall off and wind up in a hip cast. The last thing I wanted was to wear white.

Unfortunately, circumstance was such that I typically had to spend more time with my own friends than my mom's, and it was always the same routine. Just like the girls in Judy Blume's books, they all called the same boys every time. In our case, it was Daryn Saks, Jeff Gold, and Brian Brioni. The first question was always, "Who do you like?" And the second, "Well, let's say she just got run over, then who would you like?" Our teacher was never on the list, so what was the point? Why bother calling some prepubescent slobbering idiot to find out who he liked when I had a perfectly good man waiting for me in homeroom? But, still, I went along with it. I desperately wanted to fit in—even though I knew my mom was home alone, waiting for me to come home.

The more I picked up Judy Blume's books, the more I knew something had gone awry. How could I possibly have had anything in common with Margaret or Nancy or Winnie or Jill, when I couldn't even relate to my own friends? They were all just innocent children, happy and carefree, with age-appropriate bodies and parents who were grown-ups. But it wasn't like that in my house. My father seemed like a teenager himself, on the verge of discovering who he was for the first time at forty. He questioned everything, rebelled against everyone, and was determined to find his place in this world before it was too late. By the time I turned twelve, he was so tortured and confused that when he stopped coming home until very late at night, I used to imagine him walking the streets alone in the dark with his head down, thinking he had no place to go. For some reason, he felt home was no longer an option. None of us knew why, and I worried about him all the time. I worried that he wasn't happy and that it was because of me and the way I turned out. He used to promise me that I'd grow up to be something special. He used to promise me that all the time. But there I was. Just an average girl with peculiar hips. I worried that I was losing him. If only Judy Blume had written a book about the male midlife crisis, it might have shed some light on my adolescent experience.

My mother used to wait up for him with the covers pulled up to her chin, wondering what she had done wrong to make him so unhappy. All she ever did was love him, protect him, and support him while he was trying to make sense of his life. She needed someone to confide in, someone to tell that her life was falling apart, that she didn't know her husband anymore, and that she didn't have any idea what she should do to help him. She tried everything. I watched her try everything. Her friends' lives were so organized and simple. Ours was a mess. How could she possibly tell anyone the truth? My sister and I became her best friends. We all knew that we would soon find ourselves alone, and I missed my father long before he left our house. I had no idea what my mother would do without him. She seemed lost. I had no idea how I could possibly save her.

A few months ago, when I was asked to contribute to this anthology, I stumbled upon *It's Not the End of the World*. Of all the Judy Blume books I'd read, somehow I'd missed this one. The one that got away. The one that finally clicked. Had I been twelve when I read it, I would have, of course, called Judy Blume immediately. I would have told her that she was the first person who ever made me realize that I wasn't the only twelve-year-old girl in the world who already felt like a woman—a woman who already knew how it felt to be left by a man I thought was mine forever.

I would have told her that Karen Newman was me, and I would have asked her how she could have possibly known that I, too, spent hours devising imaginary near-death scenarios that I was sure would bring my parents back together.

There I am, on the edge of a cliff, hanging by a twig, while my mother and father desperately climb up the mountain to save me; but at the last second, just as my mom is about to grab me by my striped Danskin twinset, the twig snaps and I fall against the rocks, tumbling and flailing like a rubber doll, until I hit the ground and bounce up and down a few times, before splitting into five neat little pieces.

And there they are.

Clinging to each other by the side of the mountain, crying in each other's arms, looking down at their dead daughter, each one of her limbs lying just a few inches away from her torso—although, surprisingly, there is very little blood. But then, miraculously, I stand up, and they realize it was just an optical illusion and all I have are a few scrapes and a mild concussion. We climb our way back to one another, link arms, and walk back to the car shaking our heads.

Or the one where I'm in the hospital, badly in need of a kidney transplant. And there they are, fighting over who will be the donor, until they fall into each other's arms laughing about all the other stuff they used to fight about before I woke up with a missing kidney.

Needless to say, I wanted to kick myself when I read about Karen Newman's plan to have herself kidnapped. I wish I'd been able to come up with something more along those lines. I liked the idea of involving the police. But just the thought that someone else was desperate like me was enough to make me wonder if, in fact, I wasn't such an oddball after all. And was it a coincidence that Karen had an Uncle Dan who was six-foot-five and I had an Uncle Billy who was also that height? Not to mention that my family was living in Short Hills, New Jersey, at the time, and Karen lived only a few towns away. It was almost as if Judy Blume knew me.

If only I had known there were millions of girls out there who were trying to pass themselves off as happy-go-lucky, run-of-the-mill kids while their families were falling apart. If only I had known it was normal for me to want to tell my friends that everything they talked about was boring and stupid and nothing compared to what I was going through. And it was normal that they all seemed childish to me and that I resented them for being allowed to be so immature, because my childhood was being taken away from me and I wasn't nearly ready or able to let it go.

Eventually, enough time passed that I gave up the idea of my parents ever getting back together. Once my father got his first black leather couch and my mom was taking courses at the New School, it was clearly over. Had I read about Karen Newman when I was twelve, it would have certainly saved me a lot of sleepless nights, wondering what was wrong with me. It would have been comforting to know that it wasn't my hips or my taste in men that catapulted me into womanhood. I would have understood that by the time you turn twelve, you're not supposed to feel like a little girl anymore, and that if your parents don't split up, there's likely to be some other surprise around the corner that will shock you into growing up well before you're ready.

How was I supposed to know I wasn't the only one? Had I looked a little deeper, I might have noticed that my friends weren't really little kids anymore, either. Their hearts were also being shattered left and right, their innocence slipping through the cracks. We were all being forced out of our comfort zones whether or not we liked it or knew it. I guess I thought if I could get my parents back together and finally find the right underwear, I could make it all stop. But the train had already left the station.

Now I'm sitting here surrounded by dozens of Judy Blume books. Sometimes I find myself staring at the back cover of *Are You There God? It's Me, Margaret,* and I think about all the twelve-year-old-girls out there who must have read that book, girls who were new in school or whose parents couldn't agree on how to bring them up, or girls who had no idea who to ask for help in making sense of the utter chaos that is seventh grade. All those girls who thought they were the only one in the world like *that.* I wonder how many of them felt like Blubber, or how many of them knew their friends were no different than the girls who made fun of Blubber, and if reading about it made a difference in how they led their lives from then on. Judy Blume was the first woman to look girls straight in the eye and tell it the way it is. No one had ever thought to tell us that all that strangeness going on in our bodies wasn't strange at all, and no one ever talked to us about other girls. It's amazing that we ever got along without her.

I wonder if Judy Blume really knows how many girls' lives she affected. I wonder if she knows that at least one of her books made a grown woman finally feel like she'd been a normal girl all along, and I wonder, if by any chance at all, she'd happen to know where I could find a really good girdle.

———

Stephanie Lessing began her career as a writer in kinder-garten. It was at that time that she began her research on girl behavior in an attempt to figure out what was wrong with her. Her psychoanalytical approach to studying female behavior produced many acclaimed essays, including "Why Am I the Only One with an Umbrella?" and "What I Wouldn't Give for Missy Cohen's Culottes."

Prior to publishing her first novel, She's Got Issues, Stephanie Lessing designed promotional campaigns and adver-tising material for Conde Nast publications, and she often writes about her New York City experiences working at Vogue, Glamour, Self, Vanity Fair, and Mademoiselle on her blog: www.stephanielessing.com. Stephanie lives in New Jersey with her husband and their two children. Her second novel, Miss Understanding, was recently published.

Boys Like Shiny Things

| *Laura Ruby* |

"Hey Ma . . ." I called. "Here's the bus."

As we got on, the bus driver greeted me with, "Hi, Beautiful."

Ma gave him a big smile and said, "Deenie's the beauty, Helen's the brain."

—*Deenie*

Manhattan, the trendy meatpacking district. Pastis, the "it" bar of the moment. Beverly air-kisses the stunning man guarding the door against badly dressed invaders from Staten Island and New Jersey. I grew up in New Jersey, but it's not something you'd admit to here.

"He was voted one of the fifty most beautiful New Yorkers," says my friend Linda.

"Who?" I say.

"The door guy."

Beverly gets us in, as we knew she would. Beverly herself is beautiful—long blonde hair bright as a supernova, delicate features, a wide-open smile. She's dressed carefully in a flute-shaped skirt and a leather blazer that she peels off to reveal a shiny but tasteful bustier the color of champagne. It's the bustier that does it, I think. Or maybe the hair, I'm not sure. Whatever it is, the men in the packed bar step aside for Beverly as if they are making way for Heidi Klum in her teeny underwear and her enormous Victoria's Secret wings. When Beverly takes a place at the bar, they surround us, each waiting their turn for a chance to bask in her bright bombshell glory ('cause boys like shiny things).

Two Venezuelans reach her first. One of them corners Beverly and dares the other men to approach her. The other makes elaborate sweeping gestures with his arms. When he talks to you, he presses his lips against your ear. He has impossibly thick dark hair that waves back from his forehead. I like the hair, but Linda thinks it's stupid. "What's with the hair?" she says to me. "Is it alive?"

The evening has barely begun and already bombshell Beverly is text-messaging her various boyfriends while the other boys vie for her attention. Linda says a few acidly funny things and the men sense a challenge. Linda has icy Nordic eyes, a long Nordic nose, and the lush body of Salma Hayek. Her father studied physics under Oppenheimer. She is smarter than everyone in the bar. She is smarter than everyone on the planet. Her eyes sparkle like the fjords.

The men look from Beverly to Linda, Linda to Beverly. They are fascinated. They are frightened.

From the men, I get polite questions about what I do (writer) and where I live (Chicago). Do I like it? Is it really that windy? The men don't listen to the answers. This is okay, I tell myself. I'm not

here to meet frightened or fascinated men. I don't have to understand Venezuelans and their complicated hair. And yet it is obvious
that I'm neither the smart one nor the pretty one, and no one
knows what to make of me.

And, for a moment, neither do I.

My youth is punctuated by two things: trips to the library and trips
to the doctor. On one library visit, I find Judy Blume and I can't
stop reading her books. Sometimes I read my Judy books while
waiting in the doctor's office, trying to keep my mind off the intrusive and embarrassing medical things that are surely about to be
done to me. Judy seems to know all about intrusive and embarrassing things.

Judy knows a lot.

I fall into my books to pretend I am someone else—I am Sheila
the Great, I am Margaret, I am Deenie—for good reason. At the
allergist's, my arms are abused by dozens of little needles. At the
pediatrician's, it's Nurse Evil with her Pressure Cuff of Torment
and Thermometer of Doom. I have a dentist who doesn't believe in
Novocain when he drills my teeth and an orthodontist who wants to
pull half of them out because I seem to have too many. How I
ended up with too many teeth is one of life's eternal mysteries.

Another eternal mystery: why do I run like a duck?

"Laura, pretend it's a race. Up and down the hallway, okay?"

We are at the orthopedist's again. The doctor already examined
me, and I'm hoping that these insane laps around the office will be
the end of it. He watches me for a few minutes and issues his ver-
dict: "Well, that has to be the funniest run I've ever seen. But I
can't find a thing wrong with her."

My stepdad and I drive home. I have the feeling that my mother isn't going to be happy with this answer. My mom also thinks there is something wrong with the way I run, but she doesn't think it's funny. She thinks maybe I need some sort of treatment. Orthopedic shoes. Leg braces. An operation to replace my knees or maybe wind up my feet like propellers. A run that peculiar couldn't be normal. It couldn't be *right*.

So she forbids me to run until she gets some answers. I'm not allowed to play tag with the other kids the way I always do. Hide-and-seek is out, too. As is a perennial neighborhood favorite, monsters, which basically consists of us pretending to be mummies, ghosts, and werewolves who chase one another around, grunting and screaming.

The other kids don't understand.

"I'm not allowed to run," I tell them.

"Why not?" says Georgie, who lives across the street and is my best friend.

"Because my mom won't let me."

He blinks. "Why won't she let you?"

"Because there's something wrong with my legs."

"What's wrong with your legs? Do they hurt?"

"No," I admit. It sounds ridiculous even to me. If my legs don't hurt, then what could be wrong with them?

I sit on the sidelines and imagine what I would look like with my feet on backward.

"Deenie, God gave you a beautiful face. Now, he wouldn't have done that if he hadn't intended for you to put it to good use."

—*Deenie*

My younger sister Melissa is beautiful. Long and lean, with sandy brown hair and eyes a spectacular shade of green that is hard to describe: not quite hazel, not quite teal. A little otherworldly. Her skin's perfect, too, with the sweetest spray of freckles that you can only see up close. If Melissa didn't have that little bulb on the end of her nose, my mother says, she could be a model. She says this all the time.

When she says it, I think of *Deenie,* the book about the beautiful girl whose mother also wants her to become a model. Deenie finds out that she has scoliosis and will have to wear a back brace for at least four years, destroying any hopes her mother had of becoming an overbearing stage mom. Deenie, of course, doesn't take her diagnosis well, but she takes it better than her mother, who is devastated by it. And this makes it that much harder for Deenie to bear. It makes her furious. The brace, she says, makes her feel like she's in a cage.

My sister might be pretty like Deenie, but she doesn't have scoliosis. Even my sister's vertebrae are lovely, her bones sound and gorgeous. I think maybe my mom would feel better if I had scoliosis, but the only afflictions the doctors can verify are bad skin and a terminal case of clumsiness. My mother holds my face up to the light, turns it, sighing at the pimples pebbling my cheek. "When you were little, I used to think you'd be beautiful."

The trickster god Puberty had other plans. In addition to the zits, the frizzy hair, and a growth spurt that etched red marks in the skin on my hips, my right eye has a tendency to cross when I'm tired. An appointment is booked with the ophthalmologist. I may, says my mother, need surgery to tighten the muscles. I wonder if the surgeon will have to pluck out my eyeball. I wonder if I have to get a fake eye. Maybe it wouldn't cross anymore, but then it might not move at all, and wouldn't that look just as weird?

Sometimes I feel like I'm in a cage, too.

"God gave you a special brain," Ma told her. "And he wouldn't have done that if he hadn't intended for you to put it to good use."

—*Deenie*

So I'm not beautiful. But I'm smart. Melissa's the pretty one; I'm the smart one. I'm the one who gets the A's in school. I'm the one who reads all those books. I'm always scribbling in my notebooks. Smart, yes, of course. Smart girls could have bad skin and big feet and fake eyeballs. Who cared about a fake eyeball on a smart girl? The world would admire her for her brain. A smart girl could *do* things. A smart girl could get a bunch of degrees and be a doctor or a lawyer or a professor or a librarian.

What a smart girl can't do is have a boyfriend.

My mother sighs. "Are you sure you want to do this?"

I've written a letter to Nick and asked my mom to mail it. (Nick is a boy I met at camp the summer I turned thirteen.) Nick is cute. And funny. I have a wild crush on him. Even weeks after camp is over, I can't stop thinking about him. If I'm so smart, then why didn't it occur to me to mail my letter on my own and spare myself this crushing pity?

"Are you sure?" my mother asks again. She doesn't have to say anything else. She doesn't have to point out the big feet and the funny run and the crossed eye and the bad skin and the mass of hair that appears as if it is attempting to take over the planet one frizzy curl at a time. Maybe the doctors haven't found anything specific, her expression says, but one thing is clear: I'm broken. Boys don't like broken girls no matter how smart they are. Boys like shiny girls like my sister. Better to accept it. Better to fall into yet another book and pretend you are someone else for a while.

> *"If I was going to be ugly I was going to be ugly all the way . . . as ugly as anybody'd ever been before . . . maybe even uglier."*
>
> —*Deenie*

I show up at my best friend Joann's house. She has not one but two younger sisters. Her littlest sister is too young to be anything but a little sister, but her middle sister is pretty. Very pretty. Everyone says so.

Joann is not pretty. She's as awkward as I am. She's also smart. She takes advanced math classes. Maybe this is why we're friends. So we can be awkward in our advanced classes together. The advanced classes are packed with awkward people who have pretty little sisters.

Today, Joann has a gigantic gash on her chin.

"What happened?" I say.

"I had a zit," she says.

I don't understand what having a zit has to do with that gaping wound. She looks as if she's had a run-in with a pair of ice skates.

"What are you talking about?" I say.

She lifts her horrifying chin defiantly. "I cut it off."

"You *what*?"

She tells me a story about a zit the size of a small moon and how she's always getting them and she's so angry and so tired and Clearasil doesn't work and they *lie* on the commercials, so she pulled the nail clippers out of the medicine cabinet. Snip. Like that.

"The nail clippers?" I say. I cannot think about this without getting nauseous. What is it about feeling ugly that makes you want to do something even uglier?

"You shouldn't do things like that to yourself," I say.

"Why not?"

"Because!" I want to give her a good reason why not, but I can't think of one. I have to change the subject. I tell her that I'm going on a diet. "I'm 122 pounds. I want to get down to 118." When I'm 118 pounds, I will reward myself with a miniskirt.

Joann and I agree that we will eat nothing but fruit for the rest of the day.

We are still hopeful. It is amazing how hopeful we are.

"Sybil Davidson has a genius I.Q. and has been laid by at least six different guys . . . Erica says this is because of Sybil's fat problem and her need to feel loved—the getting laid part, that is. The genius I.Q. is just luck or genes or something."

—*Forever . . .*

When I am thirteen, I read *Forever . . .* I marvel at Katherine and wonder how anyone could feel comfortable being naked with someone else. What if he thinks you're ugly? What if he thinks you're broken? What if he tells you?

My first boyfriend is Albert, a seventh-grade lothario from another school. Even though he lives around the block from me, I don't meet him until my friend Kristen brings me over there. She has a crush on him. But he doesn't like her. He likes me. He tells me I'm pretty. I'm astonished. Kristen has dibs—she liked him first—but the feelings are too overwhelming for me. *He thinks I'm pretty.* How this is possible I can't even imagine. Doesn't he see the hair? The big feet? The ridiculous number of teeth? When he asks me out, I say yes immediately. We break up twenty-four hours later. I'm the one who calls it quits. I don't know why.

The next boyfriend is Harry, who is nearly three years older than me and is either gay or antisocial, or both. I go over his house and we sit at opposite ends of the couch watching TV. We do this for six months. He never once tries to kiss me. When we talk on the phone, he tells me about how he likes to hunt and gives me instructions on how to properly skin a deer. I love animals—all animals—and I don't want to hear about murdering Bambi and reducing him to a jacket and a pair of boots, but I listen anyway. I think if I listen to the stories about killing animals, maybe he'll try to kiss me. I can't understand why he won't. But then I understand it better than Albert, who did want to kiss me. I don't understand why anyone wants to kiss me. I keep hoping that Harry will try to kiss me, and that will mean I'm worth kissing. I keep hoping that someone will say something I'll believe.

I move from Harry to John to Mark to some guy I met on the boardwalk at the shore and some guy I met on the bus and some other guys on my floor in my college dorm and more guys I meet at this party and that party. I kiss some, mess around with others, all the while wondering when they will discover that I'm not who they thought I was, that I'm a screwed-up, broken, not-very-pretty person with horrible afflictions and a much more beautiful sister.

"I'm fat."

I am walking across the quad with three other people: a bitchy girl who hates me, a guy who doesn't care either way, and another guy who has given me his jacket because it's cold. His name is Rich, he's extremely good-looking, and he's paying a lot of attention to me. He's friends with the bitchy girl, and I can see that she's as surprised as I am at this whole jacket thing. Why would he give me his jacket? Unless he likes me, which is stupid. Also, crazy. I am too big, too lumbering, too clumsy. I run like a duck.

Smelling the warm leather of Rich's jacket and seeing the hateful expression on his friend's face, I am overwhelmed with feelings of awkwardness. I want Rich to like me, but you have to be pretty for such things. I don't know how pretty feels or what pretty does. I am not Deenie before her back brace—the Deenie who knows that Buddy Brader is watching when she flirtatiously tosses her head, the Deenie who lets Buddy hold her hand in the movies and doesn't even mind that much when her palms get sweaty. I'm Deenie after she has hacked off all her beautiful hair and left a few loose strands hanging down. I'm Deenie who can't stop thinking about her awful crooked spine, who can't stop shouting about it.

"I know I need to lose a few pounds," I say.

Rich tells me that he doesn't think I need to lose anything. But I know he's lying.

" . . . now would you please leave so I can change."

"Are you ashamed of your body, Katherine?"

"No . . . of course not."

"Then what's the difference if I stay?"

—Forever . . .

I am at a fraternity party dancing with my friend Annika. The music is loud and bad, the room dark and smelling of Budweiser laced with just the slightest whiff of stomach acid. The fraternity brothers ring the room swigging the beer and scoping out the girls. It's somewhat humiliating, the dancing, the scoping. We dance here because we're freshmen and there's nothing else for us to do. I don't dance the way I'd like to—that is, freely, with my arms swinging and my feet flying and the sweat pooling at the small of my back. The way I move is safe and slight. I want to be noticed but not noticed. Seen and not seen. It's the same for Annika. Her sister is three years younger and beautiful. (I'm beginning to believe that there should be a club.) We dance as if we don't want to displace any air.

I won't know what to do if I get picked by one of these fraternity brothers. I won't know what to do if I don't.

This confusion permeates all of my college experiences, even the ones I'm supposed to be good at: the school part of school. I don't automatically ace all of my courses. I have to work at it. And if I have to work at it, how smart could I possibly be? And if I'm not as smart as I've been told I am, what am I?

> *"I used to tell myself it didn't matter that I wasn't pretty like Deenie because I have a special brain and Deenie's is just ordinary . . . but it didn't help, Ma . . . because it's not true! None of it's true . . ."*
>
> —Deenie

Dave. Drew. Tim. ____ (insert name here). Rob and I circle each other for years until one day he is gone. The word "ugly" is too small.

I swear off men and take myself to the doctor—a psychologist.

When you've lived with a mom who handles her anxiety disorder by threatening to have your eyeballs plucked out and you are the smart one in your family, you eventually get some therapy.

My first assignments are to interview people. I talk to my mother, my stepdad, my aunt. I also talk to my sister, the pretty one. Turns out the label wasn't so good for her, either. She was pretty, she said, but she wasn't *that* pretty. Not stunning. Not gorgeous. And if she wasn't as pretty as she'd been told she was, what was she? She tells me that she has felt stupid and unpretty all her life.

For her, I'm furious. She *is* beautiful. And she's smart, too. Why, I yell, can't she be both?

Oh.

Well.

It takes a while, but I do start dating again. Most of the men are perfectly nice people, but I must have my last hurrah. I must find one more person who will help me punish myself for my secret ugliness. I fall hard and fast for Paul, a man I meet at a party. He's bright and funny and desperately eccentric. His eyes are so wide-set and his chin so pointy that he resembles a six-foot-tall praying mantis. I think he's perfect. Unfortunately, he doesn't feel the same way about me. Doesn't take him long to start pointing out the various imperfections. My faulty logic. My pedestrian job as an advertising copywriter. My bourgeois taste in books and music.

We sit at a bar. A man observes his blond hair, my reddish hair, and tells us that we are "salt and pepper." I turn to Paul and ask which one of us is salt and which is pepper. He rolls his flinty eyes at the stupidity, the faultiness of the question. He takes a sip of his drink and says, "You're salt, I'm pepper. Salt enhances other flavors. Pepper has a flavor all its own."

I tell myself that this is a joke.

One day, we are sitting next to each other on the edge of my bed. I say that I've recently begun to run. So far, I've only been able to make it three or four blocks at a time, and I might look ridiculous when I'm doing it, but I'm doing it.

"You're running?" he says in a tone of disbelief. "*You?*" I am wearing shorts. He takes my thigh and shakes it, showing me how loose the flesh is.

Another joke. Isn't it funny? Ha. Ha!

Paul breaks it off. He tells me that I'm not who he thought I was. He tells me that I'm just not attractive. The irony of a man who looks like a giant insect telling another person that she is just not attractive isn't lost on me. And yet he has somehow divined my secret wound and stuck his big buggy thumb right into it just because he could. It feels too familiar to me to call him on it.

I tell my mother and she is sympathetic. She says that she has always thought I was striking.

I decide to stay in therapy a little while longer.

"This time when he kissed me I concentrated on kissing him back."

—*Deenie*

Another bar, New Orleans. A man has asked me to dance. He is not my type. He is not flinty or cagey or sly. His eyes are warm and friendly and open. He's just a little bit shy. There's something about him. Something comfortable. I dance for hours, my arms waving, my feet flying, sweat pooling at the small of my back. The man keeps trying to talk to me. He likes what I have to say. I speak, he listens. He wants to hear more. When I get home from New Orleans, there's a letter waiting for me. Soon, there are others.

He tells me I'm beautiful.

He is the only man I have ever believed.

I marry him.

Here at Pastis in New York City, I twirl my ring and think about what Judy has tried so hard to say: You are not any one thing. You are many. Don't let them make you believe that this is an either/or world.

It's so simple. And so hard.

But I choose to see things Judy's way, because Judy knows. I work. I think. I talk. Sometimes I flash my husband my shiny bra ('cause boys like shiny things).

A Venezuelan wants to know what I like to do besides write.

I tell him that I run every day.

I believe it doesn't look funny at all.

———

Laura Ruby ran screaming from high school and went on to a glamorous career as a professional liar, er, copywriter for various companies. She's the author of several books for children, the teen novel Good Girls, *and the collection* I'm Not Julia Roberts. *She has been dyeing her hair funny colors for so long that she no longer remembers what her natural shade is. Visit her at www.lauraruby.com.*

A LONG TIME AGO,
WE USED TO BE FRIENDS

| *Megan Crane* |

I found out my best friend dumped me when she got married without telling me.

As breakups go, I would say this counted as pretty unambiguous. Clear and to the point, really. With boys, there always seemed to be that murky gray area where *maybe* he broke up with you and was seeing that other girl, but then again *maybe* he was actually in love with you and just had difficulty expressing the depth of his emotion, hence the hussy.

Or maybe that's just my pathology talking.

Like Stephanie and Rachel in *Just As Long As We're Together*, I thought T. and I were meant to be friends forever. We met in college. Maybe that was the problem. Everything about Vassar College in the early nineties was melodramatic. It was all cigarettes and intrigue, secrets and tragedies, one after the next in the course of an evening. In the significantly more boring years after college, T. and I conducted our relationship mainly over the telephone. We ran up excessive phone bills at our respective companies, and it was due to her influence and encouragement that I left the New York metropolitan area behind—where I'd spent my entire childhood and adolescence—and moved down to the New South following the 1996 Olympics.

T. had a truly delightful cackle and could roll her eyes with so much delicious expression that it could stop you at ten paces. The voices she used to tell stories were hilarious, and some of them I mimic to this day. She had beautiful skin and an addiction to the finer things in life. Very expensive makeup, for example. Good-quality clothes. She was obsessively neat (we did not make good roommates for precisely this reason), which meant everywhere she lived always smelled sweet and fragrant. She was the first person in my age group who bought her own house, without the help of a partner's paycheck. She could be surprisingly raunchy. She seemed to know intuitively how to do things like write resumes, kick ass in job interviews, and rise through the corporate ranks. Not only did she know how to do these things, she seemed to enjoy them, while I, conversely, hated every last thing about joining the workforce. She seemed to thrive once she'd made it to a position of authority. I, meanwhile, floundered and soon gave up on corporate America altogether. While I hid in graduate school, T. continued to flourish in her career.

T. and I used to spend hours on the phone. Literally, hours. Sometimes there were several calls a day. No detail was too small or insignificant to share, complete with analysis and asides. We reveled in the minutiae of our lives, which was probably why I should have paid more attention when this changed. We called ourselves sisters—family—and I know that I meant it. I believe she did, too.

And yet, as in any relationship, there were undercurrents of rage and jealousy. Nastiness lurked within us both, and it sometimes spilled out in petty, horrible ways. Snide comments about each other's life choices. Rudeness and underhanded machinations. A truly awful fight shrouded from memory in the haze of too much alcohol. There were other people, other friendships that threatened ours, or seemed to. There were incidents and problems that I thought were forgotten or solved. Looking back, I think they were actually signs that the relationship was ending.

Where does a relationship start to go wrong? Can you pinpoint it? Or do all relationships simply come with built-in life spans?

Was it my unhappiness in those years? Her tendency toward judgment? My need for her to be the adult? Her need for me to be the bratty child? The fact that maybe neither of us enjoyed our roles after a while, though we kept playing them? Or, maybe, all of the above?

But hindsight is always a narrative, leading to inexorable conclusions. Life, however, mostly just happens.

Maybe we let each other go.

Or, anyway, that's what I tell myself.

Here's what I know.

We hadn't really talked in a while. Which was strange in the particular context of my friendship with T. but not all that strange when you consider that I once got on a plane to Zimbabwe in the hope that a friend I hadn't seen in six years would be waiting at the

Harare airport to meet me. (She was. I'm expecting an invitation to *her* wedding any day now.)

I just assumed both T. and I were busy. I knew I was. As T. and I stopped keeping in touch, I was consumed with leaving England after five years. Then with moving from New Jersey across the country to California. I finished and defended a doctoral dissertation. I sold my first book and wrote a second. T. and I were on different continents, then in different states. While I'd certainly noticed that T. and I had lost touch, I figured it was just a phase. Distance could make even the closest friendships ease a little bit, become less urgent.

After all, friendships moved in and out of states of intimacy for any number of reasons, not all of them catastrophic. Sometimes you spoke every day, sometimes you didn't speak for months, and it meant nothing. This particular friendship had ebbed and flowed before, too. There had been other periods of zero talking between us, usually precipitated by a fight, but we'd always made up in the past.

Once, we hadn't talked for months following an angry phone call. This came on the heels of our disastrous four months of living together. I resented the fact that she just up and moved out on me, leaving me to fend for myself—something I felt unprepared to do. I imagine she resented the fact that I was incapable of washing a dish or picking up after myself. In any case, tempers flared on the telephone. I hung up on her.

Then, months later, I was upset about the direction my life was going in. I was tired of the same people and places. I was tired of me. It was easy to pick up the phone, slide back into the comfort of my relationship with T.

"Hey," I said when she answered the phone.

"Hey," she said.

And then we tumbled into the usual rhythms of our conversation.

As if nothing had happened. As if there was never any real space between us.

I assumed it would always be this way.

During the early months of this latest silence, I remember thinking that I was too stressed out and busy to deal with it, and if *she* wanted to reach out, she could. It never really occurred to me that she wouldn't.

In those previous silent periods, I'd never taken her off my list of friends altogether. Nor had I done so this time, especially since we hadn't even gotten in a fight. Quite the contrary—we'd gone on vacation together just a few months before *the silence*. Until I received the news of her wedding (many months later from a mutual friend), if I'd been asked to make up that list of friends, T. would have been on it.

In other words, if I'd gotten married in that period of time, it never would have occurred to me to do so without her.

Which just goes to show how little I knew about our friendship.

I'll admit that it hurt my feelings. But not for the reasons it should have. I should have been upset that she let me go, that on the day she'd been thinking about for most of the time I'd known her—and one she'd always planned to share with me—she hadn't considered me at all. I should have been angry at her for drawing such a significant line in the sand. I should have wondered what I'd done to hurt her so badly that she would undergo such a radical change without bothering to send me so much as an e-mail. I should have wondered why she either (a) didn't care about me any-more or (b) thought I was such a terrible friend that I didn't war-rant the sort of notification one might send estranged relatives and the local paper. I should have felt all of these things, and perhaps on some level I did. But mostly it hurt my feelings because I was faced with incontrovertible evidence that she viewed our (appar-ently lost) friendship in a completely different light than I had.

Which makes me wonder now: How much do any of us know about our friendships?

What makes for best friends, anyway? In the beginning of *Just As Long As We're Together*, Stephanie and Rachel seem bound to-gether mostly by history and geography. Which you shouldn't un-derestimate, by any means. There's a reason people differentiate between "work friends" and "neighborhood friends." Some people meet a new best friend every time they leave the house. Others maintain a select inner sanctum of close friends, keeping everyone else at a distance. Still others create entirely separate worlds to in-habit—one for work, one for family, one for home—and never allow those worlds to collide (those people always seem to have the most interesting weddings, don't they?). There are as many differ-ent ways of *having* friends as there are of *being* friends.

In my latest book, my heroine, Gus, is forced to confront many of the same issues Rachel and Stephanie must face in *Just As Long As We're Together*—many of the same issues T. and I were forced to face in real life. What happens if your friendships aren't what you thought they were? What do you do if your best friend no longer wants that title? What if you, yourself, aren't as good of a friend as you always assumed you were? I'm lucky enough to have truly great best friends in my life, but I've also lost best friends like T., and these relationships, good and bad, have been the focal point of my life for years. I wanted to try to address these experiences in my book.

In most of the lives of the women I know, friendship with other women plays an enormous, pivotal role. Sure, most of us have or want a significant other, but it takes a lot of time and energy to find The One. Most women need their girlfriends to travel down the road with them as they either seek out or wait for The One. For some women, the journey is more important than the end result, and therefore their companions become like family to them. For others, their companions are ditchable the moment a good-looking End Result appears.

I believe the enormous success of shows like *Sex and the City,* as well as the chick-lit publishing phenomenon, can be explained by the vast thirst women have to see or read stories that explore these relationships in their various forms. Our lives are made up of networks of women, stretching from the female relatives who initially shape us to the female friends who make us and break us, sometimes, as in the seventh grade, all at the same time.

Everyone knows what the courting stage feels like. You get so excited when you meet. The two of you can talk about anything and everything. You can't wait until the next time you get together, because you feel as if you could keep talking forever. You feel dizzy and a little bit giddy from the new intimacy and the laughter. The excited shock of recognition—the way you see yourself in a new person and how, through her, you see the world through new eyes.

Finding a new best friend is like falling in love.

T. wasn't the first friend I had, nor the first I lost. I wish I knew how it happens that some friends you make you just can't keep:

They are everything to you for a time, and then, suddenly and without warning, they are not. Meanwhile, though I am surrounded by the friends I've kept (and who've kept me), it doesn't seem to be anything more than luck that they've stayed around. Luck and work on both our parts, that is. These friends stretch back across the years and hail from almost every place I've lived or job I've had. Women I met along the way who I've had the pleasure to share this journey with.

Because becoming a woman, it turns out, is every bit as difficult as you imagine it must be when you're trapped in that awful sex-segregated classroom in the sixth grade, watching a movie you but dimly comprehend and being forced to pass around sanitary napkins.

(Note to schools: Please stop doing this. It's traumatizing. No one—but no one—has a pleasant memory of the Period Presentation.)

I was out recently with friends when the subject of making new friends came up. My friend's significant other was finding it hard, he said, to find people she liked in her new city. He expected that when her new job started, it would get easier, but said that what his girlfriend *really* needed was girlfriends of her own.

All the women at the table nodded sagely.

I imagined all the women I'd known across the years. The girls I'd admired, who'd made me laugh and then giggle, who'd been comrades in arms in the social battlefields of high school and college, who'd been welcome relief from the dreariness of corporate life, all of whom I'd liked at some point, some of whom I'd loved, others I'd ended up hating, still others who hated me. Of them all, I'd kept just a select few. It wasn't easy to get to know another woman, to figure out if she was like you. To see if she'd become a sister.

Which was what I thought we were all looking for. Sisters, not girlfriends. Family.

But:

Women are tough, we said, smiling at one another. *It's always a battle to find good female friends.*

In *Just As Long As We're Together,* Stephanie and Rachel's friendship is tested and ultimately changed by the arrival of Alison, the new girl in town. Stephanie and Alison become fast friends, leaving Rachel out in the cold—or so it feels to Rachel. Rachel and Stephanie fight about all manner of other things in the course of the novel, only coming to terms with what was really going on in the final pages:

Halfway there I said, "You want to talk about it?"

"Do you?" she asked.

"I don't even remember how it started."

"You told Amber that Max liked me."

"Oh, right . . . I never did get what was so bad about that."

"It was just the last straw," Rachel said. "I was so mad at you by then."

"For what?"

"Because you didn't like me anymore."

"No," I said, "you were the one who didn't like me!"

"I didn't like you because you didn't like me!" Rachel said. "You were best friends with Alison and everyone knew it."

"But you had Stacey Green," I told her. "You didn't want to be my best friend anymore."

"That's because you didn't want to be mine!" Rachel shifted her books from one arm to the other. "I felt it was some kind of competition . . . me against Alison . . . and I was always losing."

Judy Blume, *Just As Long As We're Together* (Bantam Doubleday Dell, 1987), pp. 292–293.

What strikes me when I reread this book, the one I first read long ago when I was navigating best friendships with girls I only dimly remember now, is how very much like romantic relationships these female best friendships are. They require so much care. So much interest in another's details, thoughts, and emotions. So much effort and attention. The lasting forms of these friendships ease into something like family. The other ones flare and then disappear.

These days, I don't have a best friend. I have close friends but no all-encompassing best friend. I suspect that now, having found The One, there's no longer a space for that kind of relationship. I only have so much emotional energy, after all, and if I were to expend so much of it on the maintenance of a friendship like those breathtaking ones of old, what would be left for my partner? My work? Me?

But I don't mean to suggest that you can't have both a Significant Other and best friends. I just don't think you can have a Significant Other and A Very Best Best Friend, with whom you are far too close, in a toxic sort of way.

As you grow older, I think the emotional dependency of that

kind of Best Friendship has to ebb away or there would never be any space to form the sort of emotional attachment you need to have with your life partner. Or the sort of relationship that now, in my thirties, I am pleased to have with myself. (Note to teenage self: It's true, you can *like* yourself. Really.)

But knowing that this ebbing is probably inevitable makes me wonder if some of the tensions in those vibrant, heedless, wondrous best friendships come from the fact that they aren't The Real Thing. Seventeen hours of discussing mundane details on the telephone won't take the place of a lover or a spouse, though perhaps they help fill a space. No wonder these relationships contain as much darkness as they do light—they're saddled with an unbearable weight. No wonder it's so rare that we maintain them in the same form forever.

The best sorts of friendships are the ones that adapt. The ones that flex to fit you both as you need them. That seems like common sense, but it's very hard to find, because not everyone changes at the same time or in the same way. Sometimes friendships are meant to end the moment circumstances change.

Maybe this is what T. discovered as she met and fell in love with her husband (whose name I don't even know). This was always her unapologetic goal, no matter her success: to locate her husband and make her own family. Maybe she discovered, years before I would, that things have to change when that happens. That these partings are inevitable and perhaps even necessary, and because I could not have understood why this was so at the time, she neglected to tell me. And then just disappeared.

But all of this supposes that T. was the one to make all the decisions, as if I had no part in what happened. When, in fact, I knew I was letting go of her. As each day passed, as each week became a month and I failed to act, I was making a choice. As I look back over the other best friendships I've had that also ended, I wonder if, in addition to simply having a finite amount of room for such intimacy, we also have certain periods in our lives in which we seek out people who seem to embody the things we lack. Then, when we gain those things for ourselves, we no longer need that friend in the same way, which causes a serious dissonance in the relationship. Perhaps this is why these particular friendships burn so bright and then disappear so completely.

What I desperately admired about T. was her strength in worlds that confused and scared me. She was so capable. Successful. Alternatively, I was a complete mess and decidedly unsuccessful at anything that did not involve lying on my couch eating chocolate and watching *Buffy*. As I climbed my way out of the depression of my twenties, I found that I wasn't as messy as I thought. And that as it turned out, I had the chance to be successful in my own right. When this happened, I think the pendulum swung too far in the opposite direction for our friendship. The last thing I needed was a friend who seemed to treat me as if I was the same person I'd been before. That messed-up, ruined girl I'd finally put behind me. And I think one of the things T. needed very much was to be needed.

I think we simply outgrew each other.

When I was in high school, I had a best friend who was closer to me than members of my actual family. J. and I were ridiculously, disastrously close. We called each other the Death Twins, to indicate both our bond and our oh-so-jaded outlook on life. (Which is hilarious when I look back at my preppy self, complete with pegged jeans. I was about as jaded as a wide-eyed singing and dancing Disney cartoon.) J. and I were so tight that when we drove around with her boyfriend, he was banished to the backseat so as not to disturb our bond.

Then college intervened. We separated and found other friends in our separate colleges. We fought bitterly (and one night, memorably, with our hands) and didn't speak for a long time. Years, I think.

And here's the difference between Best Friendships and Actual Romantic Relationships: In the former, you really can have space. Years of it, if necessary, and then sometimes, if you're lucky, you can find your way back.

J. wrote me a Christmas card years later, and in so doing, reactivated our friendship. We will never be as claustrophobically, suffocatingly close as we were in high school. Instead, we can be friends. At last.

I think about this a lot when I think about T. and wonder why our relationship followed the trajectory it did.

There are things that I know about myself that I would never have learned without T. in my life. Some of those things are incredibly unpleasant, it's true, but that might be what friends are for. There were times when she seemed to be the only thing between me and a great darkness I feared I might get lost in. We were silly together in a way I have never re-created with another friend and don't imagine I ever will. I miss the stories that only she knows, the jokes that only she gets. As I wrote somewhere else, losing a friend is like losing a language, and I miss the one we spoke together. I loved her with the whole of my heart, and I can't regret that. There is no reason not to imagine that some day one of us will reach out, the other will be receptive, and we will reaccess that intricate, secret world that we shared.

Although, let's hope, in a less all-consuming fashion.

It is also possible that T. and I will never reconnect, never so much as speak again, and that's fine, too. I don't wish her ill. Quite the opposite. I like to think she's out there wielding that smile of hers like a weapon behind lush MAC cosmetics. I hope the husband she chose is worth the wonderful woman I knew once, whose fierce defense of those she loved was awesome to behold.

Reading Judy Blume taught me this lesson long before I would have to learn it for myself. You can't hold on to people. Sometimes you have to let them go. Rachel knows that Stephanie and Alison are closer to each other than to her, and in *Here's to You, Rachel Robinson*, she finds a way to come to terms with it. As we all must do.

I believe that people come into your life for a reason, and it's up to you to learn the lessons they can teach you. I believe best friends teach us how to be better people, and to do that they sometimes have to leave you to do it yourself. T. taught me a great deal—much of which, I imagine, will take me years to fully understand. That's the gift of friendship. It changes, even after the friendship ends. I don't need to speak to T. again to keep the memory of her—both good and bad—in a special place in my heart.

I like to think she's out there, happy, remembering me in the same bittersweet way.

"You can have more than one best friend at a time," I said.
"No, you can't."
"Why not?"

"Because best means best.*"*

I thought about that. "What about close?" I asked.

"You can have more than one close *friend at a time, can't you?"*

Rachel thought that over. "I guess so."

"And close is as good as best!"

"I don't necessarily agree," Rachel said.

"But it's better to be friends than not to be friends . . . you agree with that, right?"

"Well, yes," Rachel said, "if you're talking about true friends."

Judy Blume, *Just As Long As We're Together* (Bantam Doubleday Dell, 1987), pp. 293–294.

Megan Crane is grateful to her best friends, all of whom suffered through her teens and twenties with her and still helped inspire her to write English as a Second Language, Everyone Else's Girl, *and* Frenemies. *Why they allowed her to sport that atrocious haircut remains a mystery.*

CRY, LINDA, CRY

| *Meg Cabot* |

She had big brown eyes, an elfin smile, soft, curly brown hair, and go-go boots . . . the kind of boots Julie on *Mod Squad* wore. The kind of boots none of our mothers would get for us, no matter how much we pleaded, because they were too expensive and too grown up for us. Even her T-shirt was new and different—*TNT,* it read across the budding mounds of what were destined (possibly at any moment) to become actual boobs: *Talent, Not Talk.*

Her name was as exotic as the place from which she'd moved— Shoshona. And she'd transferred into Mrs. Hunter's fourth-grade class at Elm Heights Elementary School in Bloomington, Indiana, all the way from Canada.

And she was about to make my existence a living hell.

I didn't know it, of course. And if someone had told me, I wouldn't have believed it. Everyone knew that bullies didn't come in four-foot, sixty-pound packages, with brand-new solid gold post earrings and Goody barrettes.

Everyone, that is, except for Judy Blume.

Too often in books, schools are depicted as nurturing, caring environments where bullies either don't exist, or on the rare occasions when they do crop up, they come from troubled homes. They're "victims," just like the children they've terrorized. Eventually, when the child the bully has been tormenting comes to understand that her bully doesn't have a daddy or lives in a trailer park instead of middle-class suburbia, she forgives and even eventually befriends the bully, and everyone gets along.

Yeah. Right.

Judy Blume is careful not to give *Blubber* that kind of *After-School Special* ending. True to life, the victim and the bully in *Blubber* do *not* become friends, the bully is never even punished for her crimes, nor is there any obvious lesson learned. While the protagonist, through becoming a target of bullying herself, comes to understand that by tolerating the bullying of others, she did something wrong, this is portrayed subtly, so subtly that the careless—or youthful—reader might miss it entirely.

Still, even if in the fourth grade I'd known there was such a thing as pretty female bullies, I was hardly the victim type. Like *Blubber's* heroine, Jill, I was as average as a kid could be—not too smart but not too dumb; not too fat but not too skinny; not too short but not too tall. I was completely normal . . . a little shy, maybe, but I got along with all my peers and had a tight group of friends, some of whom I am still in touch with today, thirty years later.

Sure, my family wasn't the most well off, and my mom made a lot of my clothes. But I attended a school populated by children of academics—college professors who valued books over designer jeans and had successfully shielded their children from the knowledge that they might be missing out on current trends, as the Internet hadn't been invented yet, and the only channels any of us got were the three major networks and PBS (and *Cowboy Bob* on local station 4).

There was nothing physically to set me apart from my peers— just as Judy Blume is careful to point out there is nothing physical that sets her bully's victim, Linda, apart from the other children in her class. Linda is slightly overweight. But there are other children in the class who are larger—who could even be classified as fat— and Wendy, the book's antagonist, doesn't pick on them. Perhaps because of the title, I've often seen *Blubber* categorized as a book about a fat girl who gets tormented by her peers. But the discerning reader soon realizes that the reason Linda is picked on has nothing to do with her weight (although her weight is the subject about which Linda is most sensitive and therefore the subject on which Wendy chooses to focus the majority of her taunts) and that the term *blubber* doesn't have as much to do with Linda's size as it does her personality—or lack thereof.

No, Linda is picked on by Wendy for the same reason that my bully, Shoshona, picked on me.

We, the victims, allow it to happen.

Oh, yes. I went there. I, like Judy Blume, am putting the blame—well, part of it, anyway—on the victim herself. In today's society—thirty years post-*Blubber* and Shoshona—it may be considered politically incorrect to say these girls asked for it. But Jill's mother's suggestion—that her daughter "laugh off" the taunts that are making her life so hellish—is still the best advice a parent can give to a child in such a situation (although obviously a call to the teacher who has allowed such bullying to go on under her very nose is also recommended). Judy Blume herself, when describing *Blubber* on her Web site, writes:

> A *person who can laugh at herself will be respected, right?*
> *But Linda doesn't laugh. And maybe that's the problem.*
> *There's something about her that makes Jill and a lot of kids*
> *in her fifth-grade class want to see how far they can go.*

Bullying is about power. And those who wield power can quickly turn on others, even those who once considered them friends—especially those who lack the inner resources to laugh at or stand up for themselves. I considered Shoshona a friend, although truthfully we had nothing in common. At ten years old, I still considered playing with Barbies the height of amusement, a pastime Shoshona looked down upon, although she didn't seem to have any better suggestions as to what else we might do while playing together. Drawing, reading, and board games were all "dumb" to her. One memorable playdate included Shoshona asking me to sit in a desk chair that spun, then twirling me around and around in it until I begged her to stop (true to form, when I asked her to stop, she wouldn't . . . until I threw up, that is. Shoshona, disgusted, stomped home, not even apologizing for making me sick . . . or, as my parents later discovered, for breaking the chair).

You might think an afternoon that ended in vomit would have dampened my enthusiasm about pursuing a friendship with a person who disdained the pursuits I enjoyed yet could think of no alternative activities, save those that caused me to lose my lunch and ruined my parents' furniture.

But that was the power Shoshona held over me—the same

power Wendy, in *Blubber*, holds over Jill. I was shy. Shoshona was not. I was willing to let others have their way in an effort to get them to like me. Shoshona was not. I, along with the rest of the girls in my class, worshipped Shoshona the way Jill, in *Blubber*, worships Wendy—the way any ten-year-old worships a natural leader—even though it turned out her T-shirt had lied: Shoshona had no discernible talents. She couldn't sing, for instance, like my friend Becky, or do backflips, like my friend Erika, or do fractions in her head, like Barbara. In fact, Shoshona was almost *No Talent* and *All Talk*.

The desk chair incident was devastating to me. Shoshona had come to my house, and she had a bad time! How would I ever live it down? How would I get back in her good graces?

I felt even worse when my attempt to redeem myself in Shoshona's eyes by having a "cool" birthday party with a *Freaky Friday* theme—everyone was to come dressed as their mother—fell flat. My friends Becky, Erika, and Barbara arrived dressed like me, in long trailing gowns with white gloves, loaded down with rhinestone jewelry, giggling like mad. Shoshona, however, didn't dress in her mother's clothes. She wore an exact replica of her mother's clothes—but in her own size: business attire for the busy ten-year-old executive. She narrowed her eyes at the rest of us in our floppy hats and too-big high heels and told us we looked like a "bunch of babies."

We were only too ready to agree with her. Being Canadian, Shoshona seemed hopelessly cosmopolitan. She had some very fancy ways compared to us Hoosiers. It was Shoshona who introduced our class to the titillating concept of "going together." She and Jeff Niehardt were going together by the end of Shoshona's first day at Elm Heights. It didn't take much longer than that for most of the rest of the class to pair up.

Everyone except for me and my friends. Like Becky, Erika, and Barbara, I didn't want to "go with" anyone.

Still, most of the talking Shoshona did was about boys. Though I had no particular interest in boys at the time, it was clear from the way Shoshona carried on that the interests I did have—Barbies and *The Boxcar Children*—were babyish and that I needed to "grow up."

This was news to me. Things had seemed to be going swimmingly for me in Mrs. Hunter's fourth-grade class until Shoshona came along and pointed out that in actual truth they were not. My friends—particularly sensitive Erika, who cried when her science experiment involving glucose didn't turn out, and beanpole brain Barbara, whose main offense, according to Shoshona, was that she was good in math, a trait that would certainly never win her any dates—were as babyish as I was. If I ever wanted to grow up, I needed to be more like Shoshona.

And I needed to get a boyfriend, pronto.

It was my reluctance to go with anybody that really horrified Shoshona. She suggested I go with Joey Meadows, a fifth grader, and even got him to ask me to go with him. Nice as I found Joey, I wasn't ready for that kind of commitment. So I gently turned down his kind (read: terrified. He was as scared of Shoshona as the rest of us were) offer.

Little did I know how this simple act would enrage Shoshona. The very next day when I arrived at school, I was no longer Meggin Cabot. According to Shoshona, I was now Maggot Cabbage and would remain so until I changed my mind, stopped being so baby-ish, and accepted Joey Meadows's request to go with him.

Suddenly I had gone from being Shoshona's "friend" to being the object of her scorn and antipathy. I was mortified.

I didn't cry in front of her. I had more pride than that. But I spent plenty of hours in my bedroom closet weeping as if my heart would break. I didn't want to be called Maggot Cabbage for the rest of my life. But then, I didn't want to go with anybody, either.

It didn't take long for my parents to catch on that something was wrong, primarily because most nights I wouldn't come out of the closet. Finally, one evening my father crawled in there with me and asked what was the matter. I explained about Maggot Cabbage and Shoshona. I listed the myriad ways Shoshona had taken over the class—swinging classmates Muffy and Monique (the only names that have been changed in this essay are those of the inno-cent) to her side; making faces at me and rude remarks, if when the class split into groups, I tried to join my old friends Becky, Barbara, and Erika, who liked and accepted me just the way I was; calling me a baby when I wouldn't play "chase the boys" on the playground at recess; making fun of my homemade clothes and nondesigner jeans; laughing at the fact that I was forbidden from watching *Starsky and Hutch*.

My father, a computer science professor who was the first in his family to go to college—on a basketball scholarship, no less—was not particularly versed in psychology, let alone child psychology. And he seemed to know next to nothing about women, having dated exactly one in his entire life—my mother.

His desire to help with my situation, however, was heartfelt. He showed me—right there in the closet—how to make a fist (never tuck the thumb on the inside. You might break it) and always to aim for the nose (if you aim for the mouth, you might cut your knuckles on your opponent's teeth).

Yes. My father advised that the next time Shoshona called me a baby or Maggot Cabbage, I should punch her in the face.

I was horrified. I had never punched anyone before in my life (not counting my brothers. But I had never hit them in the face, preferring the more sisterly practices of "Indian rubs" and pinching).

The situation had clearly progressed to a point where something needed to be done. But what, to my father, indicated a need for fisticuffs, to my mother showed a need for something else entirely. Always a woman of action, Mom placed a single phone call and purchased a single book. The phone call was to my teacher (though I begged Mom not to tell Mrs. Hunter what was going on, certain that word would get out that Maggot Cabbage was such a baby, she couldn't handle her own affairs), and the book was for me. The book was called *Blubber*.

I don't remember if I recognized myself in its pages. Certainly I, a timid child, had never been so bold as to egg anyone's house (whether or not they deserved it) as Jill, the narrator, does. Nor had I ever participated as actively in tormenting another student as Jill does at one point in the novel.

But there had been a certain girl—I'll call her R.—at a school I'd attended previous to attending Elm Heights, whom I, along with everyone else in the class, had found insufferable.

And though I myself had never joined in on teasing her, I had certainly never done anything to stop it, somewhat relishing R.'s comeuppance (she was incredibly bright, and like many bright children, came off to those of us who were of more average intelligence as a horrible know-it-all).

What I took away from *Blubber* during that first reading, at the age of ten, was that doing nothing to stop the tormenting of a classmate was, in its own way, every bit as bad as if I had been one of the ringleaders. Certainly Linda was as obnoxious and deserving of mocking as R. had been, but that didn't make what had been done to her or to R. right . . .

. . . any more than what Shoshona was doing to me was right.

I knew that I, like Jill in *Blubber*, was going to have to learn not to punch Shoshona but to laugh off her taunts. At the very least, I was going to have to stop letting them bother me.

And that wasn't going to be as hard as it sounded. I had gotten to a point where I no longer wanted Shoshona as a friend. I no longer cared if she liked me. I found her, in fact, boring. What fun is spinning around in a chair when you could mutilate Ken (who had already permanently lost an arm in a tragic war accident) or read a book?

So the very next day during art, while Mrs. Hunter's fourth-grade class was gathered around the clay table and I said something to Erika that cracked her up—but caused Shoshona to raise her eyebrows and go, "God, Maggot, could you be more of a baby?"—I did it.

Oh, I didn't punch her in the face (though, thanks to my father, I knew how). Instead, I said the phrase I'd been rehearsing since finishing *Blubber*.

"Look, Shoshona," I said. "You be you, and I'll be me. If you think what I like and what I do is babyish, that's fine. You don't have to like them or do them. But don't expect *me* to stop liking them just because *you* don't. Because I'm not you."

Shoshona, blinking in astonishment at this mild statement—which was, given that it had come from me, one of the shyest girls in the class, quite an outburst—said, "God. Okay. You didn't have to yell."

It's no coincidence that Mrs. Hunter dropped the bomb later that day that she understood there were children in her class who were going together. Never, Mrs. Hunter said, had she heard of anything more ridiculous. Fourth graders, she said, do not "go together." She added that if she heard any more reports of children going together, she would send the offenders to Mrs. Harrigan, the principal, a fate—needless to say—worse than death. When Shoshona raised a hand to protest, Mrs. Hunter looked her dead in the eye and said simply, "Shoshona. *Don't.*"

Shoshona made a face to show how unfair she thought Mrs. Hunter was being, and I watched as Jeff Niehardt sadly erased his beloved's name from the inside of his pencil box. Shoshona swore at recess that when she and Jeff turned eighteen, no one, not even Mrs. Harrigan, would stop them from going together.

I'm not sure if that actually happened, because Shoshona moved back to Canada at the end of the school year, and I personally never saw her again. All I know was, after that day, no one—not even Shoshona—called me Maggot Cabbage again.

But I've thought of Shoshona—and *Blubber*—often over the past thirty years. Not even one year later, a girl named—ironically—Judy became the target of some of Shoshona's bullies-in-training, Muffy and Monique, for wearing blue eyeshadow and sleeping during social studies. When Judy didn't bother to come to her own defense, I did, making sure Judy had someone to sit with at lunch and someone to swing with at recess. Muffy and Monique, not being anywhere near as vicious as Shoshona, soon lost interest.

Middle school followed, with a whole new batch of social misfits who were targeted by a whole new batch of bullies. The tears in the girls' room flowed freely and copiously—sometimes from Muffy and Monique, who in turn became victims themselves and eventually my friends.

But I myself was never again a victim. *Blubber* had taught me how to stand up for myself and even—amazingly—how to defuse situations for others. Soon I found myself coming to the defense of R.—the girl from my previous elementary school—when we met again in high school. R. had lost none of her insufferable know-it-allness in the years since I'd last seen her. She had, if anything, become worse. Brilliant academically but socially inept, not a day passed when her books weren't scattered from one end of the hall to the other by some smirking jock.

But this time I wouldn't stand by and watch as others taunted her. And I certainly didn't laugh at her. I invited her to eat with me at lunch (to the chagrin of my other friends), attended slumber parties at her house, invited her to the movies, and occasionally still see her, to this day. As with Jill and Linda, I can't say we became best friends . . . but I felt for her. I'd stood in R.'s shoes. I knew how it felt.

And if there was a way I could help her not sit in her closet and cry every night, I was willing to try it.

Today, whenever I need to remind myself about the massive disconnect between adulthood and childhood, I go to Amazon.com and look up the reviews for Judy Blume's *Blubber.* I can't think of another children's book that is more polarizing—parents are "appalled" at the behavior of the children in the book and at the way the parents in the book handle the situation (Jill's mother's suggestion that her daughter "laugh it off" seems to raise parental hackles, though, if you ask me, it's way better than advising her to punch Wendy in the face), while children—the ones who aren't "appalled" by the number of times Jill's mother says the D word—accept what happens to Linda and Jill as a matter of course.

Because it *is* a matter of course. I don't know if there's something that happens to some adults—especially once they've had children of their own—where they selectively forget what being a kid is really like, or if these people really grew up in such a sheltered environment that bullying never went on in their schools. I sort of think it's the former. Only Judy Blume, despite having children of her own, never lost sight of the fact that girls are *not* made of sugar and spice and everything nice.

Years after the Shoshona incident, I found comfort in a cartoon by Matt Groening (creator of the *Simpsons*) in his book *Life in Hell*. It's a simple line drawing of a group of little girls surrounding another little girl, who is weeping. The girls are chanting, "Cry, Debbie, cry." The cartoon is called "The Cruelest Thing in the World: A Roving Gang of Fourth-Grade Girls."

Unsensational and unsentimental, *Blubber* is this cartoon exemplified. Judy Blume understands that there have always been bullies and there have always been victims, and until the victim learns to stand up for herself, the bullies won't quit torturing her. No amount of parental or teacher intervention will save her.

She has to save herself.

That's what Judy allows Jill to do, and in doing so, she allowed me to save myself.

*Meg Cabot spent her childhood in pursuit of air condition-
ing, which she found at the Monroe County Public Library in
Bloomington, Indiana. Meg has published over forty novels for
younger readers as well as adults, including* The Princess Diaries *series (on which two hit feature films by Disney were
based),* Size 12 Is Not Fat, *and the* 1-800-WHERE-R-YOU *series (on which the television series* Missing, *currently being
broadcast on the Lifetime network, is based).*

*When she is not reliving the horrors of her high school ex-
perience through her fiction, Meg divides her time between
New York City and Key West with her husband, their primary
cat, Henrietta, and various backup cats. Be sure to check out
Meg's Web sites: www.megcabot.com and www.megcabotbook
club.com.*

THE M WORD

| Lara M. Zeises |

$\mathcal{I}$ *was seven when* $\mathcal{I}$ discovered the secret.

My parents had already divorced, and I spent weekends in the oatmeal box of a bachelor pad my father had filled with bland Rent-a-Center furniture. It was a one-bedroom, so I slept on a pull-out couch in the living room. Its mattress was too thin, and I could feel the metal supports poking up through it no matter which way I twisted my body. So mostly I preferred sleeping on it unconverted, even if the tweedy fabric of the cushions smelled like dust and stale cigarette smoke.

The word "sleeping" is a bit of a euphemism here. I never liked not being in my own bed, the one that had pillows broken in just so and linens that smelled like the fabric softener sheets my mother used in abundance. After my dad had retired for the evening, I'd read a book or watch some TV, trying to get sleepy, ticking off the hours before I'd be allowed to wake him up so that we could go out to breakfast.

In the dark, under scratchy eighties-style geometric-printed sheets, I'd slip my hand down between my legs, pressing the cotton crotch of my panties inward until I found the right spot. That's all I did at first, too. It didn't occur to me to move my fingers around or to remove my underpants from the equation. All I knew is that it felt good, my finger there—sometimes good enough to help me fall asleep. Sometimes so good that I'd wake up hours later, finger firmly in place, my hand hot and crampy from staying in the same position so long.

I honestly had no idea what I was doing, even though with time I did learn that panties were a nuisance I needn't be bothered with, and that if I moved my finger around a bit, I'd feel a delicious warmth run the entire length of my prepubescent body. Later, after many, many nights of experimenting with pressure and position, I rubbed long enough and hard enough and in the right rhythm to feel every muscle *down there* pull tight together, like a tiny fist, and then explode into waves of hot twitchy goodness—a surprise that left me not only breathless but decidedly awake.

So I did it again. And again. And again and again and again.

And still I had no idea what it was that I was doing. I had no names for the magic my fingers made or what those fizz-pops— now the goal of my nightly no-panty dives—were called, or if anyone else I knew was doing the exact same thing.

Until, that is, I read Judy Blume's *Deenie*.

Deenie is the story of a young girl who's so strikingly beautiful that people value her for her looks more than anything else—especially her mother, who is convinced that it's Deenie's fate to be a model. Those plans are interrupted, however, when Deenie's failed attempt to make the cheerleading team reveals that her "bad posture" is really the beginnings of "adolescent idiopathic scoliosis." Translation: Deenie's spine is growing crooked, in the shape of an S.

While the bulk of the book is about beautiful Deenie adjusting to life in her new Milwaukee brace and learning that she's more than just a pretty girl, sly Blume fits in two short passages about Deenie's favorite extracurricular activity. The first appears halfway through the novel. Deenie tells the reader that she's starting a new unit in gym class—a once-a-month discussion group where girls can ask anonymous questions of their wise teacher. Deenie's question is among the first to be chosen: "Do normal people touch their bodies before they go to sleep and is it all right to do that?"

In response, Susan Minton, Deenie's "single white female" classmate, says that she's "heard that boys who touch themselves too much can go blind or get very bad pimples or their bodies can even grow deformed." Poor Deenie worries briefly that her late-night self-petting sessions are responsible for her scoliosis, but her gym teacher soon clears up that fear.

"I can see you've got a lot of misinformation," Mrs. Rappoport replies. "Does anyone here know the word for stimulating our genitals? Because that's what we're talking about here, you know."

One of Deenie's classmates timidly raises her hand and says, "I think it's called masturbation."

Finally, my ten-year-old self thought happily. *After all those years of practice! There was a name for what I was doing!*

Masturbation!

In retrospect, I realize that what I was feeling wasn't so much happiness as relief. Someone else was doing it, too. A lot of someones, it seemed. I mean, if there was a name for it, there's no way I was alone. I couldn't be, if it was in a book.

Like Deenie, though, I instinctively knew that masturbation was a "very private subject." Not once did I try to broach the topic with any of my girlfriends, or my very liberal mother (who until I was thirteen used to pee with the bathroom door open), or my own gym teacher, a conservative male baseball coach who probably would've fainted dead away if I'd asked him about "stimulating my genitals." Even when I was a senior in high school and a friend of a friend admitted to doing it, I pretended like I had no idea what she was talking about. I was embarrassed, though Mrs. Rappoport had assured Deenie's class—and me—that masturbation was "normal and harmless."

In fact, I don't think I admitted to anyone—female or male— that I was a master at masturbation until I was a sophomore in college. And it wasn't because I was suddenly comfortable talking about the activity, either, but because I was going through a feminist "I own my sexuality" phase that deemed it necessary (in my opinion) for me to admit that not only did I touch myself but that I liked it. A lot.

Judy Blume's *Deenie* pays homage to the Natalie Wood/Warren Beatty classic film *Splendor in the Grass*. Book Deenie is named after Movie Deenie, a choice her mother made to ensure Book Deenie's beauty. Blume lets readers know on page 1 that Movie Deenie's fate is to go insane and end up in an asylum ("Ma says I should just forget about that part of the story," Book Deenie says).

What Blume doesn't mention, however, is *why* Movie Deenie has a breakdown to begin with, or that *Splendor in the Grass,* based on William Inge's one-act play *Glory in the Flower,* is a commentary on sexual mores in the 1920s. Movie Deenie is of sound mind when she falls in love with the handsome and charming Bud. But between her mother making her feel guilty for having sexual urges (God forbid she act on them) and Bud's father advising him to break up with Deenie, as she is a "good girl" and therefore not the kind he should be getting carnal with but rather the kind he should hope to marry one day, it's no wonder Movie Deenie begins to crack—and crack up. After all, it's perfectly fine for Bud to play the field, but when a distraught Deenie discards her virginity (mostly to get back at Bud for breaking her heart), she's marked as a bad girl, unredeemable in nearly everyone's eyes.

Book Deenie has a Bud, too—Buddy Brader, a cute boy on whom she has a crush and later with whom she has her first kiss. But by the time Deenie comes into close physical contact with Buddy, she's already trapped inside of her Milwaukee brace. Blume says the inspiration for *Deenie* was meeting a young girl who had scoliosis and talking to her about her brace. But then why did Blume choose to name her heroine Deenie? Did she intentionally cage the sex parts of a girl whose movie counterpart goes nuts after intercourse? Or was it simply a coincidence?

The ending is just ambiguous enough to leave those questions unanswered. Deenie, who has begged to be allowed to go to her friend's party sans brace, is chastised by her father and told she can't go unless she wears it. Ever the sly one, Deenie decides to wear the brace *to* the party but change out of it the minute she arrives. Then guilt takes hold of her—"I thought about my father and how he trusts me," she says. "I've never really lied to him and I don't think he's ever lied to me"—and Deenie changes her mind. She remains steadfast in this decision, even when Buddy Brader pulls her into a dark part of the basement and asks her, "Couldn't you take off your brace for a little while?" Book Deenie remains the good girl and tells him no, that she must wear it all of the time. Saintly Buddy replies, "Oh, well," and proceeds to make out with Deenie anyway.

In the end, the brace—now linked to Deenie's father's trust—becomes a chastity belt of sorts. This might sound far-fetched were it not for a scene earlier in the book in which Deenie develops a rash due to the metal of her brace rubbing against her bare skin. She's told by her doctor that she'll need to wear an undershirt to protect her from further irritation. Deenie takes this as a slap in the face; undershirts, she thinks, are for babies. "I think what I'll do is wear my bra under it," she says. "I'm certainly not going to school without a bra."

Frustrated and angry, Deenie takes off her brace and climbs into the tub, which has been treated with a powder that should help clear up her rash. She's bored at first but eventually finds the hot water "relaxing." "Soon I began to enjoy it," she says. "I reached down and touched my special place with the washcloth. I rubbed and rubbed until I got that good feeling."

Once again, Book Deenie and Movie Deenie have more in common than just a name. In *Splendor in the Grass,* a key scene shows Deenie bathing and arguing with her mother. In defiance, she stands up in the tub, naked and dripping wet, shocking her mother out of the room. The act is both a challenge and a statement—Movie Deenie's way of telling her mother she's no longer a little girl but a woman.

Book Deenie could certainly relate.

• • •

The scope of teen sexuality changed drastically between the time when *Deenie* was first published (1973) and when I graduated from high school some twenty years later. Yet adolescent fiction hasn't matured as quickly as its readers. While it's definitely more common to read accounts of boys flying solo, relatively precious few novels even *allude* to girls getting their groove on by themselves. (One notable exception, Meg Cabot's *Ready or Not: An All-American Girl Novel*, picks up where Blume left off; in it, Samantha's older sister Lucy not only instructs her about the pleasures to be found in a showerhead but reiterates that it's normal to have these urges, period.)

The stigma still attached to female masturbation makes me sad, not just because I am an author of teen fiction, but also because I am a girl. And let's admit it: girls don't talk to one another about beating off because they're made to feel embarrassed about the act itself. Even today, when middle schoolers are experimenting with blow jobs at the back of their school buses, most teen girls would rather die than confess they do the solo deed. After all, masturbation is supposed to be a boy's game, isn't it?

I guess this is why I always remember *Deenie* as that book about masturbation, even though proportionally the topic takes up maybe 2 percent of the entire novel. Yet just having that little bit of information—that tiny confirmation that I was far from alone—was so important to me. Not just the ten-year-old me, either. The thirty-year-old me, rereading *Deenie* for the first time in at least fifteen years, is still comforted by the knowledge that yes, it is normal, and yes, other girls do it, and no, I am not bad, dirty, wrong.

And I definitely will not go insane.

———

Lara M. Zeises writes books for young adults. Her novels Bringing Up the Bones, Contents Under Pressure, *and* Anyone But You *all address various aspects of teenage sexuality. Inspired by authors like Judy Blume, Lara strives to tackle taboo subjects in an honest, straightforward manner. She hopes her stories, like Blume's, help readers feel less alone in the world. You can find Lara at www.zeisgeist.com.*

Do Adults Really Do That?
Does *Judy Blume* Really Do That?

| *Laura Caldwell* |

Catholic schools are not exactly the model for frank discussion about sex. At the Catholic school I attended in the far suburbs of Chicago, sex was explained in one sentence by my fourth-grade social studies teacher: "When a man and woman fall in love, the man puts his penis inside the woman."

Upon hearing this, I glanced around at my classmates. Blank stares. No one seemed impressed, freaked, or intrigued. And I guess I wasn't, either. *I don't get it,* I thought. But no explanation was forthcoming, and the fact was I didn't get a lot of things. I didn't get why the state of New York had a city in it with the same name. I didn't get what it meant that my father was an attorney, although I knew I sounded marginally cool saying that.

One mysterious morning that same year, the girls in my class were suddenly taken and shuttled into the basement without explanation. I'd recently read a book about the Holocaust, and I remember having the irrational fear that we were being led to the gas chambers. The darkened cafeteria where they herded us didn't help matters, nor did the way we were silently seated in rows. But then a projector whirred and a movie sprung to life against the cement block wall.

The film was roughly fifteen minutes long, and it explained menstruation in such a complicated, scientifically sophisticated way, I'm sure it's the same film med students see during their OB Gyn training. Again, there was no discussion at the end of the film. Again, I thought, *I don't get it*. A quick, mumbled conversation on the playground later revealed that none of my friends understood much, either.

So the girls at my school did exactly what girls around the country were doing in the 1970s—we turned to Judy Blume books for the real scoop. *Are You There God? It's Me, Margaret* taught us about training bras and puberty. *Deenie* informed us about masturbation. *Forever* educated us about losing your virginity, and if you believed the book, instantaneous orgasm. We felt informed after reading the books. We felt wiser, older. We understood the world.

But then the book *Wifey* was released when I was in seventh grade. Unlike the other Judy Blume books, this one wasn't targeted for children or teens. It was, as my mother told me, "Absolutely, 100 percent, for adults only." I had a high-level reading capacity and I'd been reading, "adult" novels since I was in first grade, but I was also the type of kid who followed orders. So I shrugged, said, "Okay," and forgot about it.

Until one afternoon in Ms. Hutchinson's history class, the book was surreptitiously slipped to me like a baggie of cocaine. It was *Ms.* Hutchinson, by the way, not Miss or Mrs., a distinction that wasn't lost on me. In retrospect, Ms. Hutchinson was a staunch feminist. This only became important later, when I stopped to wonder why a group of girls were allowed to pass around and read *Wifey* during class. Surely she'd seen us. We held the book under our desks. We thought we were reading it on the sly, but I can't imagine we were that successful. So maybe she knew clearly what was going on; maybe she thought, *They'll learn soon enough anyway.*

And did we learn—about body parts and bodily fluids, about sexual positions and sexual deviancies. *Wifey* tells the story of Sandy Pressman, a deeply dissatisfied housewife in Plainfield, New Jersey. Sandy's husband, Norman, isn't interested in her talks about why she's unhappy, nor is he even remotely interested in changing their sex life. He absolutely requires the missionary position (which was unlike any "missionary" I'd ever heard about) or nothing. He tells her that if she'd just make friends with the women at their country club and if she'd just take up golf and really give it a go this time, they'd all be a lot happier. Sandy tries. She signs up for lessons and makes efforts to be more social, but the disconnect from her husband and the attempts to lead a life that feels false send her into despair.

A book about a suburban mom should have been boring as hell for a twelve-year-old, but my friends and I soon found out that Sandy was anything but dull. When her kids leave for summer camp, she gets her own summer vacation—one of sexual awakening. A motorcycle man in a stars-and-stripes helmet periodically appears on her front lawn and whacks off. She has a one-night stand with her sister's husband (who also happens to be her gynecologist). She very nearly gets pulled into sex with the husband of her best friend, who is gamely trying to go along with his wife's desire for an open relationship. She starts an affair with Shep, the old boyfriend with whom she'd been utterly smitten.

Sitting in Ms. Hutchinson's class, I was shocked and I was titillated. It wasn't just the fact that the character in the book was having sex. (Since I'd been reading adult fiction for a number of years, I'd come across some generic descriptions of sex before.) Rather, the shock came from the frank way the book dealt with sex, anatomy, and desires. At one point, when Sandy's old boyfriend draws her outside a party and kisses her, she thinks how grateful she is for the Tampax she's wearing and for how it's "holding in her juices." Sandy talks about douching with vinegar, sometimes with wine vinegar for variety. Genitalia is described in exquisite detail, including its colors, scents, and sounds. The sex is rough, awkward, acrobatic, and sometimes downright unpleasant-sounding. And yet everyone seemed to keep wanting it.

If I'd felt informed after reading Judy Blume's other books, I now felt completely stumped again. Was *this* how adults thought about themselves and their bodies? Was sex not a sweetly physical act à la *Forever?* Was it something more sinister and much more raw?

I started watching my mother and father for signs that some of the acts in the book were taking place in our idyllic ranch house. This seemed impossible. I studied our neighbors during block parties, wondering if they were cheating on their spouses or having furtive sex in the study. I stared at Ms. Hutchinson during class. What was she like in the evenings when she was at home? Did she have a husband with whom she did all sorts of crazy things? Did she *want* to do those things? (In the book, Sandy hadn't always seemed too sure.)

My friends were no help in figuring out these matters. We giggled over the descriptions and read earmarked pages over and over. No one appeared as bothered as me by the thought that this sexual activity might very well be going on around us. And the truth was that I wasn't necessarily bothered by the *thought* of the sex—it was simply the thought of all these adults I personally knew having the sex. The concept was entirely too intimate. I couldn't look at the bus driver without blushing. I couldn't look at my dentist without imagining him naked with his wife. The only adults I could talk to without the pain of this knowledge were the nuns at our school. I knew they'd taken vows of celibacy. I knew they'd never have anything to do with the sexual world, and that was a relief, because since reading *Wifey*, sex seemed to be everywhere.

Sometime during this heady period, I began to think about Judy Blume. The *real* Judy Blume. Before this, I'd given no thought to the person behind the curtain when it came to books. Laura Ingalls Wilder, Louisa May Alcott, Carolyn Keene? Those were simply names on a spine. They meant little to me. In our small pocket of suburbia, we had doctors and lawyers and plumbers and policemen. When dinner table discussion turned to "What do you want to be when you grow up?" my parents offered suggestions like *astronaut* and *president of the United States,* but never *author.*

Who was this Judy Blume? I wondered. What in the hell was her life like? Where did she come up with these ideas? For the first time, I began to think about what it meant to be a writer or an author. Did an author have to experience something in order to write about it? Was Judy Blume off somewhere having sex with her brother-in-law during a party? Had she watched a man in a motorcycle helmet masturbate on her lawn. These questions confounded me. They did not, however, propel me toward my own writing career. Actually, I wasn't much of a dreamer. When people asked what profession I'd take upon adulthood, I usually threw out a half-hearted, "Maybe a teacher?" which I knew would please my parents. But I never really thought I would actually grow up one day, much less get a job.

Eventually, I moved on from *Wifey* and from all the questions it brought. But after life dragged me into adulthood and through a law career and eventually left me with a book contract, I thought about the novel again. I knew by now that authors certainly did not have to *have* an experience (especially one like sex with your brother-in-law) in order to write about it. I knew this because I'd written a book called *Burning the Map* about a woman whose trip to Rome and Greece with her girlfriends changes everything in her life. And who gets a fair amount of action in the process.

I'd written one scene in particular, in which the character spends the night in the Roman Coliseum rolling around with an Italian man. The scene was a hot one, and the minute the book came out, I began to get questions about it: Had I been in the Coliseum after hours? Had I actually fooled around with someone there? The answer to both questions was yes, but I felt hesitant to admit that for a few reasons. The first was the fact that my experience hadn't been exactly as I'd described it in the book. Not even close. Yes, I'd met a guy in Rome, and yes, he'd snuck us into the Coliseum at night, and yes, I'd kissed him there. And that was about it. We did not spend the night. It was not a sexual watershed moment.

The other reason I felt uncomfortable was my surprise that people were asking such questions. The book clearly said *A novel* on the front, and although I'd taken a trip to Rome and Greece with my girlfriends, I truly had written a work of fiction. I'd labored and toiled to craft every character from scratch, to make the book move along based on the development of these characters and for the sheer fun of the reader. If I'd written about the actual trip I'd taken to Europe, it would have read something like this: *I went to Greece. I drank too much. I got sunburned. The next day, I drank too much. I got sunburned. The day after that, I drank too much. Oh, and I got sunburned.*

In short, I felt uncomfortable with the thought that people were thinking of me instead of my characters. And this brought me back to *Wifey*. What had Judy Blume gone through with the publishing of that book? When I met Ms. Blume briefly at the Key West Literary Seminar, I nearly asked her, but then I chickened out. I never learned the answer until recently when I picked up *Wifey* (with its new exuberant chick-lit-style cover) and read it again. In her introduction, Judy Blume describes the "uproar" that was caused by the release of the novel. Some people, she says, congratulated her on having written a *real* book at last, while others were angry that she hadn't used a pseudonym, and still others were pissed off that she'd even had such thoughts at all.

Blume also concedes the similarities, or lack thereof, with her characters. "No, I'm not Sandy, although many of the details of her life come from mine—her exotic illness, her failure on the golf course, her fantasies. And I was never married to Norman, but I knew plenty of guys like him." She discusses how fearless she felt in writing about sexual fantasies and escapades. "I just remember this burning inside, this need to get Sandy's story on paper. I was, after all, raised to be Sandy. I still identify with her. If I sat down to write

Wifey now, I wonder if I'd be able to let go the way I did then. I'm not as filled with angst today (angst is good for writers). I'm as content as I've ever been (contentment is bad for writers), though I can always come up with something to worry about." Blume concludes, "Maybe I just didn't know enough then to be worried. Maybe I really didn't care what anyone thought."

Rereading *Wifey*, I expected the book to be screaming with sex, the way I remembered it. But as an adult, I didn't see the novel that way. There are some delightfully saucy passages, that's for sure, and the language is often blunt, but I saw more of the *story* this time. I saw Sandy's anguish upon feeling unfulfilled, leading a life she is somehow not connected to. I saw the trap many fall into upon adulthood—doing what you're supposed to do, not what you want to do. I felt for Sandy's husband, even though he's a horse's ass, and I felt for her ex-boyfriend, Shep, who can't leave his wife, because he simply can't leave that life. The ending, which I won't spoil, is a wrenching and honest one.

When I'd written my first novel, I, like Judy Blume, didn't know enough to be worried, and I really didn't care what anyone thought. Because in the same way I couldn't imagine growing up and working for a living, I hadn't actually imagined that the book would ever be published. I was much more cautious when it came to the novels that followed. I kept the sex clean or I kept it out all together, afraid of the confusion that could result between me and my characters.

Now, after six published books, I'm back to not caring as much. I'm back to focusing on what a *character* would really think or feel or do, even if it involves handcuffs and a bottle of Kahlua. (Although I still draw the line at having someone sleep with her gynecologist.) I let the characters fight, even if they sound petty. I let the characters mope around the house in a bathrobe, even if it's the ugliest bathrobe in the world. I let them feel something strongly one minute and change their minds entirely the next. And in my real life, I try to let myself do the same. So maybe that's the best lesson à la Judy Blume—write honestly and live honestly.

———

Laura Caldwell, who lives in Chicago, left a successful career as a trial attorney to become a novelist. She is the author of Burning the Map, A Clean Slate, The Year of Living Famously, The Night I Got Lucky, *and two novels of suspense,* Look Closely *and* The Rome Affair. *She is a contributing editor at* Lake *magazine and an adjunct professor of law at Loyola University Chicago School of Law.*

I Am

| *Erica Orloff* |

The pinnacle of life, of glamour, of all a girl could want or aspire to in seventh grade was Jordache jeans. When I moved to America, after living abroad with my family for a few years, I returned to a world in glitter-dusted chaos. The sixties were over, Vietnam was fading in memory. And in its place were drag queens with false eyelashes like furry caterpillars, the Bee Gees, leg warmers, the Village People, Studio 54, disco balls, and skin-tight Jordache, Sasson, and Gloria Vanderbilt jeans, their labels sewn across the rear pocket. But my mother didn't understand that.

In fact, my mother, a woman well read and seemingly perfect, understood nothing about being a teenager. My father forbid makeup and dating, and my mother believed denim was . . . well, blue cotton denim. Who cared what name was sewn across your ass? While my peers were perched on Candies and spending up to eighty dollars on jeans, I was trying to figure out how to be cool with a budget under twenty bucks. It wasn't that we couldn't afford designer jeans and high-heeled clogs—my mother just didn't see the sense.

"You'd break your neck in a pair of those!"

"But *everyone* has Candies."

"If everyone jumped off the Brooklyn Bridge, would you jump off, too?"

Well, I might.

Then came Farrah. "Wings" and "feathers" were the buzzwords when you went to get your hair cut. Mom didn't understand what was wrong with my perfectly stick-straight, wear-it-in-a-ponytail plain old brown hair. When I got a curling iron, my very hair conspired against me. I seethed. All the Dippity-do, Aqua Net hairspray, and heat-barreled torture devices used to tease my hair into something mildly, remotely cool were a failure. My hair could be seared by a curling iron until it smelled like burned flesh and cemented into place with enough aerosol hairspray (yes, I helped destroy the ozone), and *still* within forty-five minutes I looked like Morticia Addams. All I needed were Lurch and Gomez.

And if Mom didn't understand what was wrong with perfectly fine limp hair, she most especially didn't understand the mothers who dressed like their daughters, shared the same lip gloss with them, and tried to be cool. My mother didn't believe in being "friends" with her daughter. Not even a little.

"I'm not here to be your friend. I'm your mother."

I understand that now, but her philosophy, a sort of parental "don't ask, don't tell" policy, also excluded any discussion of sex or boys or even the complexities of my first bra. All I knew was that I was a geek, and life was hell. And what was left after coming to this lonely assumption was a simmering anger and a hatred for all the ways in which I would never have Farrah hair and jeans with a label that said I was . . . someone.

And then I read *Deenie*. In my oppressive household (my father was a brilliant but volatile Russian who forbid dating until sixteen and thought lipstick was whorish—Bonne Belle Lipsmackers were about as seductive as I was going to be allowed to get), *Deenie* was akin to reading Karl Marx. Downright revolutionary. I hid it under my bed, having borrowed it from a friend, and read it secretly. It was subversive, scandalous. And it perfectly captured the roller coaster of adolescent life.

I still remember when oh so beautiful Deenie chopped off her hair. She did it in anger and rage and fury and rebellion. She did it in a moment when her emotions got the best of her. Its lopsided ugliness was an external sign of how she felt inside. And I, straight A's, always striving for perfection for a father who loved me but demanded brilliance, thought Deenie was the most audacious, courageous character I had ever read about. After that, I devoured *Forever*, also hiding that book beneath my mattress, certain my father would send me to the threatened convent if he knew I read about S-E-X.

But while all of junior high was abuzz about the realistic depiction of teen sexuality in *Forever*, Deenie was the heroine who spoke to *me*. Hell, I was lucky I knew what a kiss was. *Forever* was as far away as forever. I had to get through first kisses and fumbled second base, not full-blown sex. Deenie felt my pain. She was me. But it didn't make it any easier to accept my flat hair and awkward adolescence.

I remember the cover of Judy Blume's wonderful book was a girl staring into a full-length mirror. I imagined she was like me.

Staring at that mirror, hoping for some kind of wisdom to lift herself out of her anger, out of the parts of her life she hated. I would find myself wishing I could talk to her—a living, breathing character who knew me better than I knew myself. But even knowing how much anger Deenie felt inside didn't dissipate how I felt. Being a teen girl, for most of us, meant hating our hair as too curly, too straight, too mousy, too frizzy, our bodies as too fat, too thin, too muscular, too short. Or in my case, too tall. In a harbinger of things to come, our breasts arrived in accordance with the luck of the DNA draw, and they were either too flat or not perky enough. Or in my case, embarrassingly buxom.

But, like the artifacts of adolescence—class notes and hair clips, lip gloss and leg warmers—I grew up and left Deenie behind. I went to college. I married. I had a child. I divorced. I married again. I became a novelist. I got sick. I nearly died. I forgot about Deenie. Until I spent a winter in a hospital bed.

When I was thirty, I found out that my lifelong agony and stomach pains were actually an immune disorder called Crohn's disease. I lost thirty then forty pounds on an already thin frame. And then I nearly died. In the emergency room, the doctors told my new husband to call my parents because I might not pull through. My mother mentally planned my funeral on the plane ride to my bedside (she had long since turned into a friend). My hospital stay was measured by weeks, not days. The doctors tried to help me, but nothing worked. One treatment option, at that time, was chemotherapy drugs. Another option was high-dose steroids. I opted for the latter so that I might be able to have more children.

I entered the hospital a size 8, thin, five-foot-ten. After my treatment, I noticed that when I smiled, my face obscured my vision—my cheeks puffed up so much from the drugs that my eyes were swelling shut. I gained about sixty pounds in three weeks.

When they finally let me look in a mirror, I honestly thought of Deenie before her reflection on the cover of Judy Blume's book. Forget a choppy hairdo. Or even a brace. How was a woman supposed to feel pretty or whole when she looked so very sick?

For once and for all, I had to make peace with the girl in the full-length mirror. No jeans or Farrah 'do was going to fix what was wrong with me. Chopping off my hair would change nothing. This would have to be an internal fix. I'd have to learn to love my insides—who I *was*—so that the misfit on the outside didn't matter. I didn't have Deenie's awkward brace. But I was now overweight and swollen beyond recognition. I felt like an awkward, seething, sad adolescent all over again. I could almost hear the chorus of my ex-husband ringing in my ears, telling me, "Nobody will want you." And now, who would? I had gone from being so sick that my ex called me a "bag of bones" to someone who was unrecognizably plump.

Nobody will want me.

Wasn't that Deenie's lament? Who would want a girl with a brace?

Luckily for me, my new husband wanted me. It's fifteen years later, my health is much improved, and much to our *four* children's chagrin, he still chases me like I am a sixteen-year-old hottie. I do wonder about him. But more astoundingly, my inner self evolved. If the eyes are the window to the soul, I learned to face the mirror bravely and really *see* myself, the me inside, my soul, my fearless-ness, myself. Whatever the mirror reflected, sickness or health, like Deenie, I made my peace. I love who I am. As my inner world evolved, my imaginary universe expanded. I've now published fif-teen novels, and my brain never shuts down as ideas come and I get to create whole worlds at my computer. I write for teens, and it's easy to remember that world. The outsider world, the Deenie world.

Who am I? I am not my disease, nor my weight, nor even my children. I am not my clothing labels, my bank account, my car (an unglamorous "mom van" anyway). I am not the ugly words spoken to me by a man who wanted to hurt me. I'm not my books or even my beautiful marriage. It's all illusory. I am, instead, this essence in-side. I am the courage to fight back from near death. I am the dig-nity of learning to love my inner self. I am the *love* I create with my four children. I am a mother nursing a baby. I am a person who prays. I am God's child. I am part of the ever elegant and evolving universe. I am peace. I am serenity. I am blessed with compassion because of my suffering. I am grace through pain. I am kindness. I am laughter. I am all these things. *I am.*

And I like to think that if I met Deenie, she would be all those things, too.

Erica Orloff finally gave up on Farrah hair and stopped killing the ozone when she switched to nonaerosol hairspray. She is the author of Do They Wear High Heels in Heaven? *a book inspired by her long illness, as well as ten other novels for adults. She writes for teens as Liza Conrad and is the author of* High School Bites *and* The Poker Diaries.

FOREVER . . . AGAIN

| *Stacey Ballis* |

Shakespeare wrote comedies, tragedies, histories, and romances. Oscar Wilde wrote plays, novels, and poems. Stephen King writes scary stuff, and *really* scary stuff, and stuff so goddamned ultra-creepy that it makes you want to sleep with the lights on. Judy Blume, if you asked her, would probably say she writes for adults, young adults, preteens, and children. But growing up, the Judy Blume fans I knew tended to fall into one of two categories: the "After-School Special" camp, the ones who were most devoted to *Blubber* and *Are You There God? It's Me, Margaret* and that ilk, and the "Sunday Cartoon" camp, those who had the fondest memories of *Otherwise Known As Sheila the Great* and anything starring that Dennis the Menace–esque Fudge. No one inspired loyalty like JB, and whether you liked your books serious or humorous, you waited impatiently for the Troll Book Orders to arrive, to see what new Blume delights accompanied your new poster of a chimp with a kitten in its arms.

But regardless of usual preferences, no JB fan could deny that there was one book that stood out. A one-word title, from the woman who wrote *Starring Sally J. Freedman As Herself*. A couple on the cover who were clearly not in the fourth grade. An electric buzz around school, overheard snippets of shocked conversations from even the most jaded eighth graders. *Forever* was the book that got passed reverentially from older sibling to younger, usually with key passages highlighted and essential page numbers listed in the back. It was the book that we read aloud at slumber parties, whispered about in the back of the school bus, and was the single most likely item to be stolen from a sixth-grade desk. Well, that and the box of Nerds candies.

I mean, this was the book that had a penis in it. And the penis had a name. And the characters had actual sex not once but a bunch of times. And they came, whatever the heck that meant. *Forever* was the single most illicit read for almost everyone I grew up with. (At least until eighth grade, when we discovered *Flowers in the Attic,* which frankly made *Forever* look more like it should have been called *Tales of a Twelfth-Grade Nothing.*) At the time, what resonated with me the most wasn't the feeling of being in the know or the illicit content but rather the clear and beautifully rendered image of falling in love, and falling back out, and being okay. I mean, at the time, no one ever talked about anything but true love. Lifetime love. Even crushes were "I'm going to totally marry him when I grow up," not "I think he'll be a lovely few months someday." Judy Blume opened a door for me by simply depicting something real and not overly romanticized, which seemed to make it even more, well, romantic.

Today, when the subject of Judy Blume comes up with my girlfriends, everyone gets that wistful look in their eyes, recalling the rainy Sundays, packets of Lik-M-Aid or Razzles, the burgeoning love of literature, and then the look changes. The eyes go from wistful to wicked, the smiles from subtle to smirking, and pretty soon we are talking about *Forever.* The conversations we had about that book some twenty-five years ago and the questions it either answered or elicited about boys were the precursors to our eventual Carrie/Miranda/Charlotte/Samantha conversations.

As a young girl, I devoured that book, deconstructing every sentence containing reference to S-E-X. That was what preteen girls did, and I was certainly no exception. But I never would have expected that years later this book would become as important and relevant to me in my thirties as it was to me in the delicate time before I became a teenager.

I was the last person who expected to fall in love in college. I saw myself as the adventurer, the one who was most likely to take a year off and travel after school, the one who already knew she didn't want kids and did want a career and would probably not get married until she was in her mid-thirties at least. So when I found myself in the beginning of my junior year of college happily cohabitating with my boyfriend and thinking about the future, it was a surprise to everyone, including me. He proposed shortly after my graduation; we had a two-year engagement and a lovely outdoor wedding. I was a young wife and eventually became a young divorcée. Not so shocking. We grew apart, in different directions, and after eleven years together, seven as husband and wife, we decided to end the marriage. I found myself suddenly single at thirty-one, nearly a dozen years since my last date. Scary. How did it work?

How was I going to meet someone? And what the heck was I going to do with him once I met him?

Even worse than not having any clue about the dating world was not having a clue about sex in the real world. Sex in college is one thing, fueled by alcohol, hormones, freedom, and curiosity. Sex as a married person can be about deep emotional connection and safety and sometimes even obligation. But sex as a single woman in her thirties is a whole new arena, and frankly, I was terrified. Not in the least because, as often happens when a relationship begins to sour, the first thing that had gone south in my marriage was the passion, and when we made the painful decision to split, I'd been celibate for nearly two years.

Now, divorce hits everyone differently. Some jump into their newfound freedom with all the exuberance of a cannonball off the high dive, bound and determined to make as big a splash as possible. Some rack up enough dates and bedfellows to negate the years they skipped in matrimony. Others are so devastated by the experience that they completely avoid new relationships, not even willing to stick a toe in the shallow end in case it is too cold.

I fell somewhere in the middle. I was intrigued and excited by the possibilities inherent in the adventure of dating, making new connections to new people. After all, I'm a social animal, I can talk to anyone, I make friends easily, and I'm a really skilled flirter. I'd always had the "if only you weren't married" guys hanging around, and now I could take advantage of their attention. This was going to be a piece of cake. I daydreamed about the interesting ways I might end up meeting my prospective dates, fantasized about magical early connections and the fireworks of a first kiss. Mmmm. First kisses. And those tingles all up and down the spine, and hands on the side of my face, the firm hold on the lower back, the touch sliding up the rib cage, the, um . . . shit. There's going to have to be nudity.

Wanna talk about really being scared? How about being a size 28 recent divorcée about to consider getting naked with someone new for the first time in almost twelve years? The idea was almost enough to keep me firmly ensconced on my couch, with my go-to boyfriends Ben and Jerry. I mean, I watched *Sex and the City*. I knew that sex was pretty much a given for a girl in her thirties, third-date rules and all. And in theory, it was really a wonderful notion. Meet a guy. Go on a date. Like him, he gets a good-night kiss. Go on a second date. Still like him, fool around. Go on a third date. Still hasn't turned into an idiot, sleep with him. Perfect timing. Long enough to get to know someone a little bit and feel trusting, but not so long that if the sex doesn't work it becomes difficult to extricate yourself. All my girlfriends swore by it. And I'd never been shy about sex, usually considered it a very pleasant pastime, and once upon a time, I'd been considered pretty good at it. But *theoretical* sex is one thing, and *actual* sex is something very, very different.

I tried not to think too much about it. I waited the designated three-month mourning period and then did all the stuff the newly divorced are supposed to do. I signed up for JDate. I signed up for Match.com. I put a personal ad in the Chicago alternative newspaper. I told all my friends that I was officially on the market and available for appropriate fix-ups. I started making eye contact at parties. And as I began to get through the e-mail communications and phone calls, I started actively dating.

It wasn't so bad in the beginning. After all, the one thing that all of those dating opportunities provide are a lot of first dates. I went on more first dates in those first few months back on the scene than I will probably ever go on for the rest of my life. At least I certainly hope so. I dated nice guys, assholes, sweethearts, and liars. I dated short guys, tall guys, thin guys, and heavy guys. Bald, befurred, intellectual, gray-matter challenged, testosterone driven, and a couple who I am quite certain are gay, even if they don't want to admit it. I dated fascinating guys, boring guys, and guys with ADD. Potheads, alcoholics, and teetotalers. Liberals, conservatives, and nonvoters. Lots of Jews, several Christians, a couple of reformed Catholics, one Buddhist, one cantor, and a pastor. White guys, African-Americans, Latinos. For six months, I dated everyone.

Well, almost everyone.

Here's who I did not date: anyone who was remotely attractive to me in a sexual way.

Now, I have a terrible habit of wishing for things so hard that I directly affect the movements of the universe. Here is an example: I got divorced in September. By October, the frigid Chicago winds began to blow, and I began to worry about the snow. For I was a girl who had gotten very used to having my own resident shoveler in the household. Eleven years, I never had to worry about slipping on the stairs or digging out my car or finding a clear parking space. My ex was actually one of those sick guys who loved to shovel, it made him feel strong and manly, and I wasn't one to argue. I was in charge of hot chocolate with extra marshmallows, and that suited me fine. When I thought about the coming winter, I had a feeling of dread deep in my bones. That led to the fervent wishing and hoping and praying for a winter without snow. And that winter, drumroll please, turned out to be one of the lightest years for us, snow-wise, that we had ever seen. I only had to shovel twice.

Twice. In *Chicago.* I single-handedly broke the weather.

So when I realized that none of the guys I was having my endless first dates with were making it to a second date, let alone a third date, whereby I might have to deal with the ubiquitous third-date rule, I realized that perhaps my powers of wishing had backfired. I was subconsciously hoping to not have to deal with sex, and therefore the universe had only sent me guys I wouldn't want to sleep with. I realized that I was scared about what would be essentially another first time. I was revirginized. At thirty-one. What a pain in my abundant tushie!

I started trying to think happy thoughts about sex. After all, I loved sex, at least what I remembered of it. I tried to put positive sex images into the ether. I watched romantic comedies. I meditated on my classic celebrity crushes and read Colette for sensual inspiration. Thinking perhaps that the fault rested in my bed itself, once the marital resting place, I bought a new mattress and box spring, threw out all my pillows and linens, and created a bed worthy of romping upon with no residual husband aura.

I figured it had started to work when I got reconnected to a friend of a friend. We'd met a couple of times and always had pleasant exchanges. I'd always found him attractive, but I was a married woman back then. Not anymore. To my delight, he noticed my lack of a ring, and we began a careful and slow courtship. He understood my need to build some trust before jumping into bed. I abandoned the third-date rule and ended up accidentally creating the third-month rule. He was patient. He wooed me. We talked on the phone and e-mailed like mad. We held hands and kissed for long stretches on my couch. We laughed and joked and ate and drank and eventually we went to bed together. He was very sensitive to my situation, and it was fine. No fireworks, but fine. Until he fell asleep and I had an attack of the regrets, which gave me gastric distress to a degree that sent me to the couch to watch infomercials all night while he snored in my bed. A few days later, having run out of excuses to avoid him, I finally confessed that I probably still wasn't ready, and we agreed to go back to just being friends. Luckily, that worked and we stayed happily in touch.

My girlfriends told me I had waited too long, invested too much, put too much pressure on myself and on him. That third-date rule was there for a reason. It was strongly recommended that I get back in the saddle sooner rather than later. I went back to dating. Then, in an instant message on one of my online sites, I was approached by a man who I recognized as someone who worked with a couple of acquaintances of mine. We began a lovely communication, purely e-mail and phone, as he was out of town for a few months working. It was fun. And we made plans to get together on his return. We met for a drink. I wasn't really attracted to him, but I didn't find him repulsive, so when he kissed me, I let him. And when he invited himself over, I let him. And when he wanted to go to bed, I couldn't think of a good reason not to. So I let him. It was fine. No fireworks, but fine. Only not so fine that I was eager to let it happen again. He agreed that we shouldn't pursue anything further and should go back to being friends. We never spoke again.

My girlfriends told me that not being repulsed isn't the same as being attracted and that it would probably be better to try and think of reasons *to* sleep with someone in those situations. And that long phone calls didn't count as dates, and was I really not listening to them on the whole third-*date* rule business? I need to go out with someone three times, *then* sleep with him. How hard is that? They also said that I should find something that could be fun and no pressure. Okay. Fun and no pressure.

It was around then that a trainer at my gym caught my eye and my funny bone. A sweet, cute guy, with one of the best bodies I had ever seen, he was also smart and quick-witted and made me laugh. We had a casual at-the-gym-kibitzing friendship, and I never considered him for dating. But one day, when he was filling in for my regular trainer, he asked if I wanted to hang out sometime. I thought about it for a minute. He was younger than I by a few years, but I enjoyed his company and I did find him attractive.

Okay, he had a fifty-two-inch chest and a thirty-inch waist and gen-u-ine six-pack abs and an ass like a peach. I mean c'mon. Like I'm gonna pass that up.

Besides, he seemed like he fit the profile. Fun. No pressure. I said yes. We hung out a couple of times, watched movies or went out to a bar, and finally, *on the third date,* we slept together. It was fine. No fireworks, but it was fun. There was certainly no pressure. It lasted a couple of months, but I was bored and had to end it, which didn't sit as well as I would have hoped. Apparently a desire to date someone who didn't have three roommates and did have a car was shallow. My belief that a date could involve food that didn't come in cardboard containers and a movie in a theater instead of on DVD made me materialistic. I sort of regretted the whole thing. We agreed to stay friends and fell into a "here's the highlights of my life" e-mail every once in a great long while.

This wasn't working. I was back in the dating business, but it wasn't really going according to plan. I'd figured out how to go to bed with someone, just not someone who was really good for a decent relationship.

I needed help.

I needed to go back to the source. The guru. Judy Blume.

And the bible, *Forever.*

I remembered Katherine's dilemmas from *Forever.* First, she didn't know if she was ready to sleep with her boyfriend Michael and to take on the responsibility of a sexual relationship. Then she didn't know if sex had become the defining element of their relationship or if there was enough beneath it to maintain a relationship when they left for college. Then she met someone new who she was drawn to and had to decide whether she should move on without Michael and pursue the new guy.

Why was I feeling so connected to a fictional seventeen-year-old when all my actual thirty-something girlfriends were supporting me? I thought it was because they had all dated in their twenties. I thought it was because of my long stint of celibacy. I realized it was because Kat wasn't going to actually give me specific advice and then berate me for how I chose to interpret it. Kat could only lead by example. Her tale of love and loss could only be a parable for me to glean what I needed—she was a silent partner. And she wasn't going to say one frigging word about third dates, that was certain.

I returned to the text. Before Kat gives up her virginity, her mother, fearful that she and Michael are becoming too close, gives her an article about sexuality. In the article are four key questions a person should ask herself before moving into a sexual relationship:

1. Is sexual intercourse necessary to the relationship?
2. What should you expect from sexual intercourse?

3. Have you thought about how the relationship will end?
4. If you should need help, where will you seek it?

I thought about my own recent experiences. I thought about the questions.

1. Is sexual intercourse necessary to the relationship?

Well, I had a great time with all three guys in the initial stages, but the sex didn't really add anything to the bond we had created. We were definitely better before the sex in all cases.

2. What should you expect from sexual intercourse?

I'd always had fairly high expectations of sex, and in none of these cases had I been blown away. Maybe I needed to stop thinking that it was going to be fireworks right out of the gate. I know that I didn't give either of the first two guys a real chance to become anything more than a one-night stand.

3. Have you thought about how the relationship will end?

I'd never thought about the endings in any of the situations. But if I had stopped to consider the likely ending of each connection based on what I knew of them and of myself, I probably only would have slept with bachelor number one. After all, I didn't know the second guy well enough to even anticipate what would happen, and I knew from the get-go that I would probably not be able to go the distance with a younger man.

4. If you should need help, where will you seek it?

At least this one I knew. My girlfriends. My stiletto-wearing, cosmo-drinking, third-date-rule-following, Judy Blume–reading girlfriends. My endless source of support, advice, encouragement, and wisdom. The first place I could always turn for the answers I couldn't find on my own.

And, of course, to Judy. Who, even thirty years later, still has more insight into the nature of relationships than Dr. Phil any day.

I won't say that this triumvirate of "first times" were the last mistakes I would ever make. In fact, I'm quite certain I am far from the end of my mistake-making days where men and sex are concerned.

But I know one thing.

I'm far more likely to recognize Forever when it arrives.

———

Stacey Ballis lives in Chicago and currently doesn't own a single pair of leg warmers. She does, however, own a copy of the movie Xanadu, *so her recovery from the 1980s is not quite as complete as doctors might have hoped. She is the author of* Inappropriate Men, Sleeping Over, Room for Improvement, *and* The Spinster Sisters. *She continues to struggle daily with the management of her hair.*

THEN AGAIN, MAYBE I...

| Melissa Senate |

The summer I turned twelve was the "summer of Sam": 1977 in New York City. We lived in Flushing, Queens, where David Berkowitz, aka the Son of Sam, was on a murderous rampage.

"He's shooting girls with dark hair!" the kids in my sixth-grade class yelped in those final days of school, looking around with dropped jaws at the brunettes. At me, for instance.

And so that crazy summer, my mother gave her boyfriend—a well-to-do businessman who for some reason (it might have been love) fell for a welfare mother of three with no child support from their dad, who hadn't been seen or heard from in a few years—an ultimatum. Which was: *Marry me or it's over. My kids need a father. And we have to get out of here.*

We did have to get out. Son of Sam aside, at every sighting of me, the apartment building bully, a skinny kid named Mike, had begun yelling, "Melissa's growing titties! Melissa's growing titties!" Mortified, I walked with my arms crossed over my chest, until my friend Leslie pointed out that (a) it was true and (b) it was a good thing.

My mother's boyfriend, who slept on the pull-out couch every Saturday night, wasn't so sure he was cut out to be a father. "I'll put you up in an apartment in Manhattan!" he pleaded.

"It's marriage or nothing!" my mother insisted.

He chose marriage over nothing. The actual marriage would have to wait, though, since my father was God knows where and therefore not available to sign anything, like divorce papers.

While my sister (then fourteen), my brother (then ten), and I were sent to sleepaway camp for a few weeks, my mother and her fiancé went house hunting in the suburbs of New Jersey. One day at camp (Jewish Federation in the Catskills), instead of making macramé bracelets or inadvertently squishing slugs on hikes up Bald Mountain, it was deemed Holocaust Remembrance Day, which was really in April. (The Powers That Be at camp also pushed the clocks ahead an hour to give us an extra hour of daylight, so we were used to altered reality.)

We lined up single file in front of a tent and were told to go in one by one. "What is it?" we asked the kids who came out. There were shrugs. There were solemn expressions. There were awed expressions. But no one was talking.

I went in. The tent was completely empty except for something hanging at eye level, covered by a black sheet. A sign above it read: *Lift the sheet.* I lifted. It was a mirror. Along the bottom of the mirror was another sign: *You are a survivor of the Holocaust.*

I freaked out and ran screaming from the room. I couldn't handle being a survivor of the Holocaust on top of everything else going on in my life. I didn't want my mother to marry her boyfriend, who didn't think he was cut out to be a father. I was confused by my own father's disappearance from our lives, which I knew involved another woman who was pregnant with his baby. And I was scared at the idea of moving to some strange town in New Jersey. I was scared, period. And since the Son of Sam had been caught weeks ago, couldn't we just *not* move?

No. We were moving. Camp was all I had, a vaguely familiar stopover between my old life and the new one, and now even camp had pulled a fast one on me.

I broke down, screaming and sobbing. Once my counselor got the whole story, I was excused from whatever activity was next and treated to extra cookies that night at Snack. Any kid who'd ever moved, who'd ever dealt with divorce, who'd ever had a stepparent, was urged to tell me it would all be okay. I mostly got long-winded stories about how it wasn't okay. But talking helped. And in those last days at camp, someone—and I have absolutely no recollection who—gave me a book to read. It was *Then Again, Maybe I Won't* by Judy Blume, the only Judy Blume novel I *hadn't* read—because it was about a boy. I'd heard about the book, famous among kids everywhere for the main character's wet dreams and penchant for using his binoculars to stare through his teenaged neighbor's window. "Read it," I remember being told. "It's about a twelve-year-old named Tony Miglione who has to deal with a lot of stuff when his family moves."

So I read it. And reread it. By the time my mother and her fiancé picked me and my siblings up from camp and drove us to a split-level house in Fair Lawn, New Jersey, an upper-middle-class suburb twelve miles but light-years away from Flushing, Queens, I had a context for imagining my new life, which had some remarkable similarities to Tony Miglione's.

And context helped. Overnight I had a new almost-stepfather, a new town, a new home, a new school, a new lifestyle, a new body (thanks to puberty), and confusing new thoughts, which included: Will I ever see my father again? My paternal grandparents? My old friends? The me I was before? But I had no idea what to expect, what to even imagine. What I did have was Tony, who knew how to handle things. Well, *sort of* knew how to handle things, since there was the matter of his shooting stomach pains, for which he was ultimately prescribed a shrink.

The similarities:

Tony: At age twelve, he moves from a cramped two-family house in streety Jersey (aka "Joisy") City, New Jersey, to a hoity toity suburb when his dad strikes it rich.

Me: At twelve, my family moves from a cramped two-bedroom apartment with orange carpeting, peeling linoleum, and fire escapes to a nice house with a finished basement and a yard and impatients lining the hedges. There is no more welfare. No more food stamps. No more need to stand on long lines in government offices to prove that we exist so that my mother can receive assistance. My mother no longer has to work a minimum-wage job. There is no more after-school daycare. My brother gets his own room because he's a boy. My sister and I share. We cannot agree on rock star posters and therefore put up none.

Tony: He worries about fitting in and making friends, but a boy his age lives next door. They have a pool. This is the first time Tony has seen a pool in anyone's yard.

Me: The same, except the next-door neighbor is a girl named Carol. She's exactly my age. My mother pushes me to knock on their door. I'm welcomed up to Carol's room. She's pretty and nice and has long brown hair with perfect Farrah Fawcett wings. I can see the outline of a bra through her tank top. I haven't yet gone shopping for a training bra, so Carol is in the know. I want to be her friend, but she gives me a test and I fail.

"What kind of music do you like?" she asks.

"Olivia Newton-John and John Denver," I tell her. I see from her expression that I've said the wrong thing. She likes Aerosmith. Heart.

"I like KC and the Sunshine Band, too," I tell her hopefully, but it's too late. In the six years that I live next door to Carol, I'm never invited to swim in the pool. In fact, in those six years, I see her only twice in passing.

"Just wait till school starts," my sister tells me. "You'll make your own friends. Don't worry. I'm sure there are other girls who like Olivia Newton-John," she adds. And then I'm pretty sure she added a "yeah right!" when she thought I wasn't listening.

My mother's fiancé, whose name is Neil, by the way, is exceptionally generous, even if he doesn't think he's cut out to be a father (which he's not, also by the way). Labor Day weekend, the entire family piles into the car (something we never had in Flushing) and heads to the mall for a back-to-school shopping trip at Bamberger's, compliments of Neil's credit card, something my mother also never had before. I am let loose in the junior department. I have no idea what I'm doing. My sixth-grade wardrobe consisted of hand-me-down nylon shirts and blue corduroy pants, and I can't recall ever being aware of what I wore. I bring what I see the most of into the fitting rooms, like gauchos. And bras, size 32 double A, which I don't yet need, but which seventh-grade gym class requires.

"Look who's getting underarm hair!" my mother shouts out as I raise my arms over my head to test the fit of my new bra the way *Teen* magazine said you should.

"Mom!" I yelp, slamming my arms against my sides. But I'm pleased that she noticed. My mother has been applying to the local community college as a freshman. She's been busy furniture shopping. Changing kitchen wallpaper. Planting bulbs in the garden. I like the sudden attention.

That Sunday, I get my period for the first time as I'm trying on my new gauchos, which I've decided on for the first day of school.

"Don't tell anyone!" I order my mother.

"Guess who got her period!" I hear her telling Neil later. I also hear her telling my grandmother on the phone. I'm sure people can tell anyway, which makes me embarrassed to leave the house, but Tony's got it worse. He gets unexpected erections while solving math problems on the blackboard and can't turn around without using his textbook as a shield. At least I don't have to worry about that.

My brother and sister and I are each attending different schools. My brother is in sixth grade at the elementary school. I'm starting seventh at the junior high. My sister is starting high school. I'm a nervous wreck about going to junior high all alone on the first day, so my mother arranges for me to meet up with two older girls, eighth graders. I wait on my corner. Five minutes. Ten minutes. They never show (there's never an explanation). I fly down Saddle River Road on my new bike with its rainbow stripes to my brand-new school, which is smaller than my elementary school but nonetheless scary as hell. As I lock up my bike, I'm immediately the subject of a point and giggle. I'm not sure if it's the rainbow stripes on my baby blue bike or the green gauchos.

Tony's first day goes a lot better. He makes a few good friends right away, which gives me hope. During the first week of seventh grade, a popular girl named Laurie invites me to her house after school. We walk home with her friends, who walk ahead or behind us. They eye my gauchos (I have them in three colors, all corduroy) and give Laurie "stop being so nice to strays" type looks. Inside her house, we have absolutely nothing to talk about after "So how do you like it here?" We talk about her cat. My cat. I have no idea how to do this, what we're supposed to talk about. It's finally time to go home, where I throw up from nerves. My tryout for the popular club is over and I didn't make the cut. This is where having an MIA father comes in handy. What slight could ever hurt as bad?

I do make one friend, though. A very good one. Her name is Cara. Every day after school, we go to her house (hers because she has her own room). We spend our after-school hours listening to Elton John and Bruce Springsteen (Carol would approve). We memorize the words to *Stairway to Heaven* and sing it at the top of our lungs. We have everything to talk about, from boys to our bodies to our classmates to our families. Cara also has a stepfather. Her own father lives with another family in Fair Lawn; they have a daughter our same age who goes to our school. I am blown away by this. It's almost as strange to me as my own situation, my MIA father. I wonder whose situation is stranger: mine or Cara's.

My stepfather tells me and my siblings not to talk about our family business, which he considers private, like the fact that he and my mother are not yet married. Or that he's not my father. Or that my father is somewhere in the world, probably twenty miles away, living with another family, like Cara's dad. I'm not sure if Neil thinks people will talk or if he's just a private person.

Much, much, later, I'll read somewhere that our stories are our own, but at twelve, I didn't know. And I was dutiful. I didn't use the word "stepfather." I didn't talk about my absent father, who I wondered about constantly. *I have a father somewhere*, I wanted to scream in the front yard. *Just because he's not here doesn't mean he doesn't exist!*

My grandmother, my mother's mother, says during every visit, "You are all so lucky! Neil is a wonderful man! He took you out of the gutter. You should be grateful. Are you grateful?"

It's hard to learn that your story is your own when important people in your life are telling you what your story needs to be.

I said I was grateful.

I reread *Then Again, Maybe I Won't*. Tony's struggling with this, too, with being "silenced." The "perfect" boy next door, a rich kid foisted on Tony by his social-climbing mother, shoplifts, which Tony can't understand and can't talk about to anyone. Tony's older brother has "sold out" from teaching school to joining the corporate world. His mother allows her snooty neighbor to call her Carol instead of Carmella because "Carol is easier to remember." And his grandmother, who literally cannot speak (her larynx was removed during surgery) and who only communicated through cooking for the family, is banished from the kitchen to suit the new rude housekeeper.

Here, there are differences between me and Tony. But the conflict is the same. I keep it in. So does Tony. Until he finally explodes and is told to shut up. All that shutting up causes debilitating stomach pains that land him in the hospital. The cure: a therapist. Tony talks. The pains go away.

I don't talk. Instead of telling my almost-stepfather that it's my right to tell people what I want about my own self, I say nothing. Tony is not someone who says nothing. He tries so hard to hang onto himself as he was, as he *is* throughout *Then Again, Maybe I Won't*. It comforts me. But I don't know how to do it, if I'm doing it, if I'm still me.

My first major crush obliterates most other thoughts whirling through my head, which leads to the next big similarity between me and Tony (as well as a similarity for every adolescent in the world): Tony develops a major crush on his neighbor's sixteen-year-old sister, whose window he can peep into with the binoculars he gets for his thirteenth birthday (his parents are so clueless that they actually believe he wants the binoculars for his new hobby, bird-watching). The sixteen-year-old is nice enough to him but of course not remotely aware of him as anything other than her little brother's little friend. Tony is busily lusting, busily having his first erection, his first wet dream.

My crush is a seventh grader like me, but not in any of my classes. His name is Rob and his last name rhymes with Miglione. Only the first letter is different. I see this as even more reason that we belong together. I am crazy about this boy despite never having said a word to him. He is a slender, dark-haired, dark-eyed boy who has captivated me on sight. I once heard the sound of his voice and spent hours closing my eyes to hear it again.

A girl named Amy who has a few classes with Rob offers to ask him if he likes me. I say yes because I'm twelve, and this is what twelve-year-olds do, as evidenced by the girl in Tony's class (Corky) who is madly in love with him and goes to embarrassing lengths to show it. To Tony, she barely qualifies as a nuisance. That's how little she registers on his radar as a girl. It was important to know that you can, like Corky, love a boy with all your might, and that said boy will not even think of you for a single second of the day, even if you do everything in your twelve-year-old power to get him to notice you. I understand this when Amy reports back that Rob's answer was *no*.

I walk around the halls, my heart bursting with something I'm not allowed to talk about. In the cafeteria I see Cara at our table and I break down in sobs like I did on fake Holocaust Remembrance Day.

"I'm really sorry about Rob," Cara says, squeezing my hand in the girls' bathroom.

And then finally, I say it. "No boy is ever going to like me. My own father doesn't even love me."

"You don't know that," Cara says. "I'm sure your father still loves you. He just can't deal or something."

It feels good to talk. It feels good to know that my story is my own, even if I'm pretty sure I will never see my father again, never hear from him again, as though he never existed at all, like the old me. (I turn out to be right about this, by the way.)

Then Again, Maybe I Won't said in black and white and gray areas that you can hold on to who you are even when your life is turned upside down and then sticks sideways. I did that without realizing it at the time, and it's thanks to Tony. It's thanks to Judy Blume.

———

Melissa Senate is the author of several novels for adults and teens, including the best-selling See Jane Date, *which was made into a TV movie. A former book editor, Melissa writes full-time from her home on the coast of Maine. FYI: Those corduroy gauchos are in a "what were you thinking?" box in the attic along with some other seventies gems, but her copy of* Then Again, Maybe I Won't *remains front and center on her bookshelf.*

Vitamin K, Judy Blume, and the Great Big Bruise

| *Julie Kenner* |

When I look back over the course of my life (not that it has been so very long so far, mind you), three important influences shine crystal bright as if from a beacon: my family, my friends, and the books I read in my youth. Their individual influences ebb and flow, sometimes my family taking precedence, sometimes friends, and sometimes books, mixing like currents in a river so that I'm never quite sure what had the greater impact on me or why; I only feel the influences pulling me along and holding me up.

On occasion, though, I *can* see as well as feel the effect of these influences, and it's interesting to stand back, almost as an observer in your own life, and say, "Yes, this I owe to the books I read or the family I love or the friends I hold dear."

With regard to the books I write, for example, I owe a huge debt to writers such as Edward Eager, E. Nesbit, and Madeleine L'Engle, who brought magic into my world and made it real. Their work has influenced my own work in so many ways that it would probably be impossible for anyone except a graduate student to analyze and decipher (assuming any graduate student felt inclined to study my books). The positive influence of those books represents a huge debt that I can only hope to pay forward.

But it's to another writer that I owe an even larger debt. Judy Blume. To her I owe not only the intangible imprint that surely paints my own craft but something even more dear: my health, my self-respect, and my confidence in my own imagination and intelligence.

Sounds lofty, doesn't it? But it's true. At the time, I never thought, *Wow, these Judy Blume books sure are keeping me grounded.* But that was in fact the case.

It started simply enough during the summer after my freshman year of high school with a bruise and William Shakespeare. I was fourteen. The bruise was on my thigh, and the play was *A Midsummer Night's Dream.* Appropriate, I think, since so much of what happened seemed to be like wading through a dream (not a good dream, mind you, but a dream nonetheless).

All these years later, I don't remember what my exact involvement was with the play other than that I was a crew member and that I was required to slink along the various levels and crawl over and under the stage in order to place and retrieve an assortment of props. I used to fantasize à la Sally J. Freedman that one of the actors would drop out or lose her voice, and the director would be in a tizzy, wondering who could take over. And since I had been there through all the rehearsals and have an excellent memory, I would stand up and say, "I can do it."

The director, of course, would be concerned. I was (and am)

shy, and that was certainly no secret. But since she had no other choice, she would give me the part. And I, of course, would overcome my fear and excel, garnering rave reviews and being discovered by a Hollywood agent, who would whisk me away to become the Next Great Star. In the process, that pesky shyness would vanish. Life would be grand.

In case you're wondering, this never happened. But the fantasies never stopped. I'd been living in a fantasy world all my life, and I can remember being thrilled when I read *Starring Sally J. Freedman As Herself*. There was a girl like me, despite the different era and the different cultures. Judy Blume and Sally J. gave me permission to lose myself in those fantasies, and I have been doing just that ever since.

During my freshman summer, though, I was limited to that one Hollywood fantasy. I was too busy listening for cues and doing my stage job to lose myself any more deeply in my imagination. Not at first, anyway.

The summer play was being rehearsed and performed in an outdoor venue in Austin, Texas. That means, to anyone not familiar with central Texas, that I spent my time sweating in shorts and tank tops, thankful that I was on the crew and not one of the actors forced to wear yards and yards of thick muslin, tights, and velvet.

One day, after slinking and crawling around the set, a friend noticed a bruise on my thigh. I didn't think much about it—I'd been banging around the stage—and went on about my life. (Later, when I reread *Deenie* after knowing the true cause of those bruises, the similarity struck me: Deenie had been told her posture was "off" by the modeling agency, but that hardly caused a life revelation, as she seemed perfectly normal.)

A few days later, the bruise was larger, and there were others. Each had a hard spot underneath, and the original bruise had expanded to about the size of a baseball. It even protruded somewhat from my skin. Frankly, I looked a bit as if one of those tennis ball–serving machines had spewed forth hundreds of balls, each whacking me on my thighs and calves and occasionally on my arms. I was a mess. And when my friends began to express worry, I realized that I was also scared.

I did what I always did when thrust into a scary situation—I fantasized my way through it. This time, though, the scary situation seemed more real. I wasn't faced with giving an oration in front of twenty-five people or even auditioning for the school play. This time, I was faced with a body I didn't understand, doing things that didn't make sense. Bruises, I knew, were supposed to appear after you banged against something. They weren't supposed to appear out of nowhere. Something was wrong, and I distinctly remember turning for comfort to my own imagination and the familiar friends who lived in my books.

I think I reread every Judy Blume novel on my bright yellow bookcase over the next few days, but the Blume character who gave me the most comfort was Sally J. I'd first read the book several years before, and though I'd moved on to much more complicated texts (that summer, I was reading several of Shakespeare's plays along with *Crime and Punishment* and several Edith Hamilton books on mythology), *Starring Sally J. Freedman As Herself* drew me in, giving me permission to lose myself in possible scenarios about the odd things going on with my body. Sally J. was a friend; we understood each other. And when my fantasies started turning dark with thoughts of mysterious illnesses that would

erase my life, I knew that she (whose happy fantasies had ultimately been tainted by the horror of the Holocaust) would understand.

Like Sally J., I made up scenarios in my head. And my friends
helped me act them out. In our case, though, we acted them out in
reality, casting ourselves as brilliant doctors with a mysterious case
to solve. (My mother has always been physician-phobic, and while
she was aware that my legs were somewhat bruised, I was careful to
not let her see the full extent. Stupid? Yes. But I had the foolish
confidence of youth and was certain that I could solve this mystery,
both in real life and in my fantasies.)

With my friends Kathy and Cindy at my side, we traipsed to the
library and hauled down medical texts, reading about blood and
bruises, and ultimately deciding that my blood wasn't clotting properly. This was, in fact, correct, but our self-prescribed treatment—
vitamin K as recommended by the skinny college-aged kid at the
original Whole Foods Market on Lamar Boulevard—was both foolish and naive. And not just in retrospect; I knew it at the time. But
I was a scared kid, determined that my fantasies would become reality. I should have known better. Sally J. had to live in the real
world despite her fantasies, and so did I.

That lesson came more swiftly than I would have liked, simply
because the largest of the bruises kept on expanding. What had
once been as large as a baseball was now the size of a Texas grape-
fruit. My theater friends—who saw me in nothing but shorts—
were concerned. *I* was concerned. And I knew I couldn't hide it
from my mom any longer. Suddenly, I found myself in the doctor's
office, faced with scary words like "specialist" and "hematologist."

Words that were all the more scary, since I knew my mom's tendency to hold out going to the doctor until the last possible minute. Clearly, I must have hit that minute.

Something, I knew, was wrong with me. I just didn't know what. And in the days before my appointment with the hematologist, I remember pulling down *Deenie*. I'd read the book several times before and loved it. But I can't say that I'd ever fully empathized with Deenie.

Now, though, I did. And I wanted the comfort of reading about someone else who'd looked into the dark unknown of a medical issue and come out of it okay. I spent hours curled up on the couch, ignoring schoolwork and taking comfort in Deenie's nervousness when she knows that she has to go see the doctor but hasn't yet had the appointment. And, yes, I took comfort in knowing that she was cured by wearing a brace. She wasn't going to die; she just needed a treatment. So there I sat, miles and years and pages away from my friend Deenie, and hoped for a simple prescription. Five pills, I thought, and I'd be fine.

Needless to say, I wasn't blessed with my hoped-for outcome. Instead, I ended up undergoing a painful medical test and then being at the mercy of a doctor who apparently believed that a young girl had no brains whatsoever since he essentially avoided my questions (like Deenie's doctor often did) or patronized me (like Deenie's doctor often did).

What in fact happened was a very long wait in the waiting room followed by an even longer wait in the examining room. Between the two waits, a nurse drew my blood. After the second wait, a distracted doctor came in, examined me without talking, pulled my mother into the hall, and then returned to tell me to pull my jeans down and lie on my stomach. I wanted to ask my mom what was going on, but she looked too scared, and the doctor himself was too scary.

So I did as I was told. And about ten minutes later, my backside had been numbed by a local anesthesia and a needle was sliding down through my body, through my bone, and into my marrow (which, thank you very much, was not at all affected by the anesthesia). The whole thing hurt like hell, and I cried and cried, empathy for Deenie growing and growing as I remembered her mortification at being fitted for her brace and my own disgust that no one would tell her what was going on.

No one told me what was going on, either, at least not until the test results came back. Here, my memory fails. It may have been weeks that I waited. It might only have been minutes. To me, it seemed a lifetime. But when the results did come back, my mother was called out of the room and given the news, and the relief in her eyes when she returned told me plenty.

The fear, I learned later, was that I had leukemia. The bone marrow test confirmed that I didn't have cancer, and after a few more tests, my significantly-less-than-verbose doctor rendered his diagnosis: idiopathic thrombocytopenia purpura.

And that is? I asked.

A blood disorder, I was told.

Not exactly the wealth of information I was looking for, and so, like Deenie investigating her own scoliosis, I went on an information hunt of my own. In today's world, this would be no problem. Back then, that meant schlepping to the main branch of the public library and the science library at the University of Texas, then poring through books and trying to understand the medical lingo. Ultimately—through a combination of my own research, questions to the nurse, and specific questions to the doctor fed through my mom—I learned that my ITP was an autoimmune disorder in which my own body made antibodies against my platelets, essentially attacking them. The cause was unknown, thus the term "idiopathic." I learned that the disorder was chronic, that it might go away when I got older, that it was the result of my body filtering out my antibody-covered platelets through my spleen, that platelets are what makes your blood clot, and that the bruises on my legs were blood clots that had formed very, very slowly, having to rely on my minimal supply of platelets to do the work normally done by a whole crew of the little guys. Worst of all, I learned that without treatment, I could hemorrhage. Possibly to death. Since that didn't sound good, I welcomed whatever treatment came my way.

Like Deenie, I had some answers. And like her, I wasn't crazy about them, but I was happy to finally be informed.

I still hoped that the treatment would be a simple shot or prescription. I also remember thinking about the book and about the brace Deenie had to wear. I hated wearing braces on my teeth, so I was glad my illness was in my blood. Surely no one at my school would see that I was ill. Like Deenie, I first anticipated that I could keep everything a secret. After all, when the prescription made my bruises go away, all the evidence would be hidden. (In point of fact, it took over a year for the largest clot to dissipate and fade.)

Again, though, it turned out that I had more in common with my literary friend than I'd anticipated. My prescription was for massive doses of prednisone taken over a long period of time (years, it turned out, since my ITP did not correct itself quickly as happens in many cases). And since my less-than-verbose doctor didn't warn me or my mother about the side effects of the drug (especially in such large doses), I didn't expect the acne that popped up on my face and back. I didn't expect my periods to stop. I didn't expect to develop cataracts or have to guzzle Mylanta at the ripe old age of fourteen. And most of all, I didn't anticipate the effects of salt. My face soon ballooned to the point where I was unrecognizable. Simply a round, doughy Pillsbury girl. And if you think that is fun in high school, please think again.

Like Deenie, I hated the way I looked. Unlike Deenie, I couldn't have taken off my doughy, round face under any circumstances. I was still me, though, and I told myself that my friends wouldn't care. Deenie had learned that, right? When she'd decided to keep her brace on at the party instead of changing into the cute outfit she'd brought with her, she was trusting her friends to be there for *her.* And her trust paid off.

I held that literary reality close to my heart, and, in fact, it came true. My friends were nothing but supportive. And while they will now tease me about my chipmunk cheek days (my face is back to its angular lines and has been for years), never once did they say a mean word during our school years. Even better, they were quick to come to my defense against any moron who did make fun.

I took the medicine for years, finally successfully tapering off without my platelet count dropping during my first semester of college at seventeen. Those years in between were hard, but I had Sally J. and Deenie and my nonliterary friends and my family helping me through. Once I was used to the meds, I slipped back into fantasy again, becoming a world-famous scientist and solving the mystery of the "idiopathic" part of my illness. I made up wild causes and fantasized that my blood had special properties that aliens wanted, and that in order to save the world, I had to save myself from the invaders. In other words, I took a page from Deenie and Sally J.'s books and turned an unpleasant situation on its ear, entertaining myself with fantasies spun from my own medical misfortune.

When the doctor did tell me I was done with the meds, I thought of Deenie again. She ultimately left her brace behind, too. As far as I know, Deenie got to leave hers behind permanently. My illness came back with a vengeance after my first semester in law school. I had no bruising this time, so I wasn't expecting it; I'd simply gone in for a routine check. As it turns out, I had essentially no platelets. My blood wasn't just clotting too slowly, it wasn't clotting at all.

This time, the treatment was surgical—removal of my spleen (and, therefore, the major component of my immune system, which was doing such an excellent job of filtering out all those misplaced antibodies and the platelets to which they were attached). And because the situation was apparently so serious, my doctor insisted I go to the hospital right after our appointment. I begged for him to let me take my civil procedure final exam first, which happened to be scheduled for the next day. And so I went from sitting for an exam to lying on an operating table.

At that point in my life, my head was more filled with personal jurisdiction than with my childhood literary friends, but Deenie and Sally J. were still with me. I know because, following Deenie's lead, in that short period (and instead of studying for my exam) I looked up everything I could about the surgery. And in the style of Sally J., I spent the week of recovery in the hospital making up complex stories in my head. Stories that always starred myself.

I'm happy to report that the spleenectomy "cured" me. I no longer have a decent immune system, and my body still makes antibodies against my own platelets. But since my spleen isn't there to filter them out, the little platelet guys still do their job, albeit with antibodies clinging tenaciously to them.

It is possible that other organs will take up the slack left by my spleen's absence, but it's been years, and so far that hasn't happened. We did hold our breath when I was pregnant, since pregnancy can, in fact, induce a temporary case of ITP.

I was fortunate, however, and sailed through the pregnancy just fine. My platelets were monitored, and so were my daughter's. She's now four and shows no sign of having inherited her mommy's misguided immune system.

I know, however, that since it is idiopathic, it could show up in her, and I tend to freak a little when I see bruises on her legs. Our wonderful pediatrician understands and gently reminds me that kids bump into things and get bruises. And even while he reminds me of that, he keeps his eyes open for any unusual bruising and performs a platelet test if something seems amiss.

I hope and pray that she never has to face any sort of unpleasant medical situation. For that matter, I hope and pray that she never has to face anything hard in life. But, like a fourteen-year-old self-prescribing vitamin K, I know that is naive and unlikely. And, truthfully, it's not really what I want for her. Hard situations help us to grow, and I know she can make it through anything. Why wouldn't she? After all, she's got her family, and as she grows, she will have more and more friends. And, you can be sure, once she's old enough to read and understand, I'll make sure that my daughter has literary friends like Sally J. and Deenie to help her along the journey.

National best-selling author Julie Kenner's first book hit the stores in February 2000, and she's been on the go ever since, with more than twenty books to her credit. Her books have won numerous awards and have hit best-seller lists as varied as USA Today, Waldenbooks, Barnes & Noble, *and* Locus *magazine. She writes a range of stories from sexy and quirky romances to chick-lit suspense* (The Givenchy Code) *to paranormal mommy lit* (Carpe Demon). *Her first young adult novel—*The Good Ghoul's Guide to Getting Even*—was released in spring 2007. Visit Julie on the Web at www.juliekenner.com.*

IT WASN'T THE END OF THE WORLD

| *Kristin Harmel* |

When I read It's Not the End of the World *for the first time,* I was in the fourth grade. *Poor Karen Newman,* I thought. Sure, she was lucky because she was already in sixth grade (and everyone knew that the sixth graders ruled the elementary school), but her parents were getting a divorce! I didn't know anyone whose parents were divorced. *How awful,* I thought. But it would never happen to me.

Sure, my mom and dad fought a lot. Dad would work late; he'd come home and only half listen to the things we had to say; my parents would snap at each other, and I'd go watch *Mr. Ed* or *Get Smart* reruns on Nick at Nite and try to tune them out. Sometimes they would take it out on me, and I'd fill my diary with things like, "I think Dad hates me," or, "Mom yelled at me for no reason." But then we'd go on a family trip to Disney World or to see my grandparents in Massachusetts, my parents would both smile at my brother, sister, and me, and I knew everything was fine.

Poor Karen Newman. But *my* parents would never get a divorce, I remember thinking confidently as I read about Karen's parents splitting up. After all, my mom had never thrown a mocha cake on the floor just because my dad complained about the icing. My dad would never yell at my mom because my sister spilled some milk. My mom had never screamed at my dad for getting home too late for dinnertime, even though they never really talked to each other and often seemed to dislike being in the same room. So, they must be happy, right?

The summer after fourth grade, we moved to Florida. That's where Karen Newman's family was going to move at the end of the book. But they were moving there because her parents were divorced and Karen's mom wanted a fresh start. Not my family. No way. We were moving because my dad had a great new job. And besides, Mom and Dad had been happy during every trip we'd ever taken to Disney World. And Disney World was in Florida. So it only made sense that once we were living in Florida, they'd talk to each other more and start getting along again, right? Divorce wasn't even an option.

At least that's what I thought.

But divorce wasn't an option for Karen Newman, either, was it? Like me, she watched her parents fight and convinced herself that it was no big deal. She felt the tension that pervaded their home and internalized it. And so did I.

But still, I didn't see the signs. Divorce was something that happened to other families.

At first, Florida was great. Well, as great as it could be when my new fifth-grade classmates were snobs who snubbed me because I dressed like a dork. But I didn't see Mom and Dad fight very much anymore. Sure, I felt tense all the time for reasons I couldn't put my finger on. And, actually, Dad was never really home that much; he'd come in from work after we had gone to bed and be gone by the time we got up in the morning. But they must be getting along, I thought. It's not like I heard them argue. And the complete lack of talking to each other that I couldn't help but notice on the weekends? Well, it just must be that they got all of their friendly talking out of the way at night after we had all gone to bed. It couldn't be that they had run out of things to talk about altogether. And it definitely couldn't be that they just didn't like each other anymore.

Dad came home earlier than usual one night midway through fifth grade. Great, I thought. We'll finally be able to have a family dinner together! Maybe we can even go out to eat. What a treat that would be! But instead of having a great family meal like we used to, what felt like a long time ago, Mom and Dad asked me, my seven-year-old sister Karen, and my four-year-old brother David to come sit with them in the living room. Okay, I thought. Maybe we'd all sit down and play Candyland together or something. Great!

"Kids," my dad began somberly, looking at my brother, sister, and me. "Your mother and I love you all very much. But we've decided to separate."

I think my heart stopped for a moment. My jaw dropped.

No.

No.

It couldn't be happening. Not to my family.

"What does that mean?" asked my panic-stricken sister, looking from my father to my mother.

"It just means that Dad and I have some problems we need to work out," my mother explained kindly, making eye contact with each of us. Or at least I think she was making eye contact. My eyes were welling up with incredulous tears, so it was hard to see. "This has nothing to do with you three. We love you more than anything in the world. We both do."

"You're getting a divorce!" I exclaimed. I couldn't believe it! My parents were just like Karen Newman's! And I hadn't even seen it coming!

"No, honey, right now it's just a separation," my mother soothed.

"But where will you go, Dad?" I asked. I looked at my little brother, who was too young to understand. But he was following the conversation with the wide eyes of someone watching a high-paced tennis match.

"I've found an apartment close by," my dad said.

"But we'll never see you!" my sister wailed.

"Of course you will," he responded. "I'll be right up the street. We'll see each other all the time. I'll take you to dinner one night a week. And we can see each other every other weekend."

I just stared. One night a week? Every other weekend? It was just like Karen Newman's parents! And her parents got divorced soon after her dad moved out.

No, I decided. I would *not* let that happen. Not to my parents. After all, I'd seen their wedding photos. One of them was still up in the living room. Look how happy they were! That couldn't just go away! Could it?

I mean, sure, Karen Newman had tried to get her parents back together, and it hadn't worked. But maybe she just hadn't tried the *right* things. So in the name of research, I went back and reread *It's Not the End of the World*. Okay, so Karen's plans *seemed* solid. For example, bringing her diorama home from school so that her dad would have to come over and see it, thereby running into her mom and remembering how much he loved her? Pure genius. The one flaw in the plan was that in my class, we weren't actually *building* any dioramas at the moment. I didn't have any bait to lure him home.

Okay, Karen Newman Plan #2: Pretend to be sick so that Dad *has* to come see me, thereby running into Mom and noticing her stunning beauty and sparkling wit. This plan, too, was flawed, though, as Dad was a doctor and Mom was a nurse, and they could spot a faker a mile away. They were on to me the moment I held the thermometer up to the lightbulb in an attempt to simulate a fever. Hmm, it didn't work for Karen Newman, either.

Okay, on to Karen Newman Plan #3: Get Mom and Dad back together on their anniversary. Surely they couldn't help but remember how in love they had been on the day they got married, right? They had just forgotten, but I could remind them, and everything would be fine. Unfortunately, that plan crashed and burned, too. It seems that two people who are in the midst of dissolving their marriage don't really appreciate it when their eleven-year-old daughter fills the house with Happy Anniversary banners she prints out on the computer. Karen Newman's plan failed similarly. I should have known.

I can't even count the number of times I read and reread *It's Not the End of the World.* That's because when you're eleven and your parents are splitting up, no one realizes that you might have some real adult questions that you don't exactly know how to ask. Even though my mother did her best to explain the divorce to me and answer all of my questions honestly, there were some things I didn't know how to put into words. Will Dad stop loving us? Will he forget us when he moves? What will happen to us? Will we be poor? Will Dad try to take us away from Mom? I didn't know how to ask those things. But Judy Blume did. And through Karen Newman, she told me the things I ached to know.

The divorce hit me hard, just like it did Karen. Karen was in sixth grade when her parents divorced, and so was I. Why did Judy Blume choose to make her that age? I've always thought it's because that's the worst age to go through a divorce. You're old enough to absorb the tension around you and to grasp the basic undercurrents of the situation. But you're young enough that no one actually realizes that you know exactly what's going on but don't know how to ask the questions gnawing at the back of your mind. Karen Newman was the only other sixth grader I knew who was going through a divorce that she didn't understand, didn't want, and didn't know how to stop.

But Karen Newman made it through. And that was important to me, because it meant that I could, too.

I often wondered through the years what happened to Karen Newman, or rather what *would* have happened to her if she were a real girl rather than a figment of Judy Blume's imagination. There's a singular solidarity to the children of divorce, especially those of us who go through such a thing at a highly formative age, and I like to think she and I would have been great friends.

I know now, without a shadow of a doubt, that my parents are much better apart than they were together. When I was young, all I could see was that they had loved each other once, and it made no sense to me that they could suddenly fall out of love. Did that mean they could stop loving me, too? Now I know that sometimes people *do* fall out of love with each other, and that as my parents grew and matured, they grew apart, changed into different people, went in different directions. But when I was eleven years old, hurting and confused, it changed my world to know that I had Karen Newman and *It's Not the End of the World* to turn to for help.

Judy Blume, I often thought, must be some sort of oracle who knew exactly what I needed to hear. That's because for a long while it *was* the end of the world for me. Karen Newman's story ended before her parents' divorce was final. But did she know it could get worse? Did she know that her dad could leave and not look back for a while? Did she know that her father could show up just before her Catholic confirmation, an event that felt like the most important day of her life, and tell her while standing uncomfortably in her driveway that he couldn't come because he'd decided that spending time with her wasn't good for his "own personal happiness"? Did she know that she would probably internalize lots of her parents' problems and somehow feel that they were her fault? Did she know that she would spend years feeling guilty for not being as perfect as she could have been, because surely that's what must have broken up the marriage? Did she know that she would cry herself to sleep at night because she couldn't fix what was broken?

I wonder, having experienced the breakup of her parents' marriage, and ultimately her family, who Karen Newman would be today. Would she be one of those lucky kids who escaped relatively unscathed from her parents' divorce? I suspect not. Because, like me, Karen Newman felt it all. She saw her mom in pain. She saw her dad hurt. And she internalized it all, made it her responsibility to fix it, worried about the things she couldn't possibly change. And when that happens to an eleven-year-old, it shapes her for the rest of her life.

I wonder if Karen Newman has problems today with relationships. I do. There's something about realizing early on that love doesn't always work out that makes you reluctant to try. There's something about watching your parents' marriage fail that makes you doubt you'll be able to make a marriage of your own work. Would Karen Newman have found that out, too?

I left Karen Newman when we were both sixth graders, both mired in our parents' divorces. Her story had ended, and she had imparted all of the knowledge she had for me. But does the story ever really end for either of us? After your parents divorce, the shock, sadness, and confusion fade, the years wash away some of the bitterness, and you eventually learn to let go of the hope that your parents will reconcile. But in a way, you're changed forever. Divorce is a shadow that shades the rest of your life.

Today I'm nearly twenty-seven. More than fifteen years have elapsed since my parents' divorce. After several rocky years with my father, we are finally back on track. We're friends again, and that means the world to me. I am closer to my mother than I ever could have imagined; she is my best friend, my role model, and the one person in my life who I know I can rely on through thick and thin.

I don't have problems getting into relationships. I fall in love just like anyone else (even though my boyfriend choices aren't always the best, but that's another exploratory essay for another day, isn't it?). I am able to commit to relationships and I would never dream of cheating on someone—ever. But I've been cheated on. And instead of reacting with horror and surprise, my reaction has simply been one of confirmation of my fears. Rather than thinking, *That bastard!* when I once called the guy I was dating and his ex-girlfriend answered the phone in his hotel room, I resigned myself to the inevitability: *Well, it was bound to happen sometime.* Then I promptly lost even more faith in relationships and commitment. What a depressing thought that I go through relationships waiting to be let down, waiting for the man to walk away. I wonder if Karen Newman would have approached relationships with the same unhealthy skepticism.

I wonder, too, if Karen Newman would be terrified of marriage, like I am. That while her friends purchased wedding magazines and dreamed of the dresses they would wear and the bridesmaids they'd choose, Karen would feel physically ill when thinking of the prospect of getting married one day.

Don't get me wrong; I know that I *want* to be married someday. But I don't ever want to give my heart to someone who will one day choose to throw it back in my face after we've spent seventeen years together and had three lovely children together. I can't bear the thought of falling out of love with someone. But I don't know how to avoid it. And there's no Judy Blume book that covers that. There's no Judy Blume book that teaches you to mend those scars that divorce causes in the formation of an eleven-year-old's conscience and soul. There's no Judy Blume book that tells you how to cope after the storm, when your parents' divorce a decade and a half earlier has manifested itself into all sorts of problems in how you face the world. Karen Newman's story isn't nearly long enough.

But maybe there comes a time to leave the past behind as Karen realized she needed to do at the end of *It's Not the End of the World*. While Karen Newman and Judy Blume were there to hold my hand through the tough year of my parents' separation and divorce, there's no guidebook to your twenties that sums things up neatly and succinctly. There's no twenty-something Karen Newman for me to commiserate with. There's no Judy Blume character who smiles sympathetically at me from the pages of a novel and says, "I've been there, too. And I turned out fine."

If a sixth-grade Karen Newman could pull through, so can twenty-something Kristin, right? Maybe what I learned from Karen then—the skill of letting go and moving on—still pertains to my life today.

But what if Karen Newman turned out to be a commitment-phobic, relationship-challenged woman approaching age thirty who wanted desperately to be in love but was afraid to take that necessary leap of faith required for a lasting relationship? What if she lies in bed some nights and wonders if something is wrong with her? What if she subconsciously makes bad dating choices because she's simply terrified of committing to someone who might be "the one"?

No, I think Judy Blume would have found a way to write Karen Newman out of that. Surely, today she would be a well-adjusted, level-headed twenty-something with no hang-ups. Or if she *did* have hang-ups, Blume would have found a way to cleverly write a tale about how she worked through them. So you know what? I can, too. I can be my own Judy Blume. I can rewrite my own life, so to speak, so that I have a happy ending, just like Karen Newman surely had. Can't I?

Because when it comes down to it, sure, my parents got divorced. My perceptions of love and relationships got a little shaken up. I've lost a little bit of my faith in love and indeed in people. But like Karen Newman would have told me, things will get better. After all, my parents are divorced, but it's not the end of the world.

———

Kristin Karmel is the author of How to Sleep with a Movie Star *and* The Blonde Theory, *both from Warner Books/5 Spot. She gave up years ago on trying to get her parents back together, and now she's working on trying not to be terrified of marriage herself. She lives in Orlando, Florida, where she writes for* People *magazine, appears regularly on the national morning TV show* The Daily Buzz, *and is at work on her next novel. One day, she hopes to be happily married (but never divorced), but since she somewhat delusionally considers herself to be the real-life version of Carrie Bradshaw, she's also perfectly happy to embrace being single for the time being.*

FREAKS, GEEKS, AND
ADOLESCENT REVENGE FANTASIES

| *Shanna Swendson* |

When you're reading Judy Blume's novel *Deenie,* I'm sure you're supposed to identify and sympathize with the titular narrator heroine. She faces so much emotional turmoil, from family expectations to a dreaded medical diagnosis that brings challenges and personal humiliation while dashing all of her life plans. Along the way, she even learns a lesson or two. I'm afraid, though, that when I first read *Deenie* as a preteen, I found all of her problems amusing, even (sad to say) enjoyable.

You see, I was the Creeping Crud.

For those who've been out of middle school for a while, Deenie was the pretty girl. Pretty enough to be a model. She may not necessarily be the queen bee of her school, but she's got a group of girlfriends, and boys seem to like her. Deenie's classmate, Barbara Curtis, has a bad case of eczema, a red, scaly rash that covers her arms, legs, hands, and neck. Beautiful Deenie nicknames her the

Creeping Crud, and she and the other kids treat Barbara like a leper. She's the last one to get picked as a partner for gym class and usually ends up as the teacher's partner in any activity that requires physical contact.

The part about the Creeping Crud is actually only a minor sub-plot of the book, but in some respects, it's the preteen experience in a nutshell. Preteens are freaks—just ask a few of them. They'll be more than happy to point out the kids who are too *something*—too tall, too short, too fat, too skinny. They have bad acne, wear braces on their teeth, sport visible birthmarks, freckles, or glasses, or just have something about them that in some way, shape, or form sets them apart from the crowd. And it's not only physical things that make kids different—you can be too smart, too dumb, too interested in something deemed weird, or even talk with an accent. Differences are the points of weakness that other kids hone in on, the source of nicknames, schoolyard taunts, and sometimes even clique formation. Kids have a talent for finding one point of weakness or difference and focusing on it until it becomes an identity, a label that kid is stuck with, regardless of how true it remains or what else is going on in that kid's life. A girl who's labeled "the fat girl" will have more trouble shaking the label than she does losing the weight, and it doesn't matter if she's also a good singer, a poet, an A student, or a budding fashion designer, she'll still be identified as "the fat girl."

A girl's social standing at school can depend on the kind and degree of freakishness she has, as defined by others. A temporary flaw, like braces, may not be so bad. Something that might be considered a flaw, like glasses, can be turned into an asset if it's handled with style and flair—get the right frames, have an attitude about them, and incorporate them into your sense of style and you're not likely to be called "four eyes." Flaws that are considered signs of character weakness, like being too skinny, being overweight, or having bad acne, move a kid lower on the social ladder. After all, if they were worth anything, wouldn't they lose weight, gain weight, exercise, and wash their face? And, let's face it, being pretty or popular can negate something that might otherwise be considered a bad flaw in anyone else. A pretty, popular girl can get braces and glasses and hit a growth spurt that leaves her a head taller than all the boys in the class, and she'll still be popular. Deenie still has friends and still has a boy who likes her when she has a back brace, but how would that have gone for Barbara? Someone who was already a social leper would only move lower on the social ladder.

If the kids you're talking to are really, really honest, they'll admit that they're freaks, too. There's something they feel self-conscious about, something that becomes magnified in their minds until they're sure that's the only thing people notice. They're a giant nose with arms and legs. They're merely braces that can blind someone from across the room, freckles that can be seen from a mile away, or body odor that wilts plants when they enter a room, even right after a shower. Sometimes they're wrong and the freakishness is something only they notice, but more often they're right.

When you're noticing all those weird little things about yourself, of course it makes you feel better to notice the flaws in everyone around you. But while you're noticing every little thing about others, they're doing it to you, too. It's a vicious cycle, and in the culture of girlhood, any bathroom or locker room confidence between trusted friends can be turned into a deadly weapon and shared with the entire school in a matter of days.

And then there are the Deenies of the world (the prebrace version). Those are the girls who somehow manage to appear "normal." They're pretty at an age when most girls are awkward. They don't have to wear glasses or braces on their teeth. Their hair doesn't have a mind of its own and actually stays where it's supposed to—or at least looks lovely and shiny even when it's tousled. They either haven't yet developed acne or they're going to be the lucky few who escape the teen years with only an occasional pimple. They wear nice clothes that are actually in style. They haven't shot up in a scary growth spurt that leaves them taller than most of the boys in the class, but they also aren't still waiting for a growth spurt, and they don't have a layer of baby fat that still needs to be stretched out, nor are they short enough to be mistaken for being in elementary school.

The Deenies seem to exist to make the rest of us feel even worse about ourselves. They're the exception to the rule that every kid is a freak in her own way. Your parents may try to reassure you that everyone's awkward at this age, but you know the Deenies, so you know it's not true. The Deenies can make your life miserable without even trying. Though there are plenty of mean girls out there, the Deenies aren't necessarily among them. Deenie didn't do anything that was outright mean to Barbara. She didn't call her names to her face, make fun of her openly, or insult her. She just talked about her behind her back and tried to avoid her. All Barbara seemed to notice was the avoidance, and that was bad enough.

That's why the book played out like a revenge fantasy for me. It was the ultimate comeuppance for the Deenies of the world and a minor triumph for all the girls who felt like freaks because of them. I wasn't too worried about scoliosis. We had screenings in school, and as much as I was involved in ballet and gymnastics, someone surely would have noticed during all that time in a leotard while balancing on a beam if my spine had been crooked. But I did have eczema as a child (I still do at times, just in a more minor way). I got the crusty rash in the bends of my knees, the bends of my elbows, and behind my ears, sometimes even on my scalp and inside my ears. It itched, and I had to put cream on it. Sometimes I wanted to cover up the worst of it on my legs with long pants because I knew it looked nasty, and I kept wanting to bend and twist around to try to see how bad it looked, which was probably even weirder-looking than the red rash, but wearing long pants only irritated it more.

If I was ever teased about it, it must not have been enough to leave psychic scars because I don't remember it ever coming up except in the occasional bit of mild curiosity. I seem to recall some of the boys even being impressed in an "oooh, gross!" way. Other kids weren't crazy about being my partner in gym class, but that was more because I couldn't throw, catch, run, or kick than because of my eczema. There's no telling what was said behind my back, and it's hard to tell if people avoided touching me, because I've never been a particularly touchy person, but I don't remember feeling shunned. I did sometimes feel like it kept me from doing things I wanted to do. When a flare-up was really bad, I wasn't allowed to go swimming because the chemically treated water wasn't good on sensitive skin.

I couldn't get my ears pierced when all the other girls were because the backs of my ears were where it was worst, and getting a hole poked in that spot would have been asking for a serious infection, let alone whatever trouble I might have from the earrings themselves if I happened to use a metal I was sensitive to. By the time I was in junior high, I felt like I was the only girl in school who didn't have pierced ears, and I think that set me apart even more than the constant rashes did. Nobody remarked on the rash, but everyone was always showing off their cute new earrings. As an adult, I can totally see the wisdom of not having my ears pierced and have never had it done, but at the time it was a major trauma and there were a lot of tears. Getting your ears pierced was almost a rite of passage, a sign that you weren't a little kid anymore (never mind that there are babies with pierced ears). Earrings were a way to express yourself. You could get earrings to show your birthstone, your zodiac sign, or your favorite color. You could match your outfit, look dressed up, or wear fun, quirky earrings that made a statement, like a friend who wore telephone earrings because she always had a phone to her ear when she was at home. And there I was, with my plain, bare, little-girl earlobes. Every time I went to a birthday party where the birthday girl got a lot of earrings as gifts, I came home begging to get my ears pierced. Every time someone assumed I had pierced ears, because, after all, *everyone* did, and gave me earrings as a gift, I begged to get my ears pierced. My mother's answer was always the same: "You need another couple of holes in your ears like you need another hole in your head." Then she launched into a lecture about the eczema and how I'd probably have a reaction to the earrings, which would make it even worse, and did I really want that?

Because of my own experiences, instead of seeing Deenie as the heroine, I identified with Barbara, who didn't seem to have any personality flaws or anything she needed to learn. She was avoided and made fun of by the girl who was pretty enough to be a model for no reason other than a skin condition she couldn't help. And then the fun began.

The pretty girl got turned down for a modeling job (Ha! And you think you're so pretty!). She tried out for cheerleading and didn't make it (Ha! Not everything has to go your way!). She was diagnosed with scoliosis and had to start wearing an ugly brace (Ha! Now see what it's like to be a freak!). In frustration and despair, she cut off her hair, so she wasn't quite as pretty anymore. Then in the ultimate bit of wish fulfillment revenge, she came down with a bad bout of dermatitis because she was too vain to wear an undershirt under the brace. She had developed her own case of the Creeping Crud! It was an occasion worthy of a happy dance. A Deenie had been turned into a freak.

Through all of Deenie's experiences, she did eventually gain sympathy for Barbara, and by the end of the book, they're even becoming friends as Deenie learns to see Barbara as something more than a skin condition. That was the best thing ever to me. What girl hasn't idly daydreamed about forcing her school enemies—usually the pretty, popular girls—to walk a mile in her (ugly, practical, because why buy more than one pair a year when your feet are still growing?) shoes so that they can understand how she feels and maybe, just maybe, stop being so mean? It's not that you really want bad things to happen to these people (okay, maybe just a little bit). You simply want them to know what it's like having a life that isn't so perfect. You want to force them down to the level where the rest of us have to live so that they can learn some empathy, like Deenie does. If the experience makes them want to be your friend, then that's a bonus. You might daydream about suddenly becoming so beautiful that the pretty, popular Deenies of the world want to be your friend, but that's actually a lot less fun than a Deenie being forced to understand you.

I was lucky enough to avoid being labeled anything like the Creeping Crud. Instead, I got labeled another way. I was "the smart one," and that label superseded all others. If you were labeled smart, you couldn't also be pretty. That was another way I found myself on the opposite side from Deenie. In her family, Deenie was "the pretty one" while her sister Helen was "the smart one." Until her back brace forced her to reconsider her future, Deenie didn't seem to mind living up to her label and using it as an excuse to just get by in school, while her sister was held to higher academic standards.

In my schools, boys ignored the "smart" girls for the "pretty" ones—and actual grades didn't matter. A smart girl and a pretty girl could have the same grades. The distinction was based on what about a girl was noticed first. If she managed to make her mark by being pretty before anyone saw her academic performance, she was "pretty." If she showed herself in class to be smart before anyone paid attention to her looks, she was "smart." Even if a smart girl went through the preteen equivalent of *Extreme Makeover*, lost weight, got her braces off, got contact lenses instead of glasses, cleared up her skin, started dressing better, and did something with her hair, she was always going to be the "smart" girl.

In the "smart vs. pretty" wars, your brain was yet another thing that could make you a freak, something to set you apart from others. You could start seeing yourself as a giant, wrinkled, squishy brain walking around on legs, because that's certainly the way others seemed to see you. Smart girls didn't date, didn't have fun, and weren't even interested in anything that might be fun. They stayed at home on weekends (because no one ever thought to invite them anywhere), read the dictionary for enjoyment (okay, maybe, but only when getting sidetracked while looking something up), and thought everyone else was stupid by comparison (only those who gave us reason to think so).

I got stuck with the label in the worst possible way in sixth grade when I had to move to a new school in the middle of the school year. The teacher had my records before I started class, and I later found out he'd prepared the class for the new student by telling them how smart I was and how they were all going to have to work harder to keep up with me. Needless to say, I didn't stand a chance. I was labeled "the smart one" before they ever saw me (not that I was particularly pretty at the time). The kids who were the incumbent smart ones hated me as a potential rival before they even met me, and the kids who weren't considered smart were already intimidated. I had enough to feel freakish about as it was, as I was developing fairly early and already wore a bra, I started wearing glasses, and I had crooked teeth but hadn't lost enough of my baby teeth to get braces. And at nearly five foot four inches—which turned out to be as tall as I'd ever get—I was tall for an eleven-year-old. Add the teacher's preemptive strike, and I was doomed to remain friendless the rest of the school year. I did a lot of reading during that time, including most of Judy Blume's books, because I didn't have anyone to play with.

My heart broke for Deenie's sister Helen when she was dismissed by her mother as "the smart one," the one who was told not to expect anything outside her books, who wasn't supposed to fall in love, who didn't need to bother dressing well, who'd be wasting her God-given good brain if she had any fun. She seemed as trapped by that label as I often felt, and I've always wondered if she ever caught up with her poetry-writing mechanic who was going to go to forestry school. I, at least, had the good fortune to be able to be myself at home and had parents who let me be smart, pretty, funny, or anything else I wanted to try being (though I didn't test them by trying out "slutty" or "stupid").

As much as I avoided empathizing with Deenie, she was still reassuring. That brace that at first looked like the end of the world, that made her want to stay home from school so that no one would see her in it, ended up not really hurting her life in any important ways. She still had her friends and even gained more friends because of the new perspective the brace gave her. The boy she liked was still interested in her. He still kissed her, and the brace came in handy when it kept boys from groping her (I'm not sure Deenie thought that was such a good thing, but at the time I first read the book, when I was still way too self-conscious about my body to imagine ever wanting a boy to touch it, that sounded pretty good to me).

If Deenie could survive relatively unscathed with something as awful and obvious as a back brace, then I could surely survive my relatively minor freakish characteristics. Glasses, a few extra pounds, and crooked teeth weren't going to kill me. There was hope that I could break out of my smart girl mold. If a boy could like Deenie when she was wearing a back brace, there was still a slight chance that a boy might like me with braces on my teeth (alas, that wasn't the case, but I don't think it was entirely the braces that were at fault).

Adulthood has given me an entirely different perspective on *Deenie*. I can read the book now and recognize that Deenie had her problems even before the scoliosis. She was, in her own way, just as labeled and freakish as Barbara or Helen. She was stuck being the pretty one, and that limited her options. She had to live out her mother's dreams, and she wasn't even sure if she had a brain because she was never expected to use it. In a roundabout way, that back brace may have been the best thing that could have happened to her because it opened up her options. It meant she'd go through high school without a chance of being a model, and that allowed her to try something else. By the end of the book, she's considering being an orthopedic surgeon, something the pretty girl never would have dreamed of.

There's also the truth that you don't want to accept when you feel like a total freak: the popular, attractive kids who seem to have everything going for them feel like freaks, too. In *Deenie*, that inner freakishness is made visible, but for all those other kids out there, there's usually something only they know about. You don't know what's going on inside. I haven't remained in touch with my middle school peers, as I was a military brat and have moved many times since then, but I do see people I went to high school with, and my dad was a popular teacher at my high school who's remained in touch with some of his students, so I've had his perspective. I've found as an adult that the kids I thought had it all together were just as miserable as I was. They felt just as left out, just as worried that no one would like them, just as self-conscious. Some felt even worse than I did. We really were all freaks in our own way.

In other words, we all had a little bit of Deenie inside us—an inner being who wanted to break free but was hemmed in by physical barriers and outside expectations. And we also had something of the Creeping Crud there, as well, something we wished people could see past so that they could accept us as the people we were. We all rebelled against the labels we were stuck with, like Helen did when she fell for her poetic mechanic. It's a nice lesson to keep in mind but one I'm not sure the preteen brain is truly capable of comprehending. That's why we needed Judy Blume to portray that world the way it really is and kids the way they really are, to give us both the Deenies and the Creeping Cruds and force us to think about both of them.

———

Shanna Swendson survived adolescence (sort of) to become a novelist. She's the author of Enchanted, Inc. *and* Once Upon Stilettos. *She's also contributed to* Flirting with Pride and Prejudice *and* Welcome to Wisteria Lane. *Her ears remain unpierced, but she did finally get the braces off her teeth and only wears glasses when she's too lazy to deal with contact lenses.*

GUILTY'S HOUSE

| *Jennifer Coburn* |

For as long as I can remember, I've been like Winnie, the awkward white girl who lives down the block from Iggie's house. Except it's not Iggie's house anymore. Winnie's best friend, Iggie, has just moved to Japan, and her house now belongs to the Garbers, the first black family to reside on the historically homogeneous white suburban Grove Street. Winnie tries desperately to befriend the three Garber kids but winds up sticking her white foot in her mouth far too many times, showcasing her self-consciousness about race.

With naive curiosity, Winnie asks the Garber kids if they've moved from Africa. More like Detroit. She isn't trying to be a smart-ass. She simply has never seen a black person and honestly thinks the Garbers might be recent immigrants, despite the fact that they speak and dress like every other American kid she knows. How could sheltered little Winnie know she was being offensive? And how could the Garbers know Winnie's heart is in the right place when they receive a chilly welcome from the rest of their new neighbors?

Winnie and the Garber kids stumble into a friendship, despite the bumps they experience along the way. One day while Winnie is visiting the Garber house, Mrs. Landon, the town busybody, places a racist sign on their front lawn. Winnie is so embarrassed that she looks at the black father and flees from the house, bawling with guilt. Does Winnie have anything to do with the sign? Of course not. But when she runs off in shame, I know exactly how she feels. She and I both suffer from the same malady: White Guilt.

The first time I'd ever heard this term was on the nineties comedy show *In Living Color*, in which the irreverent Wayans brothers and crew satirized a number of social and political issues. In one episode, they used the term "Whitey Guilt." I pointed at the screen with recognition and told my husband, "That's what I've got. I've had it my whole life."

Unlike Winnie, I was not raised in the suburbs but in Manhattan, where the lesbian movers who helped haul furniture into my mother's and my Greenwich Village apartment called themselves Mother Truckers. I saw African-American and Puerto Rican people all the time, in every walk of life. On my sixteenth birthday, I shared a taxi with a dignitary from the Middle East while we both made our way from the United Nations downtown. I was no stranger to diversity. My grammar school was attended by the sons and daughters of Koreans who sought political asylum, Pakistani doctors who were visiting Beth Israel Hospital, and a host of artists, musicians, and writers in every color. I did not live in Winnie's sheltered environment. Yet I shared her awkwardness and guilt over what other white people had done.

Right around the time Alex Hayley's *Roots* aired on television, our grammar school decided to teach us about slavery. With every whipping, sale, and indignity, I sank lower into my wooden chair, feeling utterly ashamed of my heritage. Was I Southern? Not even southern Italian. My maternal ancestors were in Milan at the time when slaves were being auctioned off in the United States. My paternal line traces back to Russia, where Jews were being forced out of villages and terrorized in droves. No one in my family was even remotely involved in the slave trade. So why did I feel so guilty about what these white people had done? I asked my friends if they were experiencing the same overwhelming grief over our social studies lessons. I wondered if they were lying awake in bed every night thinking about black children being sold to different plantations, being torn away from their parents. "Nah," a friend replied with a shrug. "My family's Chinese. We didn't have anything to do with that. Plus, it was a long time ago. Anyone who was selling slaves is dead now."

My friend's answer didn't help.

Like Winnie, I decided to appoint myself ambassador to all black people. Not that she or I ever consciously thought about it this way, but we both wanted to personally make up for all the wrongs and injustices that had been visited upon African-Americans. Part of it was benevolent, but another part was purely selfish. I wanted to differentiate myself, show black people that I had nothing in common with those awful white slave owners—that even though we shared the same pale skin color, I wasn't like them. I smiled too widely at my black classmates. I offered them bubblegum (in the variety pack because *that's* how committed to diversity I was!). I went out of my way to prove I was a different kind of white person—the kind without prejudices.

As the Garber kids' friendship illustrated to Winnie, trying to showcase your lack of racism is, in fact, a form of prejudice. Focusing on how race is not an issue makes it one. By doing backflips to show how hip I was to black folks, I made everyone painfully aware of my race self-consciousness. I'd clumsily borrow dialogue from black characters on television shows, greeting black people with, "Hey, hey, hey!" like Dwayne on *What's Happenin'* or replying that a suggestion was "Dyno-mite" à la JJ from *Good Times*. When black folks visited my lemonade stand, I so badly wanted to make reparations for slavery that I never charged them for drinks. Naturally, this made them more than a little uneasy about drinking my concoction, but what I was trying to say was "My brother, you have more than paid for this lemonade." Winnie and I both struggled with wanting so badly to differentiate from racists that our actions were another form of racism—the type where well-meaning guilty white people see group before individual. They see an opportunity to enhance race relations before they see the person.

A lot of white people try to casually slip "black talk" into conversations with African-Americans they meet. While talking about one topic, they force a tangential comment about a jazz or gospel concert they recently attended. Or they might reach into their mental Rolodex to share a thought from their "good friend," Shaniqua Jackson. I've done this dozens of times, thinking people must be really impressed with how unprejudiced I am.

My roommate in college used to laugh about how people always tried to interject Latino names and subjects into their conversations to show her how hip to the Puerto Rican scene they were. (See how cool I am, with my Puerto Rican college roommate?) The problem was that Evelyn wasn't terribly impressed with people telling her how much they loved Tito Puente (Cuban) and burritos (Mexican). So am I really demonstrating my *enlightenment* by assuming that a black person would be interested in Shaniqua's musing on Dizzy Gillespie simply by virtue of the color of his or her skin?

While taking an African-American history class in college (a class I would never dare skip, despite a spotty attendance record everywhere else), I listened to a group of young black guys talking about how insulting it was when white women clutched their purses as they passed on the sidewalk. Again, I decided I would be the white person who changed all of that. When African-American men passed me, I would let go of my purse, which I normally clung to. I would make eye contact and smile brightly, hoping they would catch my message: "I'm not afraid of you, my black friend. Look at my purse, dangling freely off my unprotected arm. I have no fear of you snatching it from me, for we are all sisters and brothers in the rainbow of equality."

As you might imagine, this was not often the message received. Rather than link arms with me to sing a quick round of "Kumbaya," some guys viewed my overly friendly gestures as a come-on. My stomach tied in knots of guilt when I had to reply that I didn't give my phone number to *any* guys I didn't know. "Oh dear God," I'd silently plead. "Don't let them think I'm a racist." But some did. On one such walk down the street, after declining to give my number to an African-American male, his friend informed him, "See bro', I told you white chicks are a bunch of cock teases." I felt damned if I smiled, damned if I didn't. My mistake—like Winnie's—was in treating black guys differently than their white counterparts. If two white guys passed me on the sidewalk, I'd look right past them, clutching my purse a little tighter than usual. If a white guy asked for my number, I would have politely declined, rather than going into a whole song and dance about it. I wouldn't have changed, hyperanalyzed, or agonized over my actions. The fact that race was driving me was what made me a racist.

When I was in my late teens, my cousin Debbie told me that we were actually one-eighth black. I could have danced hip-hop all night! Debbie confided that our grandmother, Rose Cohen, a first-generation Brooklyn Jewish immigrant from Russia, was not actually the child of my great-grandfather, Boris. Our great-grandmother, Fanny, had a black lover who she would visit every month when Rose was a young girl. My great-grandmother had never told Rose this. And Rose never caught them kissing. There were no paternity tests. But Grandma Rose said that she "just knew" that the black man was her father. To top it off, Debbie said that Fanny's black lover was the runaway slave Crispus Attucks.

Fanny and Crispus might have simply been Chaucer enthusiasts who shared books—or drug buddies who shared needles—but we didn't care about silly things like facts. Grandma Rose said she thought they were lovers, and that was all the proof we needed. Rose "just knew," and that was good enough for us! We were black. Talk about an emancipation. Finally, I could free myself from the shackles of guilt that came with being the same race as those nasty white people who kept slaves and made black folks sit at the back of buses. Of course, this was a little tough to swallow with my stick-straight blonde hair, pointy nose, and green eyes, but Debbie told me after three generations of being diluted by genes of "the white man," my blackness didn't show up as well as, say, Shaniqua Jackson's.

Deep down, I think Debbie and I both knew we weren't black, but we loved the idea so much that we still cling to the possibility. When I recently asked our oldest living relative, Aunt Bernice, about this, she said she couldn't be sure. "So Grandma may have been black?" I asked.

"The term is mulatto," she replied haughtily. The fact that she could not definitely deny that we were part black kept hope alive.

Recently I went to see *Glory Road* with my eight-year-old daughter, Katie, who is a reviewer for the "Rated G" section of our local newspaper. The paper hires about a dozen kids who they send out to children's movies, theater, and events so that they can share their unique perspective with other children. Katie was sent to review the true story of America's first all-black starting basketball team to win the NCAA Championship. Set in the civil rights era, the film explored themes of racism in a pretty realistic way for a kids' movie. As characters used racial epithets and verbally abused black players, I sank lower into my seat. I found myself looking around the theater to gauge the reactions of African-Americans who were also attending the preview. I wanted to give them a little "peace out" sign and show them that these two groovy white chicks would've had *nothing* to do with the nasty crackers who beat up the basketball player in a diner restroom.

Naturally, they were all watching the movie, not looking to connect with an audience member seeking absolution for the sins of her father (who very well might have been a quarter black!). As we walked out of the theater, Katie said to me, "I feel really embarrassed to be white." My first reaction was to tell her that I did, too, but I refrained and instead asked her why. "Those white people were so mean to those guys for absolutely no reason," she said. "Why were they so rotten?" Katie asked. I had no answer.

How do you explain the concept of purposeful humiliation to an innocent child? How do you teach her to live her life with integrity and not saddle herself with guilt when you are still seeking forgiveness from every African-American person you meet?

Plenty of people don't understand where I'm coming from on this issue. My husband says he and his family are good people and have never discriminated against anyone. That's fine for him, but what do the Winnies of the world do with their White Guilt?

Like Winnie challenged her mother to stand up to Mrs. Landon, we need to do the same and then some. We need to make sure our kids get off Grove Street every now and then—and not freak out when they notice race. When Katie was three years old, we went to Chicano Park Day together, where she quickly noticed, "Everyone is brown here." The people who heard her weren't offended, as it was the simple observation of a child. My whole body tensed as I fought back the impulse to apologize. A few people chuckled. No one seemed upset that my child noticed their skin color. It wasn't the noticing that was offensive; it was when the awareness resulted in different treatment that pissed people off. Katie's innocuous comments were no big deal; it was the long-winded explanation that followed that surely caused a few eye rolls. "Yes, Katie, some people are brown and some are white, but what really matters is what's inside," I said for the benefit of people around me. Looking back, I'm shocked that no one shoved a spicy burrito in my mouth to shut me up. It was so patronizing, I want to slap myself.

As I reread *Iggie's House* recently, what struck me was how unresolved Judy Blume left the story. In some ways, it bothered me, because I wanted to know whether the Garbers sold their house. I wanted this resolution in some ways to assuage my White Guilt. If they stayed, the happy ending gave me some solace. In real life, though, race relations is an ongoing process—one in which we don't get a nice, neat ending wrapped in a bow.

Jennifer Coburn began reading Judy Blume books in the fourth grade, the same year she was first called "weird" by a classmate. Her mother told her that weird was simply a word used by boring people to describe interesting ones. Both Mom and Judy Blume helped her survive adolescence. She is the author of The Wife of Reilly, Reinventing Mona, Tales from the Crib, *and* The Queen Gene. *She is currently working on a gossip-lit book about the vile world of kids' sports.*

A Different Kind of Diary

| *Elise Juska* |

I was four years old and dancing in California when I first realized I wasn't invisible. My parents and I were in a restaurant, waiting to be seated, standing beside a massive tank of bright tropical fish. I barely spoke when I was little, spent most of life hiding behind my mother's knees, but that night in the restaurant I was dancing with total abandon. Maybe it was the perceived shield of the fish tank, or the anonymity of being on the other side of the country, or the fact that in the past week I had seen the Disney Electric Parade, eaten a chocolate-covered banana, and petted a llama. I couldn't help but dance. Until a woman came over, a stranger, looking at me and smiling.

"How wonderful," she said, and I stopped.

Like most shy kids, I had a rich inner life, crowded with characters both found and invented. For years, I taught an imaginary class of students for whom I set up parent–teacher conferences, wrote and graded papers, devised lesson plans, and lectured passionately to my empty living room. I devoured books and felt connected to the characters I met there, fell in love with Peter Hatcher, lived vicariously through Sheila the Great.

And I wrote stories, stories that were about me and not-me—a more interesting, more dramatic me. The narrators always had the things I didn't: older brothers, pets, braces, and families who argued with one another. In my dinner scenes, forks were always clattering onto plates, chairs were scraping floors, and kids were bolting from their houses in fits of feeling, the back screen doors flapping like wings.

The parents in my stories were usually divorced, unlike my own parents, who I'd never once heard fight. The concept was so alien that they didn't even use the term "fight," instead softening it to "raise your voice," in the same way "hate" was diluted to "strongly dislike" and "shut up" to "please be quiet." To not fight was, as I understood it, a measure of a good relationship; it was how a marriage was supposed to be.

What little experience I had with divorce was gleaned mostly from studying the parents' names listed in the Glenside Elementary School address book. I was fascinated by the single parents, mothers usually, who always seemed to have vaguely exotic names like Natasha. I imagined them the kinds of mothers who wore lots of makeup and ordered Chinese takeout. My other source was Judy Blume's It's Not the End of the World, in which Karen's parents (who fought constantly) were divorcing.

"I'm your father," Karen's dad said, "and I'll always love you." He'd taken Karen and her brothers to Howard Johnson's, which seemed to me the kind of place kids with divorced dads went to eat. "Divorce has nothing to do with that," he said.

Karen's life seemed filled with drama and secrets. She didn't want anyone knowing her dad had moved out, that he was living in an apartment, that her brother Jeff had run away. Though I couldn't relate with the facts of her story, there was something about it I understood intuitively: the impulse to keep things hidden.

When I was eight, I was given my first diary. I loved it, not just because I loved writing, but because of its aura of secrecy: the leatherette cover, the pages edged in gold, the tiny toothy key on a red string.

April 11, 1982: Today started out pretty good. Getting dressed was a real pain! I couldn't wear either of my outfits or my new clogs! I ended up wearing something decent. For Easter I got a book and this diary.

Now, it is January 2006, and I am in the attic trying to organize my childhood. I am sifting through the bags and boxes—grade school notebooks, scrolled posters, soft paperback books, hundreds and hundreds of typed, unfinished stories. The attic air is thick and dusty, warm even in winter. The floor is a grid of wood beams and foam insulation. A silent fan crouches by the window. As a child, this attic seemed gigantic, dangerous, site of Mom famously falling through the floor and Dad discovering her leg poking through the hallway ceiling. Now the space feels small, lonely. Dad has moved his stuff out, to his new apartment. Mom is purging the house of everything she doesn't need. I was charged with doing the same— an impossible task, since the same impulse that made me keep everything in the first place prevents me from throwing it away.

I start paging through the red diary. I'm not surprised to have found it, but I am fascinated by its details: my third-grade handwriting so careful, as if accustomed to being graded, and extra straight, as if restraining itself from veering into the forbidden cursive. The earliest entries are in berry-colored ink, infused with exclamation points and capital letters, all the color and fervor I never showed on the outside.

April 12, 1982: I have a feeling that today is going to be good! I have on a new outfit. Maybe the good thing about today is that Timmy Chun will like me.

There's a buoyancy in my tone, upbeat even when disappointed, like I was when I returned after school that day: *DRAT!* I can't help but smile, knowing I must have borrowed this from something I'd read. Even in my diary, I wrote myself like a character in a book. *Timmy Chun doesn't even consider me for love anymore!*

• • •

To be in elementary school was to be surrounded by secrets. The most immediate were the who-likes-who's, revealed with great drama and suspense inside the rubber tires on the playground. The school was across the street from my house, visible from my bedroom window, but on the playground I was in a different world. My favorite spot was the swings: within the long, exposed stretch of grass and concrete, they were the one place I felt invisible. I could rise up off the ground, disappear. The tires were second best, though they were an escape of a different sort; there you were hidden but not unseen. Within those fleshy inner walls I was never more aware of where and who I was: eight years old, my own wide eyes mirrored in the girls' eyes around me, boys pressing in from all sides.

The tires looked like a row of chubby horseshoes, cut in half and upside down. They were wide enough for up to four of us to huddle inside, our skinny backs snug against the tires' rounded curves. If you were nervous, you could rip at loose strings of rubber like hangnails; if you were brave but not too brave, you could pen your name on the walls. Though the tires were a girls' domain, it wasn't unusual for a boy's head to appear suddenly in the opening, upside down and wild haired, or for a boy's feet to go stampeding overhead, sometimes jumping so hard the rubbery ceiling came crashing inward.

A playground session of guess-who-I-like could be stretched to last all recess long, with the boy's name revealed in the last dramatic seconds between hearing Mrs. James ring the bell and lining up to go back inside. In the end, the secret was less about the boy than the mystique of knowing something no one else did. Once the secret was out, it lost its appeal.

In third and fourth grade, anything I had to offer boy-wise was strictly hypothetical. I barely spoke to anyone, much less boys, much less one A. J. Giglio, who was Italian and silky haired and funny. Though my crushes (see: Timmy Chun) might vary from week to week—based usually on some fleeting glance in the cafeteria or inadvertent brush of a jacket sleeve against my arm—I maintained a base loyalty to A.J. A few times I'd seen him laugh so hard he almost choked.

A.J.'s best friend was Joey Healey, boy extraordinaire. Joey was beloved by all, an all-around genuinely stellar student–athlete–human being. He yelled, "Great catch, El!" after I, by some miracle, managed to hang on to his deep fly in kickball. I once heard him say he would sacrifice his life for his parents, a notion that astounded me, not so much that he would do it but that he held such a firm position on the issue. He had the emotional maturity to sign "love" on all his Valentine's Day cards, but in fourth grade his heart belonged to Jeannie Kim. Jeannie was my friend and the envy of every girl at Glenside Elementary. Not only was she Joey's girlfriend but, I also happened to know—had a mobile of satiny pink and purple clouds and stars hanging above her bed.

> *April 14, 1983:* Oh, things have changed so much! There's so
> much LOVE going around. CRUSHES and BREAK-UPS.
> Nobody thinks much of me except my brains!

• • •

The culture of elementary school secrets went beyond the playground confessionals. To not know things was the fundamental plight of being a kid. There were the specific mysteries, the Santa Clauses and the Tooth Fairies, debunked one by one with a kind of bittersweet pride. And, there was the show with the theme song "where everybody knows your name," which I listened to drift upstairs as I lay in bed on Thursday nights, dying to see what this place was. And there was the secret life of adults, my parents especially, of which TV shows after my bedtime seemed a major part. All I saw of my parents' relationship was polite, predictable. They never yelled, never cried. Their moods rarely varied. They kissed twice each day: before Dad went to work and before Mom went to bed.

To me, this was all part of the mystique of the adult world, the prospect—part threat, part promise—of all that I would know when I was older. Though the specifics were vague, I had full confidence that at some point "real life" would start happening to me. I believed in a kind of prewritten story: I would meet a boy, probably at the age of the teenagers at Glenside Pool, who sat on one big blanket in a tangle of bikinis, gold chains, black box radios with spiky antennae. I would turn eighteen (and with that, outgoing and confident), fall in love, get married, drive a car, and have a credit card. But mostly, I would stop feeling things so much. What I observed most about adults, my parents especially, was that they were in control of their emotions. Maybe it was like getting tetanus shots; feel a thing once, then it lessens.

But this certainty I reserved for a distant future. At eight and nine years old, I turned to books to illuminate what I didn't know. *Where Do Babies Come From,* which I read the week I had the chicken pox, flushed and stressed and itching. The *Your Child At* series—*Your Child at Eight, Your Child at Nine*—which Mom read every May, then reported on what I could expect in the coming year. And any book by Judy Blume: *Deenie, Tiger Eyes, Then Again, Maybe I Won't,* and the handbook of adolescence, *Are You There God? It's Me, Margaret.* In the crusade for information, Judy Blume's books were essential reading; they brought to light everything that wasn't talked about and that I was dying to know. They demystified kissing, maxi-pads, spin the bottle, scoliosis. They revealed the nerve-racking inner life of boys, via Tony Miglione. I finished them feeling informed, sometimes scared, mostly reassured, but more than anything, grateful. At the school book fair, there existed an unspoken alliance that no kid would let on there was sex in *Forever.* There they sat, a pile of sex for the taking, available to anyone bold enough to carry one up to a parent volunteer. I wasn't, of course, but would later skim a contraband copy with the relevant scenes dog-eared and highlighted. I felt guilty about this (my mother volunteered at the book fair), but as kids we had few secrets of our own, and those we did have, like the boys' names in the tires, lost their power once told.

"Ten," Mom told me, "is a great year."

I was standing in her bedroom doorway, teeth brushed, wearing my new blue nightgown. It was the week of my tenth birthday, and Mom had just finished reading *Your Child At.*

"Ten is a great year," she reiterated. "You'll love being ten." I processed this information with great excitement, instantly adopting it as my new mantra—*ten is a great year, I love being ten*—and that entire year, even when I had a bad day, I would cling to this knowledge as truth. Yet standing in the doorway that night, I also felt a creeping sense of worry. Reassured as I was by what the book said, I also knew what it implied: as great as ten would be, it was unique, and temporary, and other kinds of years lurked beyond it.

May 17, 1983: BIRTHDAY! TURNED 10!

My handwriting is getting looser, the y's more fluorishy and brazen. I even drew fireworks flinging off the tops of the letters, like a cat's whiskers, and looking at them now I feel like crying. Maybe it's the exuberance of it, or the memory of that long-ago worry I know I wasn't admitting on the page. Diary in hand, I feel now what I must have felt then: a preemptive nervousness, about what's coming.

• • •

Feb 2, 1984: I think I'm finally into this boyfriend/girlfriend business. I think A. likes me. He said "hi" and "see you" walking home from school today.

Feb 17, 1984: Greg gave me a valentine that said You + Me = Valentines, and a little dog who said "Okay?" He gave Cara S. one just like it. He likes Alyssa Schiller in 4th grade. Joey wrote "Love, Joey" on his cards. I still like A.J. He likes Jackie.

LATEST LIKES
A.J. likes Jackie
Rachel likes Timmy
Kate likes Evan (little)
Kate likes Pete (littler)
I like A.J.
Sascha likes Evan
Evan likes Sascha
Matt F. likes Jenny
Cara likes Greg
Jessica likes A.J.
Laura likes Mike H.
Greg likes Alyssa
Alyssa likes Greg

• • •

By fifth grade, we were spending less time in the tires. Maybe we were getting too big for them; more likely, they were starting to seem childish. Instead, the girls converged by the water fountain, or the bike rack, or in the biggest and most formal setting: the Girl Scouts meeting. Weekly meetings of the Scouts were held in the cafeteria, some suburban Philadelphia approximation of a camp-fire. Instead of a grove of trees and smoked marshmallows, wooden chairs formed a half-hearted circle by the hot line in the lingering haze of that day's Philly cheesesteak w/ff or sloppy joe w/fruit cup.

I had no interest in the outdoors, no patience for making pot holders, but the Girl Scouts felt like a duty both extracurricular and somehow personal: a measure of your moral fiber, your fundamental girlness. So I did what I was supposed to, joining hands and moving my lips to songs about trees and friendship, but my heart wasn't in it. Until the day our troop leader announced: "For the next month, you'll be keeping a diary."

Our leader, Mrs. Beasley, had jack-o'-lantern teeth and took in stray cats, both of which struck me as earthy and immaterial. She also wore a kerchief that tapered to a point at the nape of her neck; to me, the ultimate qualification for being leader of the Scouts.

"For the next month," she said, "I want you to write in it every day."

I went home eager to get started. I would approach the diary like any other written school assignment—book report, letter to my Danish pen pal—adapting my tone to suit the form. In a marbled copy book, I wrote unabashed passages about staring in my bed-room mirror willing my chest to grow, wondering when I would get my period, and hoping a boy would kiss me, preferably A. J. Giglio. It was mostly truth, with a notch of exaggeration. Though I might not ordinarily have written about bras and periods, this was an assignment, and these were the kinds of details I thought a diary should contain. I was simultaneously acutely aware of writing for an audience and unaware of that audience except in the most abstract sense. It didn't once occur to me to censor myself. Writing was the one thing that made me feel completely safe.

We turned in the diaries, and the following week, after dragging our chairs into a circle, Mrs. Beasley announced: "I have something I want you all to hear." Like a jack-o'-lantern's, her smile could swing from goofy to frightening in seconds. "This," she said, and to my horror, my diary emerged from her bag, "is what I'm looking for," and then she began reading from it out loud. She didn't name the author, but it was obvious who'd written it. I felt my face redden as my mournful ruminations about bras and boys were unleashed in the warm, stagnant cafeteria air. Worse, they were unleashed in the voice of Mrs. Beasley, who was reading them with extra poignancy and emphasis, leaning on particularly embarrassing passages as if to say: *These are the kinds of private thoughts you should all be writing.*

I knew, even through the fog of my humiliation, that Mrs. Beasley wasn't mean-spirited, just misdirected. She was hoping the other girls would be inspired to the same level of excruciating intimacy, that my secrets would be the key to unlocking all of their hidden selves. It even occurred to me, sitting there, that maybe I was being selfish for feeling upset, that this kind of sharing was what being a true Scout was all about. But the longer I listened, the more her praise made me feel paralyzed, exposed, the written equivalent of dancing in front of the fish tank. The other girls shifted and giggled, no doubt relieved they'd had the good sense to keep their secrets to themselves.

More than twenty years later, as I gaze around the attic at the still-unopened bags and boxes, I know the Girl Scout diary isn't among them. That afternoon, after the meeting, I went home and threw it in the trash—not just the kitchen garbage but the metal can outside. If I destroyed it, it never happened. If I didn't talk about it, it didn't exist.

• • •

The year I turned eleven, *Your Child At* ended. I was about a week into my eleventh year when, still having heard no report, I asked Mom if she'd read the next installment. It was nighttime and I was standing in her bedroom doorway, the same spot I'd stood one year earlier, but now my bedtime was a half hour later, my nightgown replaced by my dad's old oversized St. Joe's T-shirt. When Mom broke the news that there was no *Your Child At Eleven*, I felt a mild panic. Though I'd never had any delusions about eleven being as great as ten, it hadn't occurred to me that I might have no information to go on. Maybe this meant I wasn't a child anymore; after ten, life gets too confusing for even the author to explain.

From what I knew so far of eleven, this seemed possible. I was already recalling the previous year like some distant golden age. Not only had ten ended, so had fifth grade and Glenside Elementary. We were moving on to the far more complex playing field of Elkins Park Middle, the confluence of four different elementary schools, buses, locker combinations, changing classes, algebra, foreign languages. Our little universe, in which Joey Healey was hero-king, would soon dissolve into unfamiliar faces, into designer labels, and boys and girls who clung to each other's hands and back pockets in the halls.

Here I would be confronted with things I couldn't have predicted, revealed at moments I couldn't have foreseen. Like the morning I saw no less than fifteen hickeys covering the neck and chest of Lisa Furst when changing in the locker room before gym. Like the Saturday my mom and I were shopping at Gimbels and I looked up to see Mrs. Wilson, my fearsome Home Ec teacher, in whose class I had labored anxiously over one misshapen lightbulb pillow for weeks, standing behind the register. We didn't acknowledge each other. Her name tag said Debbie.

• • •

In retrospect, it seems an act of providence—or maybe perceptiveness on the part of a knowing aunt or family friend—that I was given *The Judy Blume Diary* that year.

"This is a different kind of diary," Judy Blume wrote in her introduction, and I saw instantly that this was true. Instead of feeling covert, the diary had an aura of openness. It was bigger than a paperback and the cover was rainbow striped, like my favorite shirt. *The Place to Put Your Own Feelings*, it said—not just A Place but *The* Place, like some formal admittance into adolescence. It was spiral-bound, keyless; to write in it, I realized, would require a degree of trust.

"Sometimes," Judy Blume wrote, "just writing down your feelings makes them easier to understand." The presence of her voice inside the diary felt comforting, as did the chorus of quotes from her characters filling the margins at the bottoms of the pages:

Karen, Deenie, Sheila, Sally, Margaret. Black-and-white photos of other kids, real kids, were sprinkled through the seasons: playing in leaves in October, swimming in July. In June, a girl wearing hoop earrings rested her chin on both palms, eyes sliding to one side of the camera, as if uncomfortable getting her picture taken. In November, a girl with long brown hair sat on the ground with knees pulled to her chest, head buried in her folded arms. I recognized these kids; they reminded me of me. Still, the sensitivity of the diary was intimidating. If Judy Blume's books were places to get answers, seek clarity, it seemed her diary was the place to admit confusion and lay your feelings bare. But to me, just the word "feelings" sounded raw, embarrassing.

"I hope it's an interesting year for you," Judy wrote at the close of the introduction. "A year of challenges and choices and changes." I was sure she was right, but I didn't want any of these things. I was with Karen, who said in January: "I wanted everything to stay just the way it was." I wanted to be ten again—*ten is a great year, I love being ten*—but the changes and challenges were coming whether I liked it or not.

January 30, 1985: All the romances in books I read all seem like, "What are you so upset about?" and I think I'll never be so crushed over a boy. But if Trevor likes Rachel I don't know what I'll do.

March 14, 1985: Today I saw Dominic Brown kiss Melissa Licht and Jill Holland kiss Mike McCrea. I wonder if they're going out or if that popular group all just kiss each other.

April 13, 1985: I think I underestimate myself. I always think I'm not popular. But I saw my name on a list of people. If you weren't on it you weren't "anybody." Maybe I am popular? Well, I am too shy. I would never ask someone to play with me, be my partner. I'll have a tough time getting dates.

April 19, 1985: We're having a dance. I've never been to one before. The kid I really like will be there. I'm pretty sure his name is either Toby or David. If he's there ~~I hope he dances with me.~~ Or, at least, talks to me. I can't dance.

In the attic, I resign myself to getting nothing accomplished. I call my dad, then my sister, read them lines until we're laughing so hard we can't speak. I tab entries to read to my mom when she gets home from work. I keep turning the pages, sometimes laughing so hard I'm crying; I can sense my private, imaginary world preparing to collide with the real one, moving toward the point where the books ended and my own story began.

May 17, 1986: I am thirteen. I don't feel any different. All the books about boyfriends and girlfriends that I read are around my age. What's wrong here?

I didn't know then how my stories would play out. I didn't know that I would kiss a boy when I was fourteen, say "I love you" when I was seventeen, say it and mean it when I was nineteen, get my heart broken when I was twenty, and twenty-seven, and twenty-nine. That it doesn't hurt once, but keeps hurting; that as you get older, the feelings don't fade. That to speak your feelings, even to argue, isn't always a bad thing; sometimes it's important, necessary. That one Wednesday as I was sitting down to a bowl of pasta, I would get the phone call from my parents that went like this: "Dad and I have been having some problems . . ."

I was twenty-eight. I had moved away from where I grew up, had jobs, students, serious boyfriends. Yet I instantly recognized this call. I had read it in a book long ago. I had written it a thousand times.

"I love you," Mom said, and I felt devastated because I knew then how serious this was.

She passed the phone to Dad. In the pause, I picked up the bowl of spaghetti, crossed the kitchen, and threw it in the trash.

"We're still your parents," Dad told me. He sounded uncomfortable, slightly rehearsed. "This doesn't change that."

And I thought: Are you kidding me?

What do you think I am: Twelve?

In a way, I was; a decade and a half evaporated in the course of that five-minute call, and suddenly my primary role in the world was no longer *girlfriend* or *teacher* or *writer*. I was defined, most importantly, as *daughter* again. The years rewound, and I felt like I had as a child: speechless, faced with all the things I didn't know.

• • •

In *The Judy Blume Diary*, the photo at the beginning of March was always my favorite: empty swings hanging over pools of thawing mud. They're the good swings, the black rubber kind that fit snug against your hips. Now, as the attic starts to get dark, I put the diary back in the box where I found it. I go downstairs, pull on a coat, and cross the street.

Glenside Elementary looks small, like a toy school. The classroom windows are papered with cut-out snowflakes. It's a Saturday; the playground is empty. Most of the equipment is shiny, modern, bright yellows and blues. Only the old swing set is still there, like a relic from another time.

I get on a swing and start pumping. The metal chains are cold, squeaky on the upswing, made of loose rusted links. Since my parents separated four years ago, they have been honest about their marriage, telling my sister and me all they know now, trying to keep us from repeating their mistakes. "Say what's on your mind," they tell us. "Always remember to communicate." I wonder now how much I intuited when I was younger, if the necessity of raising your voice was something I sensed without being told. If, maybe, it was the presence of words unsaid that drove me to bang on a type-writer, scribble in journals, fill up my toy box with stories. Yes, for everything I didn't know as a child, there were some things I saw with a startling clarity, like the last entry I read:

May 21, 1986: It will be fun to look back at journals like this one when I am older. I think this is one of those things that you dig up from a box in the attic and laugh over. Actually, I think this might make me sad. It might make me wish I were right back where I am now, sitting here and writing with a marker that's running out of ink.

I swing higher and watch the outline of my feet against the sky. Though all afternoon I'd been looking backward, feeling protective of the little girl I was, she was looking into the future, feeling protective of me. At thirteen, the exclamation points were far less frequent, the bright inks dulled to blacks and blues, but the spirit of my sign-off hadn't changed: It's *10:20*, I wrote. *Tomorrow will be a good day.*

I let go of the swing and hop off, landing on a patch of crunchy winter grass. Buttoning my coat, I start back across the playground, past where the old tires once sat, past the stairs where we lined up after recess. I remember one day in fourth grade, after we'd formed our ragged lines, Mrs. James made an announcement. Someone, she said, had vandalized one of the stalls in the boys' bathroom: *JH + JK.*

A gasp traveled through our ranks: intrigue, excitement, and quick deduction.

Joey Healey and Jeannie Kim!

"Until someone admits to doing it," Mrs. James said, "we're staying right here."

There was only a moment's suspense before Joey raised his hand.

"It was me," he said, stepping forward as a murmur of admiration rippled through the crowd. "I wrote it," Joey said, and you could see even the teachers' faces soften, torn between needing to reprimand him and maybe, just a little, admiring him, too. In the spectrum of elementary school, his was a serious offense, but he had exposed his guts, brought his true feelings to light, and this was, we all knew, an act of courage.

In kindergarten, Elise Juska discovered two antidotes to shyness: the swing set at Glenside Elementary School and her father's Smith-Corona typewriter circa 1968. On the swings, she belted out Meatloaf's "Two Out of Three Ain't Bad"; on the typewriter, she pounded out stories. Her first one, "15 Candy Sticks for Mother," resides on a shelf in the Glenside Elementary School Library. More recent stories and essays have appeared in Harvard Review, Seattle Review, Salmagundi, Calyx, Black Warrior Review, Good Housekeeping, The Philadelphia Inquirer, The Subway Chronicles, The Hudson Review, and other publications. Elise is the author of the novels The Hazards of Sleeping Alone and Getting Over Jack Wagner, a Critic's Choice in People magazine. She is a graduate of the creative writing program at the University of New Hampshire and now teaches fiction writing (to nonimaginary students) at the University of the Arts in Philadelphia and the New School in New York City. Her third novel, One for Sorrow, Two for Joy, was published in June 2007.

ARE YOU AVAILABLE GOD?
MY FAMILY NEEDS COUNSELING

| *Kyra Davis* |

People have all sorts of ideas about why *Are You There God? It's Me, Margaret* should be read by pubescent girls. Some feel that preteens will relate to Margaret's anticipation about getting her period. Personally I was never all that concerned about menstruating until I actually started to do it, at which point I began praying for menopause.

Then there's the issue of peer pressure. Obviously that's a concern for every child as well as for most adults, and undoubtedly Margaret's anxiety over wearing the right outfit and being liked by the right people hit close to home for a lot of readers; but not so much for me. See, I was fortunate enough to be blessed with an inflated sense of self-worth. Throughout my life I've managed to maintain my own unique sense of style, and I've always befriended the people I enjoy hanging out with rather than the people who might elevate my social status.

So when I finally started reading Judy Blume's renowned novel at the tender age of eleven, I didn't expect to identify with Margaret all that much. But that was before I got to the part where Margaret started to address the dynamics in her family. I remember being curled up in bed reading about the tension that existed between Margaret's parents, whom she loved, and her grandmother, whom she adored, and all of a sudden I *was* Margaret. I knew exactly what she was feeling. I understood the burden of trying to maintain positive relationships with beloved family members despite their unwillingness to have relationships with one another. Margaret's parents tried to dispel the tension that existed between Margaret's grandmother and themselves by moving to another state. My mother and stepfather tried to escape the animosity by refusing to spend too much time with my grandparents even though they literally lived right next door. I'm not sure which solution is worse.

When it comes to childrearing, there are two types of people. First, there are those who want their descendants to do better than they did. These parents don't want their children and grandchildren to experience the pain and/or disappointment that they experienced in their own lives and thus they try to create a different path for their children to follow. Then there are those who feel that they have lived life the way it is supposed to be lived. They want their children and grandchildren to do the same, and they do everything they can to encourage them to follow in their footsteps.

Margaret's parents belonged to the first category of people. Both of them were raised in religious homes, and they experienced firsthand how religion could be used as a divider. They saw it as a beacon of intolerance and judgmental behavior. It was incredibly important to them that Margaret not experience the pain that religion had caused them, so they did everything in their power to shelter her from it.

Margaret's grandparents (both maternal and paternal) felt that their lives had been greatly enriched by their religion. For them the idea of not raising a child with the beliefs that they held so dear was unthinkable. Margaret's maternal grandparents disowned their daughter for the offense of marrying a non-Christian. While I'm not a Christian, I certainly know many people of that faith who would say that was a very *un-Christian* thing to do. But once we meet Margaret's maternal grandparents, we realize that perhaps they were simply trying to exercise a form of tough love. They wanted to do whatever they could to convince their daughter to return to the faith even if they had to lose her in order to do it. After all, what's a few decades of bad feelings compared to an eternity in the pits of hell?

Margaret's parental grandmother took another route. She wasn't thrilled with the idea of her son marrying a non-Jewish girl, but she was unwilling to cut her child, or her grandchild, out of her life. However, she was also unwilling to give up on the idea of said grandchild embracing the Jewish religion and identity as her own.

So basically everything Margaret's parents and grandparents did for her was out of love, which is ironic since what that love manifested was a lot of anger and bitterness. Funny how love does that sometimes. God knows that was the case in my family. My grandparents were not happy with my mother's choice in husbands. My stepfather was my mom's second husband and her third serious relationship (my father being the second serious relationship, although she was never married to him). I think it's fair to say that my mother's first two choices in life partners left a lot to be desired. She married for the first time when she was nineteen, and the man she chose was brilliant and totally insane. I mean we're talking about a guy who collected buckets full of tadpoles from a pond in a cemetery with the intent of selling them to a pet store. That in and of itself would have been weird, but what was worse was that he never actually got around to selling them, so for a while there my mother was living in an apartment that was literally overrun with bullfrogs.

My father didn't share my mother's first husband's passion for exotic pets; he was interested in more mundane things like music, women, and drugs. In fact, the only thing that the two men had in common was a high I.Q. and an aversion to moderation.

So it shouldn't be surprising that my grandparents had a hard time taking my mother's word for it when she said that Richard (my stepfather) was the right guy for her, especially when he was so very different from anyone else in our family. It's not just that he wasn't Jewish; his whole approach to life was dramatically different from what any of us were used to. And while he and my mother have some things in common, on a whole they are very different people. In contrast, my grandmother and grandfather were two peas in a pod. It's not uncommon to hear a friend talk about someone they know who has a "perfect marriage," but it's almost unheard of to hear someone refer to *their own* marriage as perfect. But my grandparents did exactly that; furthermore, they actually believed it was true. As far as they were concerned, they had discovered the secret formula for marital bliss. What they couldn't understand was why my mother rejected their formula. She wanted to brew up her own concoction, and that just didn't make sense to them.

Let me be clear here—my grandparents didn't think everyone had to be *exactly* like them in order to be okay. Before Richard entered the picture, my grandparents used to pay for my mother to take me on elaborate yearly vacations. We went to Bali, Tahiti, Kenya, the Caribbean, and other wonderful exotic places all because my grandparents felt it was important that my mother and I be familiar with and appreciative of other people's cultures, philosophies, and lifestyles. But poor Richard wasn't different in the right way. It would have been okay if he had been Chinese. My grandparents *loved* the Chinese. How many times did I hear my grandmother grumble, "How anyone could think that the Chinese are inferior to the rest of us is beyond me!" But poor Richard was Irish, and while that didn't hurt him, it didn't gain him any bonus points, either.

They also would have been easier on him if he had been an intellectual. If he had been a Jewish Eurasian intellectual, my grandparents would have thrown a party, but a Buddhist, atheist, agnostic, or secular Christian intellectual of any ethnicity would have been fine. An intellectual son-in-law would have been an appropriate addition to a family who named their dog Socrates. But my stepfather wasn't an intellectual, at least not according to the Jewish definition of the word. Worse yet, he went to church; only on Christmas Eve, but even that was a little more than what my grandparents were comfortable with.

It would have helped if Richard had been a self-made man; *that* would have been even better than being an intellectual. My grandparents had started off with *nothing*, but they came from an immigrant family, and like so many immigrants, they worked their asses off until they had a significant amount of *something*. But my stepfather wasn't a self-made man. He came from a middle-class family and took a middle-class job as an elementary school teacher. We liked teachers in my family, but it wasn't enough to compensate for the whole Christmas Eve thing.

Furthermore, my mother and Richard had clearly built their relationship on different principles and ideals than those that my grandparents used while building their own. Richard and my mother weren't a team who always presented a united front. Rather they were partners who clearly cared for each other but also frequently disagreed and compromised in order to make the business work. So when my grandparents got to know my stepfather and saw the way my mother and he interacted, they assumed that my mother was settling. They didn't think Richard was a bad person, they just didn't think he was the *right* person for their daughter. It doesn't really matter if this was true or not; what's important is that this was their *perception* of the situation. The very idea of my mother settling for anything less than what they shared with each other was unthinkable, especially when you consider the fact that I was in the picture. I was ten when my mother married Richard, and my grandparents definitely didn't see him as a positive influence.

The really sad part, the part that I didn't allow myself to see until I became an adult, was that Richard really wanted them to like him. In my mother's family the thinking had always been *if someone likes us, great; if not, then the hell with 'em.* Richard doesn't think like that. He's one of those aim-to-please guys, and he wanted to be welcomed into the fold. I think he had entertained fantasies of us being a *Charlie and the Chocolate Factory* kind of family minus the extreme poverty and passion for caloric desserts. Sadly, his yearning to be loved pushed my grandparents further away. They saw it as a form of neediness, and my mother's family doesn't do needy.

All of this would have made things difficult even if we lived miles away from each other. But the distance between my mother's and grandparents' house could be covered by foot in a matter of seconds. Perhaps this is the reason why Richard and my mother briefly considered the idea of moving to Australia. But due to financial and other pragmatic reasons, they decided that moving to a different house, let alone a different continent, wasn't a logical option.

I'll never forget the day when Richard and my mother told me that we wouldn't be spending all the holidays with my grandparents anymore. We're talking about approximately fourteen days a year. I couldn't get over the fact that we lived next door to these people—these people who had practically *raised me*—and yet we couldn't even spend fourteen days a year with them. I can recall standing on the step of our sunken living room trying to make sense of a situation that seemed patently absurd while my mother and Richard stood on the slightly elevated floor of the adjacent dining room trying to explain it all to me. My grandfather had built that floor. He had built the entire house for my mother and me. Now we were going to tell him that there were certain days when he wasn't going to be allowed to step inside the doorway that he had made?

Of course, in retrospect I understand. My grandparents were angry with Richard and my mother for not taking their well-meaning advice, and who wants to spend every holiday surrounded by anger? Once upon a time, holidays had been about family togetherness. Now they had turned into this bizarre tightrope act in which I had to decide what part of the holiday I could spend with my grandparents and what part with my mother and her new husband. The holidays that we did spend together were almost worse than the ones we spent apart. Seriously, how was I supposed to react when my grandmother came over for Christmas and presented my Catholic stepfather with an article from the newspaper's editorial section arguing against the divinity of Christ? What could I say when the present my grandparents reluctantly shoved under the Christmas tree was a board game titled Chutzpah?

I didn't have an answer and neither did Margaret. Judy Blume was incredibly daring when she decided not to provide her readers with a neat little ending or clear-cut conclusions to conflicts that realistically were never going to go away. However, what she did give her readership was a protagonist who was stronger than the angst within her family. Margaret recognized the problems, but she never really wallowed in them, and perhaps more importantly, she learned the art of compartmentalization.

Like Margaret, I never doubted that my mother and grandparents loved me. I heard it in their voices every time they said my name. I felt it in every hug. The mistakes they made couldn't overshadow the love they gave. As a child, that's what gets you through the messiness of a dysfunctional family, and lets face it, *all* our families are at least a little dysfunctional. It's really just a matter of degree.

Like Margaret's grandmother, my grandparents eventually came to accept my stepfather (albeit begrudgingly). I think their feelings about my mother's marriage were similar to my feelings about my hair. I'm never going to be completely happy with it, but I'd still rather work with it than shave it off.

So throughout the bulk of my teenage years, my grandparents managed to treat my stepfather with the same kind of civility and courtesy that Margaret's paternal grandmother showed her daughter-in-law. And like Margaret's grandmother, my grandparents frequently reminded me of my Jewish ancestry, although unlike

Margaret, I'm actually glad they did since my Jewish identity has always been important to me. By the time I graduated high school, it became clear to everyone that they needn't have worried about my being unduly influenced by either my stepfather or my grandparents' resentment of him. Like Margaret, I was always my own person and I made up my own mind about things.

So by the time I had reached my early twenties, I figured I had this whole family thing figured out. When I got married, I made it my mission in life to win the approval of my in-laws. Since I had spent years watching my stepfather fail at this task, I figured I knew exactly what not to do. I would not reveal the things about myself that could potentially piss them off. The trick was to be evasive. For example, when my father-in-law pronounced that Bill Clinton was the reincarnation of Satan, I refrained from telling him that I still had a Clinton/Gore bumper sticker glued to my car. My in-laws were Christians, but fortunately for me, my husband's previous girlfriend was a Muslim, so by comparison my Jewish faith seemed comfortingly familiar to them. When I eventually got around to giving birth to a son, I congratulated myself on being able to offer him such a cohesive family dynamic.

But that was before the divorce. I tried to make my marriage work, but nothing I did made a difference. It didn't matter if my husband and I discussed our problems or swept them under the rug; either way, things were bad, and they were rapidly getting worse. So when my child turned two, I filed. When I signed those papers, I thought about what I was about to lose: not my relationship with my husband—that had ended years before I finally decided to make its death official; nor was my divorce going to adversely affect my finances—my husband had already spent everything we had, so there was nothing for me to risk. No, the only thing I would lose by signing those papers was the bond I had built between me and my in-laws. The cohesive family that I wanted to give my son would be gone forever. At first I assumed that my now-ex-husband would be the one to actively facilitate the continuation of the relationship that had existed between his family and our son during our marriage. But my ex had too many personal demons to fight. His parental visits became sporadic and short. If it was that hard for him to maintain his own relationship with his son, I certainly couldn't expect him to maintain the relationship between his son and his grandparents. Clearly that burden would fall to me.

The problem with burdens is that they're . . . well . . . burdensome. No one wants to hang out with the woman who "broke (their) son's heart," and no one wants to hang with people who think you're guilty of such a thing. Still, when my former sister-in-law called and offered me and my son plane tickets to fly across the country to visit their side of the family, I accepted. I reasoned that it was the best thing for my child.

Margaret's parents once made the same offer. They welcomed Margaret's mother's parents into their home more than a decade after they had disowned their daughter. In the book, that visit turned out to be a disaster. And now I've lived the disaster firsthand. My mother-in-law got a migraine the moment I stepped off the plane, and it didn't go away until they dropped me off at the departures terminal a week later. The name of my ex-husband and the word "divorce" were studiously (and predictably) avoided. What I hadn't been prepared for was the way that many of my offhanded remarks would be misinterpreted. Early on in the trip, my mother-in-law asked how things had been going for me, and I made the awful mistake of telling her that they were great. The looks of bitter disapproval on everyone's faces quickly put me in check. So from that moment on, when someone asked how I was, I said "okay." "Fine" was too generic, "bad" was a pathetic plea for sympathy, and "good" was the perceived equivalent of saying that I was celebrating the end of my marriage. I was careful to refrain from using the term "social life" in reference to myself. Instead, I had a "supportive network of friends." This semantical tap dance was incredibly exhausting, and despite the fact that it was their sensitivities that made it necessary, it was clear that they, too, found it wearing. I don't think anyone was upset when it was time for me to say adios.

On the way back to California, I missed my connector flight. I remember clinging to my son's little hand while the Southwest agent broke the bad news. I literally broke down in tears. "I just want to go home!" I sobbed. "Please, can't you help me make this vacation end?" The people at Southwest were very helpful, and when I eventually got on a plane headed homeward (in a very roundabout fashion), I, for the first time in my life, coughed up the five bucks necessary to get the flight attendant to spike my tomato juice with vodka (of course, my son accidentally knocked it onto my lap before I had a chance to drink it).

I vowed that I would not take that trip again. But would that be fair to my son? I think about how Margaret's parents handled the family strife. They never flat out told Margaret that they were leaving New York in order to get away from her father's mother, but they were so obvious about it they might as well have. Margaret's maternal grandparents never said that their love was conditional, but they made it clear that it was. I think of the perverse pleasure

Margaret's father felt (and only halfheartedly tried to conceal) when his wife's parents behaved in the awful manner that he had predicted. Each individual family member loved Margaret, but they put their own petty grievances before that love. I'm not going to do that to my son. So no more crying fits at the airport. Whatever tensions may at times exist between me and my ex-husband's family, they are not as important as the fact that we are all good people who love my son and want the best for him. Everyone on my ex's side of the family (including my ex) will have an important place in my son's life for as long as they want it, and if they want to fly out to see him, I will happily put them up. I won't allow the painful memories of my divorce to undermine my ability to get along with people who I continue to care about. I am determined to show my son that children like Margaret aren't the only ones who are capable of behaving in a mature fashion; occasionally grown-ups can manage it, too.

———

Twenty years after graduating from junior high school, Kyra Davis *is still waiting to become a grown-up. Her novels include* Sex, Murder and a Double Latte, Passion, Betrayal and Killer Highlights, *and* So Much for My Happy Ending. *Her novels have received good marks from such publications as* Publisher's Weekly *and* Cosmopolitan. *Nonetheless, Kyra has yet to work up the courage to submit her work to her eighth-grade English teacher. You can learn more about Kyra at www.kyradavis.com.*

THE MOTHER OF ALL BALANCING ACTS

| *Beth Kendrick* |

Picture a journal covered in faux fur (leopard print!) and Ren and Stimpy decals circa 1994 . . .

Dear Diary—

My mom = total bitch! All my friends are allowed to date. All of them! And today, Derek Whalen asked me and Emily to go to the movies on Saturday. Of course I said yes—hello, he's a SENIOR!!! But then I made the mistake about actually telling the truth about something for once, and Mom says I can't go. She says no dating until I'm sixteen! Bitch! Well, I don't care, I'm going anyway. I'll just tell her I'm going with Katie and Amanda and she'll never know the difference. But someday, when you're old and re-reading this, I want you to remember what it's like to be fourteen. Because Mom does NOT. When I have a daughter, I'll let her date whoever she wants, whenever she wants.

I was fourteen, I was furious, and, as it turns out, I was lying.

Now that I'm "old," I do remember what it's like to be an adolescent—the highs, the lows, the constant, cringing embarrassment brought on by everyone around me—but I have to say that no fourteen-year-old daughter of mine will ever be allowed to date some frosh-preying senior. Mind you, I don't actually *have* a daughter, but if I did, sixteen seems a little young to be dating. Maybe college. Maybe grad school. Or, I know: how about *never*? Convents have come a long way—I bet some of them even have DSL and high-definition TVs these days.

And Mom, the woman I so callously dismissed as a cold, unfeeling, well, b-word, knew exactly what she was doing. Despite my attempts to deceive her, she busted me on my attempted date—there might as well have been a SWAT team swarming the movie theater—and grounded me for the rest of my natural life. Which was just as well: Derek Whalen turned out to be a scuzzy serial cheater with a rather dismaying tendency to shoplift. And he much preferred my friend Emily anyway—*she* had breasts.

My mom was never exactly like my friends' mothers, much to my chagrin. She didn't let me stay out 'til 2 A.M. or wear midriff-bearing tops or drink wine coolers at home because "at least you know we're safe and not out driving drunk or getting date raped." (I tried that argument many times; it cut no ice.) She didn't let me stop taking AP math classes or start taking the occasional "mental health day" from school just because that's what the cool kids were doing. As a former Shakespeare professor who didn't believe in wearing lots of makeup, eating junk food, or spending all our disposable income on designer clothes, she was the bane of my teenage existence.

From my fourteen-year-old perspective, my mom just didn't know how to blend in or how to have fun—defined, of course, as "letting me get my navel pierced"—and I vowed I wouldn't turn out anything like her.

So in the fine tradition of stubborn suburban girls, I spent my adolescence rebelling. I enrolled in a college two thousand miles away from home, I made dating choices based on weighty criteria such as "coolness" and "hotness," and I took off for a semester in Italy even though I couldn't speak a word past *ciao* and *grazie*. I did everything I imagined my mother wouldn't have wanted me to do in high school.

And, of course, I turned out just like her.

Somewhere in my early twenties, I stopped burning up my credit card at the mall and started scouring vintage boutiques and T.J. Maxx for bargains. I took out my navel ring because it interfered with my research projects in grad school (small metal rings embedded in your flesh plus giant spinning magnets in an MRI machine—turns out, not a good combination). Just last week, I found myself in the organic food section of the grocery store, frowning down at food labels as I sought out healthier choices. I've even caught myself using her trademark expressions: "Marry in haste, repent at leisure," "When you rub elbows with the rich, all you get is holes in your sleeves," and the ever-popular "If you'd spent as much time working as you did complaining, you'd be done already."

I've gone over to the dark side. And I love it.

Because now that I've survived the churning chaos of adolescence, my mom no longer has to be the enforcer. Somewhere along the way, as I kicked and screamed and demanded my freedom, she let go and gave it to me, in increments so small I could barely see the safety net receding beneath me. Mom went from being the spoilsport who sabotaged my dates with Derek Whalen to being the benefactor who slipped me a few extra bucks when I failed to budget and ran out of cash in Rome. She parented me through those tumultuous years when I most needed the solid foundation of maternal bedrock, but now she is my best friend. And for someone who I once derided as hopelessly unhip, she sure knows how to have a good time.

Mine is the only mom I know of who has seen every episode of *Sex and the City* and *The Sopranos*, and who has such great taste in clothes and shoes that I feel compelled to borrow them without asking. She's always eager to try new food, new hairstyles, and new adventures. Just last month, she called me on her cell phone to inform me that she and my dad were on the road to Vegas—a spur-of-the-moment weekend of gambling and romance. In the space of a decade, she's gone from my oppressor to my role model.

So now we have all new problems.

Mom's no longer safeguarding my chastity; now it's, "When are you going to stop collecting all those stray dogs and start having children?" She's no longer fending off the Derek Whalens of the world; instead, she and my husband gang up and tease me about my (allegedly) high-maintenance ways. We're still all over each other's nerves, just in different ways. In the midst of the dishing and laughing and good-natured bickering, I sometimes stop and marvel: *who is this woman, and what did she do with my mother?*

Judy Blume, as usual, has the answer to all my mother–daughter questions. She perfectly captures the dual nature of motherhood without over-the-top drama or fanfare. As an adult rereading her books, I'm astonished at the transformation I see in her maternal characters. Just as I can't believe that my mother is the same person she was when I was in high school, I can't believe that the mothers in *Tiger Eyes, Forever* . . . , and *Starring Sally J. Freedman As Herself* are the same characters I read as a child. I know that these are the same books, but somehow they're completely different.

As the go-to young adult author for girls worldwide, Judy Blume was in the unusual position of writing for a teen audience while parenting teens of her own. When she wrote *Forever* . . . , she had to consider the issue of sex and romance from both the parents' and the child's perspective. It would have been easy for her to minimize the parental figures and sidestep all the inherent moral dilemmas, but she didn't. The mothers in her books are fully drawn, actively involved in their daughters' lives, and dealing with flaws and conflicts of their own.

When I read Judy Blume in middle school, I skimmed right over the mothers' dialogue. At that age, I viewed parents as an obstacle that kept the heroine from attaining her dreams. Davey's mom in *Tiger Eyes* was (I thought) selfish, self-defeating, and a little frightening as she sank into a fog of depression after her husband was killed. Katherine's mother in *Forever* . . . was embarrassingly clinical and kind of sneaky, trying to break up her daughter's first passionate love affair. And Sally's mom in *Sally J. Freedman* was just a freak—seriously, who doesn't let her kid change in a bathhouse?

But now that I'm nearing thirty, I'm struck by how real the mothers are in these books. They're not saints, they're not demons; they're just human. You can feel them struggling to hold their lives together as they deal with problems with their husbands and children. I wanted to cry for Davey's mom, Gwen, who is trapped between her paralyzing grief and her guilt about not being there for her children when they most need a parent. She's neither mean nor selfish; she's sacrificing her dignity for her children. To move in with her in-laws who constantly upbraid her for not being smart enough, rich enough, responsible enough—*that's* maternal love. When I reread *Tiger Eyes* this year, Gwen sort of took over the book for me; in many ways, she's the most fascinating character. She and Davey's father got married too young and had a child too young, but despite financial hardship and familial disapproval, they kept their marriage strong and their family close-knit. After her husband's murder, she found the strength to work through her sorrow, start dating again, and move back to the house she'd shared with her husband. She didn't take the path of least resistance; she just did the best she could and made the decisions that she thought gave herself and her children the best shot at long-term happiness.

Sally J.'s mother, Louise, is an equally complex character. On one level, she's frightened and paranoid, always terrified that her children will catch exotic diseases or be snatched away from her. On another level, she's courage personified—in an era when women were encouraged to stay close to home, she packed up two children and moved clear across the country, leaving her husband to work in New Jersey while she oversaw her son's recovery from nephritis in Florida. As a child, I was swept away by Sally's cinematic fantasies and indignant that her wet blanket of a mom always ruined her fun. But as an adult who's watched one too many evening newcasts, I have to admit I now empathize with Louise. It's a scary world out there, getting scarier every day (Sally's parents didn't even have to worry about the proliferation of Internet predators and promiscuous pop stars). It's easy to condemn a mother for playing it safe and raising a daughter who can only indulge her adventurous spirit through fantasy, but when you consider that Louise nearly lost her only son to a disease that was poorly understood at the time, you can understand why she might not be keen on encouraging her children to take unnecessary risks. Though she says that "little girls don't need to be adventurous," she leads by example and shows her daughter that sometimes a woman's gotta do what a woman's gotta do. She's a paradoxical mix of strength and submission, pioneer and homemaker.

Diana, Kath's mother in *Forever . . .* , is an intriguing mix of Gwen's stalwart independence and Louise's homebody reticence. She married young but pursued a career as a librarian. She values her looks and tries to dress stylishly but refuses to spend her life "keeping herself up" for her husband. When her seventeen-year-old daughter falls in love with a nice boy from a nearby high school, she probably understands exactly what Kath is going through, but as an adult, she has the foresight to see the relationship for what it is: first love, destined to burn brightly, then flare out. Diana shows equal amounts of support and restraint as Kath tries to race down the path to adulthood; she doesn't want to encourage Kath to become sexually active, but she won't forbid it, either. She is, first and foremost, a parent, not a friend, and focuses on what her daughter *needs*, not just what she *wants*. In a mother–daughter heart-to-heart, Diana confesses that she regrets marrying so young, which probably has a lot to do with why she discourages Kath from following her boyfriend to college. She wants Kath to have more opportunities than she did, and isn't that what all mothers want for their daughters?

• • •

At their core, *Tiger Eyes, Forever . . .* , and *Sally J. Freedman* are all books about teenage issues, but to an adult reader, the parents' story lines seem to almost overshadow their daughters'. I'm bringing an entirely new set of experiences to these novels now, and my reward is a fresh set of story lines that I missed the first time around. I'm sure that in twenty or thirty years I'll read these books again and completely identify with all of the grandparent characters. That's the wonderful thing about Judy Blume—you can revisit her stories at any stage of life and find a character who strikes a deep chord of recognition. *I've been there, I'm in the middle of this, someday that'll be me.* The same characters, yet somehow completely different. Just like my mother, who just called to tell me that if I'd spent as much time writing this essay as I have procrastinating about it . . . I'd be done by now.

———

Beth Kendrick spent her high school years writing *painfully bad poetry and pining after boys who preferred her beautiful best friend (which only inspired more bad poetry, creating a vicious cycle) before growing up, cheering up, and deciding to write romantic comedy instead. Her novels include* Nearlyweds, Fashionably Late, Exes and Ohs, *and* My Favorite Mistake. *She also relived the funnier moments of her adolescent angst in her series for teens,* The 310, *which she published under the name Beth Killian. You can visit her Web site at www.bethkendrick.com.*

THE WIENIE GIRL'S GUIDE TO MAKING FRIENDS

| *Berta Platas* |

I was the wienie girl, way back when. I've changed a lot. People who know me today can't believe that I was once a timid, geeky kid, but thirty years of living will do that to you. Okay, so it's more like thirty-five.

In elementary school I was so shy that I never raised my hand in class or talked to anyone new during recess. Ask questions about a math problem I didn't understand? Forget about it. I was doomed to count on my fingers. Judy Blume changed that for me. Not the counting on my fingers part. I'm still a math moron. Judy Blume taught me how to make friends.

Shy doesn't always mean lonely. The friends I had until fifth grade were imposed on me by the nuns at my parochial school in Pittsburgh, where Catholic Social Services sent my family after we arrived in Miami from Cuba. I sat next to girls who were supposed to help me learn to speak English, and even with the language barrier, we got along well. I played Barbies with my sister and wild games of tag and hide-and-seek with the neighborhood kids, all the while picking up the language rapidly, as only little kids can.

But disaster struck at the end of fifth grade, when I found out we'd be moving all the way to New York City. I thought I'd never have a friend again. I'd had enough change in my young life to know everything would be alien in New York. I said good-bye to the neighborhood I knew and loved. Our landlady had lent me her copy of *Wuthering Heights*, and in total drama queen mode, I bade wistful farewells to our blue-collar Irish/Polish neighborhood, envisioning the moors, whatever those were. I wafted up and down the steep hills of my neighborhood, thinking *I'll never see this rosebush again*, and *Mr. Szyklow's dog will never follow me to school again*.

I even sighed over Randy, the guy in homeroom who had a crush on me and gave me my first Valentine ever. I read it so many times that I can still recite the little Hallmark poem inside, and the signature, "Your friend forever which is Randall." Sigh.

We arrived in Manhattan in the summer, which gave my sister and me a little time to get used to the area before school started, but we were miserably lonely. The days were hot and sunny, and we could hear the neighborhood kids playing stickball outside, but we weren't allowed out while our parents worked. It wasn't long before we were bored with each other, and this was in the bad old days of daytime television, before the Cartoon Network.

The day our mom first took us to the public library was a thrill I'll never forget. I'd never been to one before, and the building seemed huge. The smell of mildewed paper hardly registered as I walked, amazed, through room after room lined with books and filled with rows of double-sided, freestanding wooden bookcases. The sight was as thrilling as the first glimpse of sand and water on our yearly trips to the beach.

We'd heard scary warnings about the city's dangerous streets, but the children's section was deep in the center of a building full of books. What bad guys would go there? My sister and I felt safe, hidden in the stacks. The public library opened new worlds, though I never talked to the other kids we encountered there, heeding the warning of the so-called dangerous people who were out to get children and newcomers.

I'd drag home bags of books at a time, giddy with the sheer number available, the loneliness lost in stories about other places and other times. I loved most books, with the exception of any story set in the late twentieth century that featured a girl with friends. As I'd feared, I was friendless, and heroines like Nancy Drew drove me to despair. She had *two* best friends (although I always wondered if George had ulterior motives).

There weren't any self-help books on friend-making that I knew of, and when I asked my mother for tips, she said, "Just go up to people and introduce yourself." Right.

I thought about how I'd done it once before, but that was in kindergarten. Who remembered that far back?

By now, school had started, but everyone at Our Lady Queen of Martyrs, my new parochial school, seemed to have known one another forever. I sat alone in class feeling as if everyone was looking at me, feeling like an intruder. Recess was held in the quiet residential street in front of the school, and when pedestrians walked past, I would stand near the groups of laughing girls, smiling and nodding as if I was one of them, and then hurrying away, afraid that they'd noticed what I'd done. I stood alone, the alien dork. The wienie girl.

They'd jump rope and play games that I didn't know, including deliciously complicated hand-clapping rhymes that I couldn't possibly learn. It was like watching a show, and I was the only audience.

At the end of the day, as we rushed out of the building, the girls would chatter about after-school activities: playing in Fort Tryon Park, going to Girl Scouts, music lessons and dance. My sister and I went straight home, under orders to stay inside until my mom got home. When we weren't sick of each other's company, we played elaborate games of make-believe with our Barbies.

I'd left behind my tiny plastic cowboys and Indians and Tonka trucks in Pittsburgh, thinking I'd outgrown tomboy stuff. When I missed them, I wondered, what next? Thumb-sucking? I needed to move ahead. I needed a plan. I was clueless.

I pictured myself kidnapped by aliens. Maybe one of them would be totally cute like Bobby Sherman. Maybe I read too much science fiction and watched too much TV.

My mom saw us struggling and tried to get us to be more outgoing. One year she signed us up for baton twirling. We spent most of the time marching in formation. I learned then that I wasn't cut out for a military career. Another year it was swimming lessons in what seemed like a huge municipal pool with peeling aqua-colored paint. My favorite part? The dead man's float. I used it with glee at the swimming pools of motor courts up and down the eastern coast on our annual trips to Florida, freaking out the tourists.

Mom's efforts broadened my horizons, but the skill I longed for, the one that eluded me, was how to make friends.

One cold, rainy autumn afternoon, I was at the library filling my bag with fantasy novels and threw Jane Eyre on top to reread because we were having English weather. I was also looking for a book I'd overheard a classmate recommend to her friend.

It was *Are You There God? It's Me, Margaret* by Judy Blume, the book that all the girls on the playground were whispering about. The nuns said it wasn't for the likes of us. I was looking forward to knowing what all the buzz was about—not that I'd have anyone to discuss it with. I was disappointed that it wasn't on the shelves that day. There were lots of other Judy Blume books, though, and I grabbed one. Testing the Blume waters, so to speak.

The chance I took paid off. *Then Again, Maybe I Won't* changed my life. It wasn't my first choice, since it was told from a boy's point of view, and who wanted to know how boys think? I was very young.

I was hooked from the first page. The hero, Tony Miglione, was moving, and boy, did I understand about moving. He felt many of the same emotions I had when we found out we were leaving Pittsburgh and moving to New York City—fear, excitement, resentment, and nostalgia for things that still surrounded me. Tony could have been my brother.

I knew those awful fears he described, that you'd never see anyone you knew again, that you wouldn't know where the best candy was or the place to buy a magazine or what TV channels to watch.

Tony's family had gotten rich and moved to a mansion, while we'd moved from a big house to a tiny apartment. Of course, we weren't alone. *Everyone* in New York lived in tiny apartments. I wondered how people could stand to live in the city. I had to walk to school every day with my sister, and our parents hammered the "no eye contact" rule into us. Eyes on the sidewalk and you'll do okay. Those bad guys were supposedly lurking everywhere. So I didn't look up except to see if the streetlight had changed. This was before the 1978 pooper scooper law, and there were other, more immediately disturbing reasons for keeping your sight on the sidewalk.

Vidrio inglés, English glass, was what my father euphemistically called dog poop, which was pancaked on every sidewalk and street surface. So I dodged doo and schlepped (a new word—these New Yorkers had their own language) to school and back every day.

Not everything about our new neighborhood had been upsetting. I was delighted to find that OLQM had lots of Latinas and thought it would help my chances of making friends. Dead wrong. Two girls in my class were friends with each other, and though I wanted to be their friend, they teased me constantly. Bullied, actually.

Once when I was in the bathroom sitting on the toilet, I was desperate to go, but extreme bathroom shyness dictated that I couldn't start to pee until absolutely everyone had left the restroom. This usually made me late getting back to class, but I didn't care, even though Sister Regina Miriam gave me the evil eye as I walked to my desk. She never scolded me, though, so she must have understood.

That day, when I was finally alone, my poor bladder at last got some relief. Just as I let go, I heard giggling from above. I looked up, and there were my tormentors, looking down at me. They were standing on the toilet seats of the stalls on either side of me and were looking down at me over the top—and I was on the toilet. I don't know what I thought they could see around my pleated tartan wool skirt or why they'd care.

They laughed when I looked up. I wanted to scream, but if I did, the nuns would come running, and then they'd see me, too. So I yelled "get out" over and over until they finally left, still laughing. They never got into trouble, and I don't know how I avoided a urinary tract infection because I swear I didn't pee in a public restroom for a year.

On that rainy October weekend when I dove into *Then Again, Maybe I Won't*, I lived with Tony Miglione as he moved, and I wished that my family's reason for moving was that we'd suddenly gotten rich.

Then I read the astounding chapter in which Tony made friends with the kid next door. Somehow, in all of the other books I'd devoured before then, I'd never read an account, told from the point of view of someone my age, of someone walking up to another kid and making friends.

Tony had spotted his neighbor Joel playing basketball. They avoided each other; they nodded nonchalantly. I knew all of those steps. I was trapped in them.

And then Tony walked up to his neighbor and said, "Hi." And then they started hanging out together.

I remember sitting up and thinking, that's it? Hi? How could I have missed that? Never mind that my mother had given me exactly the same advice years earlier. This was in print. This made it click. I read on. Surely something awful would come of it. They'd get into a fight or something. Nope.

Tony was a good friend but not a wuss. He didn't lie to keep Joel out of trouble when he shoplifted. Aha, I thought. A good friend stands up for herself. I wished that Tony was a girl and lived in my building.

As I read, I picked up boy knowledge that I never thought would be useful, though it was certainly interesting. Boys liked to watch girls undress. They had thoughts about sex, just like girls.

What stuck with me, though, was those five lines of text where Tony Miglione made friends with his next-door neighbor, those five lines that changed my life.

I had a new modus operandi now. When I returned to school after the weekend, I watched kids in action. These were all people who thought I was invisible. I watched them as if I were a scientist studying ants run little errands to and from their mound.

One kid had the basketball. He threw and missed. Another kid caught it on the rebound. Can I play? he asked, holding the ball. Sure, the kid with the ball said. And then both of them played, until another kid showed up and blocked one of the throws. No one got mad at him. They played around him, and then he got the ball. So now three kids were playing. Interesting.

Nearby, the toilet twins were skipping rope with a whole crew of girls. I was no pro at skipping, so I think it would have taken less courage to jump out of an airplane than it did for me to walk up to those girls. I knew what to do. I had Tony's Rules of Order.

I remember my first words to them, "Hi, is this the line? Can I play, too?"

The girl waiting in front of me turned and smiled. "Sure," she said. And the girl twirling the rope on that side said, "You're named Berta, right? Is that a nickname?"

She knew my name. I wasn't invisible after all. Then it was my turn to jump, and thankfully I didn't trip over my feet like I did when I skipped rope alone. They sang a song about the name of the boy you'd marry. When they got to the S's, I skipped out. I had a crush on a boy named Sergio. Everyone wanted to know the name of the boy. They guessed all the wrong ones, and I laughed and said no, and then realized that we were actually talking. I was one of them.

I didn't know the names of the girls I was talking to, but we all ran inside when recess was over, and the next day at lunch they waved me to their table when I entered the lunchroom. My friends.

I ended up being close to my toilet tormentors, until we moved again, this time to Charlotte, North Carolina. It was bad enough to leave the big city I'd gotten used to, but now we were headed to the Deep South. Totally different, I thought. What would they be like?

They were like girls everywhere, and my new friend-making skills worked. Like tying your shoes, I just did it; fast or slow, sloppy, tight, neat, or double-knotted. Once I knew how, I did what the occasion called for, with no second thoughts. It's sad if you don't know how to tie your shoes and have to wait patiently for someone to do yours while you watch enviously as other kids do their own. I was self-sufficient.

There were other instances in Judy Blume's books, once I pried them loose from other readers and read them for myself, that gave me the feeling that one of the world's deep truths had been revealed. What other girls thought about their bodies, about how to talk to boys and how devastating a pimple or a divorce can be to a kid, but also that kids are a lot stronger and more resilient than adults think they are.

Tony Miglione's story was the first time that I'd ever read fiction written for me and about me. About kids, written the way kids think. And it changed my life. But it was only the beginning. Judy Blume had other things to teach me.

Later, when I read *Deenie,* Ms. Blume's controversial book about a beautiful girl diagnosed with scoliosis and forced to wear a hideous brace, I discovered that other parts of my life were normal, too. In a matter-of-fact way, with no details, Ms. Blume explained that masturbation was normal. It was excellent information. Who else wrote about it? No one I'd ever heard of.

Years later, when I was in high school, a bunch of girls at a school party talked about "doing it" as opposed to "not doing it."

We were not talking about sex with boys. We were huddled in an out-of-the-way school bathroom, waiting for a girl to finish using the lone stall, and someone laughed and said she was probably doing herself.

In retrospect, that girl in the stall was probably like I had been and was just waiting for all of us to shut up and troop out of there so that she could pee in peace. If so, she was doomed.

The minute Diane said "doing herself," you could have heard a pin drop on the little hexagonal ceramic tiles. We all stopped fluffing our big eighties hair and stared.

Someone else said, "That is so perverted."

And I said, "No it's not. Just read *Deenie.* It's in the library." So then, of course, I was labeled the perv, for volunteering that I knew about it.

It turned out *Deenie* wasn't in the school library. I looked later. And it wasn't in the little moldy-smelling public library on the other side of the volunteer fire department building. I must have read it in New York. In ninth grade, I didn't follow news about censorship. I didn't know that *Deenie* had been banned from many libraries. I don't think it was banned from ours. I think it was stolen by someone who wanted to know but was too embarrassed to check it out and get caught reading the book.

I hope those girls found *Deenie* later. I hope the poor kid in the bathroom stall was able to come out. I picture her, skeletal remains in her party dress, all bare bones except for her withered but extended bladder.

When I think back to sixth grade, I think of my period starting, of my first crush, of the nuns in their long black habits with oversized rosaries at their waists. I remember how painful it was to be invisible to the other kids. And I think of Judy Blume, whose stories unlocked the untold secrets of life and whose name will always mean friendship to me, now and forever.

———

Cuban-born chica-lit author Berta Platas *is not done growing up or learning from Judy Blume. In the years since junior high, she's developed coping mechanisms to help overcome the creeping wienietude that often overtakes her. One of them is writing. Another is hanging out with her really cool daughter, who is also a JB fan. You can visit her at www.berta platas.com and judge for yourself.*

BRAVE NEW KID

| *Diana Peterfreund* |

My parents taught me to swim when I was three years old. I have hazy memories of visits to the neighborhood pool, of splashing around in cool blue water, inflatable wings firmly affixed to my arms. By the time I moved to Florida, at age four, I loved the water. I loved playing in the gentle Gulf of Mexico surf, taking swimming lessons with my kindergarten class, learning to do handstands in the shallow end of our backyard pool. My little brothers took to the aquatic life as well, and our childhoods were punctuated by summers in which you hardly ever saw us out of our bathing suits.

Many years later, I learned that my mom was afraid of the water.

This little factoid threw me like a nasty spill on a Slip N'Slide. First of all, how could anyone be afraid of swimming? It was so much fun! Besides, we lived in Florida, where beach trips and backyard pools were a way of life. How could she avoid it? She'd always gone in the water when we were younger—hadn't she? Okay, maybe she'd stuck to the sandbars and the tide pools, or sat on the steps near the shallow end, or even hung out on the nearest chaise lounge and watched us from the edge of the splash zone . . . hey, wait a second!

My mother tricked all three of us. Unwilling to let us inherit her fear, the way we might inherit her love for black-and-white movies (me) or her appetite for steamed clams (my brothers), she'd sublimated her phobia and embarked on a campaign of legerdemain so thorough that we all turned into dedicated water babies. Clever woman. Sneaky but smart.

And not alone in her deception. I've since heard many stories about parents who act especially gung ho toward their progeny about activities that the adults themselves would not touch with a ten-foot pool skimmer. On one hand, props to the parents for endeavoring to make their kids better, faster, and stronger than they were. On the other hand, liar, liar pants on fire.

Though now that I'm older (and an avid scuba diver, care of my dad's insistence that all three of his kids get certified) I appreciate my mom's efforts to protect me from her own phobias, at the time I felt almost betrayed. She'd convinced me that swimming was a blast (and roller skating, too, come to think of it) only to disown the activity once she'd gotten me hooked. She'd impressed upon me how easy it supposedly was and then later let it slip that she didn't actually know from firsthand experience.

Discovering that the adults in your family don't really have all of the answers is a scary experience. If we're very lucky, we learn about little things like water phobias long before it ever comes to light that our folks don't have answers for the Big Problems. In our youth, it seems as if they just aren't willing to share the truth with us, but as we grow older, we begin to see that the truth is *they don't always know*.

In *Starring Sally J. Freedman As Herself,* the ten-year-old protagonist learns this while treading the dividing line between childhood and adolescence. And with the realization that her parents either don't have the answers or won't give them to her, Sally learns that she needs to find them herself.

Sally's father clearly adheres to my mom's moral imperative that it's just dandy to deceive your children in the name of saving them from your own neuroses. When his wife (who, like my mother, doesn't swim) expresses her fears about flying, he says, "I wish you wouldn't talk that way in front of Sally. How will she ever learn to be adventurous?"

Louise Freedman reveals her vastly different approach to parenting when she responds, "Little girls don't need to be adventurous."

And Sally proves that she's our kind of heroine by butting in with, "But I want to be adventurous."

Like Sally, I wanted to be adventurous. It was an oft-touted law in the Peterfreund household that one did not suffer wimps; my dad recited FDR's "The only thing we have to fear is fear itself" speech until we'd do pretty much anything just to get out of earshot. My parents practiced what they preached. What could be scarier, after all, than sticking your babies in a pool you'd rather avoid altogether? Whenever we got scared, we faced it, and whenever we didn't know the answer, we figured it out.

Little wonder, then, that I identified so strongly with Sally. We both had daddies who wanted us to be brave. In fact, of all the fictional girls I encountered, Sally was probably the most like me on every level. I reread *Sally J.* over and over again, always marveling at the way Judy Blume had perfectly captured my life. I was growing up forty years after the events in that book took place, and the movie stars, fashions, and telephone technologies had all changed, but little else differentiated our generations. Unlike most of the heroines I'd met in books, Sally dwelled not in New York, Boston, or Prince Edward Island but in Florida, just like me; she was Jewish, I was half; and, most importantly, we had the same overactive imagination. We each worried about the health and safety of our families, marveled at the mysteries of *boys*, made friends and lost them, and tried to cope with a world that seemed to grow increasingly complex and frightening every year. Growing up isn't easy, no matter what generation you belong to.

When I first read of Sally's world, I was her age, and for all the talk of girls growing up too quickly nowadays, I shared her level of naiveté. I didn't know what "love and other indoor sports" (the sign-off Sally swiped from her older babysitter and favored for her personal correspondence) meant any better than she did. And though, as Sally's uncle says, "Little pitchers have big ears," there always seemed to be some key word that Sally and I were missing in order to fully translate the things that the grown-ups didn't want us to hear.

And we hadn't yet figured out what was so interesting about the stuff they didn't want us to know. Sally's father has to remain behind with his dental practice when the rest of the family winters in Miami, and when he at last comes to visit them, Sally can't comprehend why he spends his first night in town at a hotel with Sally's mom. Her older brother admonishes her: "So they can do it . . . you're so dumb." But just as with the "indoor sports" that Sally thinks of as dodgeball or volleyball, she can't imagine that there's anything her parents can't do just as well in their efficiency apartment, "right here in the Murphy bed."

Of course, since my father was a gynecologist, I had a greater understanding of sex than both Sally and most of my contemporary playmates, though much of it was still lost on me. For instance, I was not privy to the humor behind my young cousin's stated intent to become an orthodontist and join my father's medical practice. The "work both ends at once" jokes never stopped, but I thought it sounded like a good plan. (As a matter of fact, I still do. I find orthodontics and pap smears equally distasteful and think you might as well get it all over at once. If anyone knows of a practice like this, sign me up!)

Unlike Sally, I knew what her mother meant when she claimed that "nice girls" only get pregnant after marriage. When Sally inquires after the unwed pregnant teen (named Bubbles, unfortunately) in her building, her mother practices characteristic avoidance: "I don't want to talk about that." But as Sally notes immediately afterward, "Everybody else in their house was talking about it." And at the same time, they are all celebrating the delicate condition of Sally's aunt. Forty years on, I was also mystified by the various reactions to news of pregnancy in the family. Why was it that one announcement generated merrymaking while another spawned worried whispers?

Like Sally, the social cues went straight over my head. All she knows is that it's a very shocking thing for her orthodox teen neighbor to get pregnant with a *"goy."* Later, she fantasizes about throwing this apparently scandalous news back in the faces of her uppity neighbors, who are wont to compare her choice of playtime activities to their own daughters'. "I know all about your Bubbles," she imagines saying. "She did it with a *goy* and got a baby . . . so ha ha on you."

Of course, the true scandal of the case, and the one that stuck most firmly in my mind for almost two decades, is the fact that the girl's parents proceed to disown and sit *shiva* for their daughter. Sally's grandmother, Ma Fanny, who has until that point in the novel supported Sally's mother in most of her fear-mongering, breaks from tradition, for at last her emotions have been truly roused. "They should only know what it's like to *really* lose a child!"

Sally, always the adventurous one, asks her grandmother if she lost a child, and when it is confirmed, asks, "Is it a secret?"

So many of the complex issues in her life have been shrugged off or sidestepped by the adults that it is little wonder Sally assumes that anything she doesn't yet know is something she's not supposed to. But Ma Fanny's candor breaks down the wall. No, it's not a secret; Ma Fanny just doesn't like to discuss such a painful subject. At last, the unvarnished truth. And because she was willing to share that tidbit in such an honest manner, we can't help but feel as if she's the one with the moral high ground in the Bubbles case.

It is in moments like these, when a parent foregoes the position of "for your protection" and admits that something is difficult, or painful, or frightening to him or her, that a child begins to realize what it means to be an adult—to be truly *grown up*. There are times when, perhaps just briefly, you are treated as an equal. *You're afraid? Well, I'm afraid, too.*

Judy Blume said, "Sally's world is the world as I perceived it, at age ten. A world of secrets kept from children, a world of questions without answers." When I was a girl, the times my mom and dad dropped the parenting act and told me how they really felt were golden glimpses into this magical realm of adulthood, where every joke made sense and every worry might not have a solution, but at least you knew you weren't alone in thinking so. It was cooler than being given a wineglass full of cranberry juice to toast with, more exciting than messing around in your mom's makeup drawer. Pretending to be a grown-up was one thing; when adults actually confided in you, you almost were an adult, too.

"Grown-ups always keep things to themselves," Sally complains to a playmate while discussing their concerns about their respective parents—Sally is afraid her father will die in New Jersey, and her friend's mom has descended into alcoholism after the death of her husband in World War II. "But it's better to share your problems with a friend, don't you think?" For Sally, sharing comes to symbolize a sense of equality. But for a family dealing with the aftermath of a war that so thoroughly devastated their Jewish community on both a military and civilian level, sharing the truth with a child is a tall order, indeed.

In 1945, Sally is seven, and all she understands about the announcement of the end of World War II is that it's a good reason to put on a dress, shoot fireworks, eat junk food, and stay out too late. Sally doesn't understand her parents' joy or their hope that the European branch of the family might have survived the concentration camps. While the war might have colored her early childhood, it didn't do so in any meaningful way. She latches on to the most dramatic of the overheard stories; lamp shades made of a Jewish person's skin and the possibility that Hitler and his cronies are hiding out in Argentina (or upstairs from her condo) provide fodder

for games of make-believe but carry no more weight than the latest
Esther Williams film. As a kid, I myself was dimly aware of the fact
that my grandfather (who'd been in America during the war) had
lost almost all of his European family in the Holocaust. Once, I met
my father's cousins, who had spent the conflict in an elaborate
hideout scenario, and my childlike brain subsequently confused the
details of their experience with the story of Anne Frank. Like Sally,
I filled in the blank spots that my folks either wouldn't or couldn't
share with snippets of popular culture—though I don't think I ever
imagined a scenario in which my favorite movie star saves the in-
mates of a concentration camp through a timely application of syn-
chronized swimming.

As ridiculous as this seems, it is often a child's innocent attempts to uncover the truth and understand the world that reveals
a more honest perspective, untainted by the indoctrination of
adulthood. Truly brave parents recognize the capacity in their children for confronting questions that an older generation can't. Truly
successful ones recognize when a child chooses to take a step into
this unknown, beyond the paths forged by parents, and begin to
grow up.

For Sally, genocide on another continent isn't half as perplexing
as the injustice and racism she sees on a daily basis right there in
Miami. During her first trip down to Florida, she is perplexed
when a black family must leave her train car as they cross into the
South. Her mother neatly sidesteps her questions about racial segregation, so Sally goes to her other expert source: her father. After a
run-in at a pair of public water fountains marked "COLORED
ONLY" and "WHITES ONLY," she is determined to get an answer
from him about this confusing issue and writes him letter after let-

ter until she is satisfied. Their exchange marks one of the comedic high points in the book but also serves as an encapsulation of Sally's nascent search for truth.

"What would happen if a person with dark skin, like a Negro or a Seminole Indian, took a drink from our fountain?" she asks her father in a letter. "Do they really have different germs? Since you went to Dental College I'm sure you know these things." After being thwarted by her mother, Sally has clearly decided that flattery is a clever technique.

"Dear Sally, In your last letter you raised some questions that are very difficult to answer." Dear old dad proceeds to tap dance like Fred Astaire.

But Sally is having none of it: "You forgot to tell me if people with dark skin have different germs in their mouth."

Finally, hoping to end the conversation, Dad responds: "As for germs in people's mouths, we are all the same."

Which brings Sally back to her original point: "Then why does the Five and Dime have two fountains, and why do they drink only from theirs and we drink only from ours?"

At last, he capitulates, and rather than merely tossing big terms like "outright segregation" at the poor girl, opens the door for her own exploration and growth:

"Dear Sally, Your questions are very hard to answer. At the moment it is simply the way things are. I doubt that they will remain that way forever, but for now, you have to abide by the rules. I'm glad that you're questioning those rules, though." The people of Sally's generation questioned those rules so much that by the time I read the book, they didn't exist anymore—as law, at least.

Sally's father serves as the character who most often assists Sally on her path toward adult understanding. Whereas her mother chooses to dismiss Sally's queries as inappropriate for little girls, her father can always be counted on to deliver the straight dope. This dichotomy becomes increasingly apparent to Sally as the book progresses and she begins to understand which parts of her own personality come from which parent.

When her mother balks at going on a trip to Cuba because of her fear of flying (the fear her husband had earlier asked her to hide from their daughter), Sally's father tries to cajole her into it, a move that infuriates his wife. "I'm not Sally! You can't convince me by calling this an adventure." Of course, Louise eventually does accompany her husband to Cuba, where she has a blast and even admits that she would be willing to fly "once in a while . . . in good weather." Watching her mother confront this fear probably does more to convince Sally that it's okay to try than all of her father's blustering about "being adventurous."

Can the very act of putting on a brave face actually make a person question the fear that he or she holds? Perhaps once my mom had successfully convinced her three children that there was nothing to be afraid of in the water, she began to wonder if she was, after all, correct about that. She wasn't about to run out and join my little brother in his free-diving classes, but maybe she'd swim a lap or two in the pool. One time, in the Florida Keys, my mom even went snorkeling, and what's more, said it was *fun*. I was so proud of her! Whereas Sally's mother uses her own dislike for swimming as her reasoning behind not wanting to force her kids to swim, my mother utilized her fear as a motivation to make sure her children loved it.

When her mother's fears seem to be gaining ground in Sally's outlook, her father takes her aside for a heart-to-heart. As with the earlier revelation from Ma Fanny, this conversation with her father gives Sally the opportunity to understand her familial relationships from a more mature perspective. "Your mother worries a lot. She can't help it . . . she loves us all so much . . . but I don't want you to grow up worrying that way." Laying out the difference in parenting philosophies is a watershed moment for Sally, and she shows her maturity by not turning the moment into an opportunity to pit one parent against the other or even to choose which style she likes best. When she does go on the trip, she pays homage to both her parents' points of view by pronouncing the adventure "scary but fun." At the end of the book, Sally writes, "I am in-between my mother and my father . . . about a lot of things." Sally recognizes that both instincts have a place in the role of parenting. She needs protection while wading into the waters of adulthood, reassurance that her parents will try to protect her in whatever way they can, but also the knowledge that when she's finally ready, they will trust her to swim out on her own. Her father may have taught Sally to be adventurous, but he also taught her to question things she didn't understand, and as her sojourn in Miami ends, she realizes that there are many things to question. Her parents aren't perfect; they possess fears and worries, just like her, and they don't have all the answers. But they have given her the tools with which to find them herself.

My own parents value hard work and bravery. After all, it took a lot of both to get them out of the poor coal-mining town in which they were raised. We were encouraged to confront our fears because my folks knew that only in doing so would we develop the courage we needed to create our own adult lives. Parents dream of giving their children the best life possible. They want them to have every opportunity, even the ones they didn't have themselves, to be better educated, better provided for, more successful, happier. They want the next generation to sidestep the mistakes they made, overcome the pressures that clouded their judgment, and be free from the fears that may have kept them from the exhilarating splash into the deep end. Perhaps that's a good enough reason to keep a secret or tell a little white lie. Or maybe it can best be accomplished by admitting your fear or even confronting it while your children look on. Just like Sally, I realized there were many reasons that my parents kept the secrets they did, and even more important reasons that they told us everything we needed to know when we were ready.

———

Diana Peterfreund has been scuba diving in the Great Barrier Reef, spelunking through sunken caverns in New Zealand, and, most importantly, white-water rafting with both her parents down the River of No Return. Her biggest fear is losing her taste for adventure. She graduated from Yale University, and in 2006, got her dose of thrills by releasing her first novel, Secret Society Girl. *Its sequel was out in 2007. Diana lives in Washington, D.C.*

Breaking Up Is Hard to Do—
Especially with Your BFF

| *Lynda Curnyn* |

Recently, I lost my best friend. No, it was nothing like that. She's still alive and well and living nearby in Manhattan. In fact, a few months ago, I met her new boyfriend, a man I could see her marrying, though I know she'd clobber me for saying that. Gianna has always shrugged off the idea of marriage, but ever since I've seen her with her new man, me thinks the lady has been protesting too much—and trust me, I know this lady pretty well.

We met on the snowy slope of a neighbor's lawn at the age of nine, two sleds coming head to head at the bottom of the hill. It makes perfect sense to me now that our friendship began with a crash. In some ways, we've been reverberating with it ever since.

These days I wonder if that crash was some kind of omen. After all, I had read all about the rise and fall of friendships from a friend who I have known just as long as I've known Gianna: Judy Blume. Gianna and I were like Stephanie Hirsh and Rachel Robinson in

Just As Long As We're Together. Best Friends Forever. If such a thing exists.

Before I even met Gianna, I knew all about "best friends." Before the age of nine, I had pledged best friendship to no less than four girls without batting an eye. It never occurred to me, as it did to Rachel Robinson, that "best means best." Admittedly I felt a twinge of *something* when I declared Amy Goldberg my best friend, knowing I already had a best friend in Carmela Castillito since first grade. And my declaration to Amy came not two weeks after Ruth Colby had announced to her entire family that I was her best friend, and a mere two days after Hannah Fisher had nominated me for that role. The truth is, on some level, I did my best for all of them. I was the Chewbacca to Amy's Princess Leia at her *Star Wars* birthday party. I was the buffer between Ruth and her domineering mother who was forever following her around with a cuticle scissor or a hairbrush. And I may have been a replacement for Hannah's absentee mother who was always mysteriously at the beauty parlor whenever I came over for a playdate.

Of course, I didn't speak to any of them after I moved to a new town at the age of nine. Except for Carmela. I guess you could say that all the other "best friends" I had were really just crushes. But Carmela was my first love. And perhaps because she was my first, she was destined not to be my last.

I was six when I met Carmela. Her house was around the corner from mine, which made Carmela someone I could walk to school with. According to my parents, Mr. and Mrs. Castillito were "right off the boat," which was supposed to explain why Carmela's grandparents lived in the spare bedroom, why Carmela's little brother was allowed to ride his Big Wheel around the streets in barely more than brightly colored briefs, why Carmela was allowed to have pet chickens and we weren't (I suppose that was kinder than telling me that the chickens weren't so much pets as they were fresh poultry).

Despite these differences, or maybe because of them, we became the best of friends. I would even say we were as close as sisters, which made sense, since neither of us had a sister of our own. And since I attended practically every christening, communion, and birthday party the Castillito family threw, I truly felt like an adopted daughter. I was even given chores when I went over Carmela's house. Except in the Castillito's exotic household, chores included picking tomatoes from the garden and rolling out pasta dough and squeezing it through a crank into long strings of linguine. Pretty soon the family was asking me to translate business letters, medical reports, or anything that came in an "official-looking" envelope. Not that Carmela couldn't read English, but I think they somehow trusted me, even at the age of eight or nine, as someone who might know something about something (I gave that impression anyway). Just think of me as the Irish consigliere to the Castillito clan. I was in tight.

So tight that I was sure, after we said our tearful good-byes as the moving truck stood ready to tote away my family and me to what seemed like a foreign country, that we would stay in touch. After all, we were best friends. The forever kind.

But I discovered that forever might be too much to ask, even of a best friend.

Yes, there were letters. Lots of them. And long phone calls, when our parents permitted us to take over the telephone lines for hours. We even visited as often as we could. In fact, at the age of twelve, I experienced my first kiss behind the catering hall where Carmela's first godchild's christening was being held, with none other than Carmela's (hot) cousin, Sergio.

But by then I already had a new best friend in Gianna. If I was being unfaithful to Carmela, it was only because I was trying to remain true to the girl I was becoming. As I moved into my teens, Carmela's world started to seem, well . . . silly. Her letters, which still came despite my meager responses, seemed positively provincial, with tales of babysitting her godchild (I think Carmela aspired to motherhood from her first menstruation) and family betrayals, like the time her cousin Teresa didn't ask her to be a bridesmaid in her wedding.

I should have seen that as a foreshadowing, as Carmela's own wedding was our undoing. Mostly because I committed what probably seemed to Carmela like an act of treason: I turned down her request to be a bridesmaid. By the time she asked, I was a struggling graduate student living in New York City. In fact, getting the call from her was a surprise; we hadn't spoken in such a long time, probably years at that point. Now faced with the prospect of blowing money I didn't have on a dress I didn't want to wear, I was eager to bow out. Besides, I was just testing my newly honed feminist wings, and something in me adamantly resisted the idea of having to cloister myself in a cloned dress like some sort of Stepford Wife in Waiting. I have since learned that there are more selfless reasons to don a hideous dress in the name of friendship. However, at the time, I turned her down flat, citing economics.

It was the ultimate betrayal. Yes, I was still invited to the wedding (Carmela was nothing, if not gracious), but we never spoke again. Even her family shunned me. The girl who was once the family consigliere was now dead to them.

I will never forget Carmela, my first best, my first love, though I'm heartily glad I didn't wind up with her. But I learned a hard truth from my breakup with Carmela. And that was that best friends *could* break up.

That reality haunted me when faced with the idea of breaking up with Gianna. We have known each other for nearly three decades. She was the sister I always longed for but never had. We couldn't break up . . . could we?

On some levels, history was already repeating itself. Because my new best friend was eerily similar to my old one. Like Carmela, Gianna is first-generation Italian American. Like Carmela, Gianna grew up in a house with her parents, her grandparents, and a baby brother who at least knew better than to ride around the neighborhood in his underwear. Though there were no chickens in Gianna's yard, there were rabbits. And, forgive me for saying this, but somehow the ultimate demise of those rabbits seemed even more painful than that of the Castillito's chickens, I suspect not just because the rabbits were cuter but I was getting older. I was learning that nothing lasts forever. Not even best friends.

When I first met Gianna, I was the new kid on the block. Worse, I had a (bad) Toni Tennille (as in Captain and Tennille) haircut and a waistline, I discovered upon being teased for the first time in my nine-year-old life, that made me just as worthy of the El Chunko title as Stephanie Hirsh.

But if I had trouble making friends, I don't remember it. Mostly because Gianna paved the way for me. Gianna had lived in our town since she was a baby. She knew everyone.

And when she blossomed from a freckle-faced beanpole into a sultry siren at age twelve, suddenly everyone wanted to know her. Well, every boy did anyway. By the time we got to high school, Gianna was one of the most popular girls in school. As her chubby, affable sidekick, I became popular by association. If we happened to find ourselves a part of the "cool crowd," it was because Gianna was dating the hot guy at the head of it. If we scored rides to the beach on beautiful summer days, it was because the driver (usually male) considered Gianna a good friend.

Strangely enough, I wasn't jealous of Gianna. In fact, I was happy enough to enjoy all the best that high school had to offer from the relative safety of the sidelines. Yes, I wanted boys, but they were a little scary, especially to a plump teen who was more used to being teased than wooed.

Of course, there was a downside to sitting on the sidelines of a so-called fabulous high school life. And that was that I lived in Gianna's shadow. As an insecure high school student, I took comfort in this role. But as a woman, I recently realized, it could be suffocating.

If Gianna and I had survived the closeness we shared as young girls, it was because life had put some comfortable distance between us after high school. I went off to college while Gianna went to work. Gianna spent most of her twenties living on Long Island before joining me in Manhattan. It wasn't until we traveled to Italy together in our thirties that our teenage past caught up with us.

I'm told that the best way to find out if you can survive marriage with a prospective spouse is to take an overseas vacation with him. I think you can apply this to best friends, too. Of course, our trip to Italy wasn't the worst of times. How could it be? We were two single women on a whirlwind tour of Milan, Venice, Florence, Positano, and Rome. In some ways, we complemented each other as travel partners. For instance, I'm not much of a picture taker, preferring instead simply to experience my surroundings. Still I was grateful for the photos Gianna, an avid photographer, brought home for us. While Gianna preferred to "wing it" when it came to the daily itinerary, I spent time poring over guidebooks for information. And while I barely spoke a paragraph's worth of Italian, Gianna was fluent.

Which should have been a good thing. And it was. Most of the time. Except my lack of foreign-language skills forced me to be socially dependent on Gianna in a way I hadn't been. At least, not since high school.

Suddenly I found myself on the sidelines again, watching as Gianna tested out her Italian on just about every man who crossed our paths. Sometimes this was fun. Like when the two older gentlemen on the train treated us to dinner, each vying to buy us the better entree or glass of wine. Or when we found ourselves in a karaoke bar outside of Venice being serenaded with Beatles songs by two otherwise-Italian-speaking lotharios.

Other times, I felt like I was playing a game in which I didn't know the rules. I had to rely on Gianna for cues, which wasn't so easy. In Milan, we nearly missed seeing *The Last Supper* because Gianna was too busy testing out her Italian on the caretaker of our hotel. In Naples, I was forced, by humiliation more than anything else, to get into the backseat of a car that belonged to a man I instinctually didn't trust because Gianna insisted he was friendly enough. There were the waiters who heaped her dish fuller and poured on the charm and I dare say, affection, simply because she spoke their language. In one restaurant, the enchanted waiter even slid most of the pasta from the serving bowl onto her plate before he realized I was sitting there. By the time we got to Positano, Gianna seemed to have forgotten the English language altogether, not even bothering to translate for me anymore and leaving me to figure out what was going to happen next. The straw that broke this camel's back was when I found myself on a boat I thought was headed for Capri, only to find myself stuck on a deserted island while Gianna and her latest paramour wandered off down the rocky coast for a romantic tryst.

Needless to say, by the time we got to Rome, I was ready for a divorce. And since one of Gianna's beaus had followed us there, I figured I could at least try for a trial separation. I was tired of being on Gianna's vacation. It reminded me too much of high school, where I existed in her world. Now that I was an adult and had found my own independence, I discovered we had very different interests. For one thing, I came to Italy to see Italy, not just the men. So when Gianna told me that Stefano would be joining us for dinner our first night in Rome, I professed a desire to tour a church on the other side of the city.

And that's when everything exploded. Gianna declared me selfish for wanting to go off on my own. "Selfish? Me?" I replied, amazed that she could see it that way. I couldn't believe she thought so little of me that she thought I actually enjoyed being a third party to her International Dating Festival.

I think it was that realization that brought me to embarrassing tears, surprising me with the depth of pain I'd felt living in Gianna's shadow. I was reminded of that fat girl in high school, willingly banished to the backseat of the car, watching Gianna sitting in the best seat, with the best guy. The only saving grace was that I was certain I was no longer in danger of being that girl anymore.

I went to the church. To be honest, I no longer even remember which one it was, only that I got down on my knees in one of the pews and prayed for peace of mind. And I'm not a praying kind of gal. I took my time on the way home, deciding against the metro, meandering back to our hotel along cobblestone streets, taking in the crumbling facades, the crowds of people.

By the time I reached the hotel, I felt like myself again.

Gianna, however, was a wreck. In fact, she was practically dangling out of the window of our upper-floor room, apparently looking for me.

"Thank God, you're back. I was so worried about you!" she declared once I made my way up to the room. Then she went on about how she was afraid I was lost, how scared she was for me. But the whole thing didn't ring true somehow. I was a grown woman. Did she really think I wouldn't be able to get by on my own?

It was then that I realized she was all dressed for a date, though her date was nowhere in sight.

"What happened to Stefano?" I asked.

Stefano was delayed for reasons that seemed mysterious enough for me to distrust him. And in the conversation that ensued, I learned that despite all the romance she shared with him, Gianna didn't trust him very much, either. And that's when I realized something new about the woman I had known for over twenty years.

When it came to men, Gianna had a few fears herself.

Suddenly I wondered if I had been as much a crutch for her in high school as she'd been for me. Just as I felt safe watching life and romance go by from the backseat of a car, maybe she felt just as safe having me there. With her best friend at her back, nothing could go wrong with the boy she was flirting with in the front, right?

I went to dinner with Gianna and Stefano that night. Mostly because I couldn't abandon my oldest friend to a man who now seemed more dangerous than dangerously sexy.

But once back in New York, our relationship was forever changed. Mostly because I was determined not to be that girl in the backseat anymore. Until Italy, I didn't realize I always gave in to what Gianna thought best out of habit. And old habits die hard.

I had to learn to say no to the all-night dance parties. Dancing was something Gianna loves, not me. I no longer desired to sit through blockbuster movies featuring the hunk du jour simply because that was Gianna's pick. Rock climbing? No way. Competitive sports? Not my thing.

These days, we spend less time together. On bad days, I wonder if my compliancy was the glue that kept us together. On better ones, I know this isn't true.

Just a few months back, Gianna called to tell me she met someone new. She sounded different this time. He sounded different this time. For one thing, he wasn't her classic bad boy. In fact, just the reverse: Jackson is a bonafide hero who was voluntarily down in the rubble in the days that followed 9/11. For another, it's clear he genuinely cares for Gianna.

I am so happy for her. I'm happy for me, too. Because the truth is, now that she has a boyfriend, I find our relationship is easier. As if I no longer have to be her everything. Maybe it was my problem thinking I *had* to be everything. Perhaps because we've both been single so much longer than we'd ever expected, we've gotten into that habit of being there for each other. I offered her a place to stay when the heartbreak of losing a man she loved made her not want to go home again. And she was at my side when I buried my father a few years ago. I will always worry that her impulsive nature will keep her from planning for her financial future. Or that she'll never give up smoking, despite the risk to her health. She will always worry that I worry too much.

I suspect we will be friends forever. Best friends? Sometimes we are, but most of the time, we can't be. I think Stephanie put it best when at the end of *Just As Long As We're Together* she declared that "close [friends] is as good as best." Even Rachel has to concede to Stephanie's point, if, as Rachel says, "you're talking about true friends."

Yes, we're talking about true friends. Because despite our differences, I know for sure Gianna is one of my truest.

If you don't believe me, just read Judy Blume.

———

Lynda Curnyn is the author of four novels and several short stories. When she's not writing books, she can be found hanging with best friends in New York City. Say hello at www.lyndacurnyn.com.

The Importance of ABC's

| *Kayla Perrin* |

Ask any sixth-grade schoolgirl and she'll tell you that size matters. Like, majorly.

Totally.

Big time.

Size—it's the key to dating the cutest guys.

No, not *their* size—yours.

Your breast size.

When you're eleven going on twelve, like Margaret in *Are You There God? It's Me, Margaret,* it's the thing that matters most in your life. Do you have breasts or not? And if you do have them, there's an even more important concern: are you an A, B, or C?

A—perfectly respectable. You're well on your way to womanhood. B—wow, aren't you rounding out nicely? C—hmm, a little risqué for someone in sixth grade. No, make that *very* risqué. Adolescent boys walk by you in the hallway and gawk. You're the subject of all sorts of racy rumors. Just ask Laura Danker, Margaret's big-busted sixth-grade classmate. No, you don't want C's (or, God forbid, D's!). Being too big is possibly worse than wearing a training bra, because at least you can stuff a training bra to the size you like. But you can't hide those titillating C's.

Or maybe C's aren't *that* bad. At least you've got breasts. Pretty breasts that other girls envy, even if they start rumors about you. Maybe the worst thing of all is being flat-chested in a sea of girls who are blooming like daffodils in spring.

Regardless of your cup size, one thing is certain. When you're a sixth-grade girl, you want more than anything to fit in. Like Goldilock's trying out the Bears' hospitality, you don't want a chest that is too big or too small. You want one that is just right.

I should know. Like Margaret in *Are You There God? It's Me, Margaret,* I suffered the frustration of being a late breast bloomer. And just like Margaret, I moved after fifth grade and had to start a new school in sixth grade. Having to make a whole new set of friends is daunting enough without going through the drama of puberty at the same time.

I was desperate to fit in. To be as normal as the other girls who were talking about getting their periods and having to wear bras. And yet I had no breasts to speak of. I stared in the mirror every day, looking at my flat chest, wondering when-oh-when I'd grow breasts. Oh, I had those little beans that were developing in each nipple, but they were taking a damn long time to grow into something decent.

Like Margaret, my breasts just weren't growing fast enough, and I knew I had to take fate into my own hands.

I would have to fake it.

Trust me, there's a lot of pressure in faking it. But then, if you survived sixth grade, you probably already know that. Faking it is not as simple as sneaking one of your mother's bras. You have to choose the right one—an old one she won't miss, and you hope to hell that the cups are small enough to manipulate to meet your needs. This certainly won't work if your mother is stacked like Dolly Parton, but thankfully my mother wasn't.

When I knew I couldn't stand another day of going to school and seeing other girls with bras visible through their shirts, I finally got the guts to take action. I went through my mother's things, delicately lifting black lacy bras, sturdy white ones, and even some with no straps. It was all very complicated, but I finally decided on one of the sturdy white ones. It was the best one to hide what I'd be filling the cups with. I practiced putting it on and stuffing it with a little bit of Kleenex. I practiced over and over again until I was ready. Then, one Monday morning, I hid the bra in my school bag and took it to my junior high, where I immediately went to the bathroom. There, I locked myself in a stall, pulled my shirt off, put on my mother's bra, and, just as I'd practiced, I used some toilet paper to fill in the empty cups.

I had no clue what size bra my mother even wore, but now I know it was a C cup. C cup was way too big for me, of course, but I discovered that my diligent practice paid off. I filled the bra with a little toilet paper and it was fine.

I was nervous that first day. Would everyone know I was faking it? Would someone say, "Hey, Kayla—you grew breasts over the weekend!" But no one did, and my first day of faking it was a success.

Of course, at the end of the day, I had to repeat the bathroom ritual so that I'd go home sans bra. Because God forbid my mother saw me wearing it. Now that I'm a woman, I'm sure my mother would have done nothing but perhaps have a little chuckle over my ingenuity, but then, as an emotional preteen desperate for breasts, I figured if my mother caught me, it would be the end of the world.

I mastered faking it but felt entirely uncomfortable about it. Like Margaret in sixth grade, I just wanted the real thing already. I can tell you, *Are You There God? It's Me, Margaret* touched me like no other book did in junior high. I read about Margaret, suffering my very same predicament, and I didn't feel alone. I knew that although I desperately wanted to cross that line to womanhood so that I wouldn't be different, there were other girls going through exactly the same thing. Maybe other girls in my very class were faking it, too, just like I was. But even if the only other girl going through my drama was Margaret, that was enough for me.

I loved *Are You There God? It's Me, Margaret.* And I adored Judy Blume. Her stories touched me right in the center of my emotional core. I read her books knowing that someone understood the trials and tribulations of grade school kids, and even more important, someone *cared*.

And that's huge when you're young and often feel alone.

I quickly got used to living the lie of having breasts in sixth grade. The tricky time was gym period, but I mastered the art of covering up so that no one would wonder what exactly was in my bra. God forbid a nosy friend like Margaret's nosy friend, Nancy, would notice my bra was more Charmin than womanly flesh.

But here's the thing about living a lie: one day, that lie is going to come back to haunt you. That's something you don't think about when you're twelve and simply want breasts.

My day came when my class went to see the Philharmonic Orchestra.

Imagine this—you're in the first row of the audience, enjoying the orchestra's music, and the conductor suddenly asks, "Can I have a volunteer to conduct the orchestra?" Your hand flies up and you wave it around excitedly like all of your friends do. You want to be picked, because being picked means you get to be the Cool One, at least for a little while.

And cool you are, because the conductor chooses you.

So you happily head onstage and conduct the orchestra, paying only half attention to the cameras around you. You don't care about the cameras; you care about bragging rights.

A short while later, you learn that the cameras are from the local news station. Which means that you're going to be on the six o'clock news.

Normally, a reason for excitement. But now you start to panic. You can think of only one thing.

I'm wearing a bra!

Dear God, please don't let my mother watch the news. Please let her be doing something else. Like shopping for new shoes.

Of course, your mother is home when you return from school. And you can't stop worrying. You keep wondering if you'll really be on the news. And what you can do to distract your parents from watching.

But tonight is not your lucky night, because when six o'clock rolls around, your father turns the TV to the local news station. Of course, the newscaster announces that one of the upcoming stories will feature students who were at the Philharmonic Orchestra.

Your father turns to you and says, "Hey, isn't that your class that went to the orchestra today?"

You need a hole to crawl into. A very large and dark one . . .

You can hardly breathe during the news broadcast, because of course they show the clip of the student getting to conduct the orchestra. And of course you just know that your mother is going to squint her eyes at the TV screen and ask, "Kayla, are you wearing a *bra*?"

Your life is over. You just know it.

Dear God, please let me die a quick and painless death . . .

But your parents are far too excited at seeing you on TV to say anything else. Still, you're sure your mother is going to ask you about the bra. You promise yourself you'll never wear one of your mother's bras again.

Neither your mother nor father says anything. And that's when it finally dawns on you that for most of the news clip, the camera caught you from behind.

Like the moment when Margaret first starts to get her period, this is proof that there is a God after all.

Still, the drama of almost getting caught faking it is enough to make you completely uncomfortable going to school the next day with your mother's confiscated bra. Yet you don't want to be braless. What if Nosy Nancy notices?

So you get the courage to ask: *Mom, pretty please—can I get a training bra?*

Thank God, your mother takes you shopping the next day. Finally, you have a bra you can proudly call your own.

Even if you don't quite have the breasts yet.

I don't remember how long after that incident I actually grew decent-size breasts. But I do remember that nearly-being-discovered-as-a-fraud-by-my-mother was my most traumatic "breast" incident before I became a teenager. Like every girl comes to realize, you'll grow breasts sooner or later, and I grew respectable B's.

B's were fine through high school and even into college, but then I started to notice something. The girls who'd felt awkward because they were too big in grade school and high school were loving their larger breasts now.

And so were the guys.

And not in that immature grade school way but in a way that a woman could now appreciate.

Personally, I was involved with my childhood sweetheart, so it's not like I needed bigger breasts to get me a guy. But still, whenever I went to a bar or a club, I saw how guys checked out the women with C and D cups.

They say blondes have more fun? Well, girls with big breasts have *the most* fun.

Suddenly, I wanted a larger cup size. I had no clue I was about to go through Breast Drama Round Two, which would last a lot longer than Round One had.

So what's a girl in her twenties to do when she wants to be a C but she's only a B?

She invests in a push-up bra.

Because in your twenties, it's all about cleavage. The more cleavage you have, the more of a woman you are. And practically everything a girl in her twenties wants to wear is form-fitting with a plunging neckline.

So there I was in my early twenties, once again looking in the mirror, staring at my breasts that wouldn't grow.

B's were fine through school, but now I was a woman. I needed C's.

I discovered Victoria's Secret and a whole host of other lingerie shops. I figured out how to master the push-up bra so that I'd looked like I'd been naturally blessed with an enticing C cup.

But it still wasn't quite the same as having the real thing. Not that I could do anything about it. And if God wasn't going to give them to me naturally, I'd have to do without because I certainly wasn't buying any.

Then I got married to my childhood sweetheart, and a miraculous thing started to happen.

I started to grow bigger breasts.

Right along with bigger hips.

I was cooking regular meals, even making dessert. The pounds started to come on, and suddenly I had to graduate to a bigger bra.

Now this is how you know that breast size is of vital importance to women (well, admittedly, at least to me). Because even though I wanted to lose weight off my hips, I didn't want to work out *too* much—because I didn't want to go back down to a B.

My C breasts looked magnificent. Put them in a push-up bra and it was *Kaboom, baby!* Guys noticed me more. Yes, I was married, but I still felt sexy. Who cared if I had some love handles? I had great breasts!

Maybe my husband cared. He never said that the extra pounds were too much, but alas our marriage fell apart.

But I still had great breasts, thank you very much.

Which looked fabulous in a bikini on South Beach, where I went to drown my sorrows after that unexpected trip to Splitsville. In fact, an older woman stopped me one day when I was wearing this stunning silver bikini and told me I should be on the cover of *Ocean Drive* magazine.

I got lots of attention from guys, and one even asked if my breasts were real. For a now thirty-year-old going through a divorce, this was the ultimate compliment.

Finally, I'd arrived. I had great breasts, and certainly I'd never have to worry about them again.

Wrong!

Enter Breast Drama Round Three.

While in Miami, I met someone else, fell in love, and had a baby a couple of years later. Throughout the pregnancy, my breasts looked magnificent. And when I gave birth, I actually dropped fifteen pounds but *still had the breasts*. This was the Holy Grail of body image—slim hips and big boobs.

And then I started to nurse. And nurse.

So here I am, yet again staring in the mirror, looking at my naked breasts.

I'm not so happy now.

When I'd gained some weight and a cup size, my mother accurately said, "I bet you don't want to lose the weight because you finally have bigger breasts." Wow, I'm not sure I'd even admitted that to myself when my mother said that to me, and I could only give her a sheepish smile. I didn't even know she realized that I wanted bigger breasts (but she obviously saw me wearing all those push-up bras and put two and two together). Now, nursing and in full-on "mother mode" in baggy sweats and a T-shirt without a bra, my mother said, "Your nipples used to be so much higher."

And just like that, I realized that I had boob drama again.

How had this happened? Don't we go through enough distress over our breasts as adolescents, then as teens, and as women in our twenties? Do we really have to go through it *again*?

I had attained perfection, only to lose it. Sure, my breasts were still large and looked great in a bra. In fact, now they were closer to D's than C's.

And yet I was miserable.

I couldn't stop looking in the mirror, lifting my breasts to see where the nipples *should* be.

I wasn't prepared for this—the reality that my breasts would *start to sag.*

Now, I love my little girl to death and wouldn't trade her for anything, but I can't help thinking about the injustice of having to lose perfect breasts because you didn't opt to bottle-feed.

Dear God, when will all this breast drama end?

Or will it?

It seems the whole world is obsessed with breast size. Women on Dr. Phil complaining that they have sagging skin instead of breasts after losing weight or that their babies sucked them right back down to prepubescent boobs. You only have to watch one episode of your favorite TV show to see that breasts are so important to women. Many have opted for faking it. And not just with push-up bras but with permanent synthetic materials. Alas, it seems that breasts are now more important than they ever were.

And mine—well, it seems my glory days are behind me.

Okay, so they're not the worst ones out there. They're still full. They still look great in a bra. But thanks to my mother, I'm aware that they don't look as hot naked as they used to.

Now in my mid-thirties, it's clear to me that the more things change, the more they stay the same. No matter how old we get, how accomplished, women will always have issues with their breasts.

I can imagine Margaret now, in her mid-thirties, still talking to God.

Are you there God? It's me, Margaret.

Please tell me this breast thing is a joke. A cruel prank, God. Tell me I'm going to wake up and see that this is all a nightmare.

I mean really, God. I finally got great breasts at fourteen, and I looked fabulous in college. My breasts got me lots of boyfriends— well, at least lots of offers. I was hot. And I felt great. I snagged the man of my dreams, got married, and then settled down to have a family.

I give of myself every day, God. I try to be the best mother I can be. I cook and clean and take care of my husband. I even have a fabulous career. I can't deny I'm living the American Dream.

So why is it that now, when everything is right in my world, I have another body image crisis to deal with at the age of thirty-four?

I nursed two babies back-to-back, and I've learned what nursing does to a woman's breasts. I did what was best for my babies— I didn't want to deprive them of the benefit of mother's milk. But now I no longer have the beautiful C-cup breasts I used to have. My breasts, God, are sagging.

Dear God, I have droopy breasts.

My parents still don't know I talk to you, and neither does my husband. But God, I'm wondering if you could please restore my breasts for me. They don't have to be C's again. I'd be happy with a B cup. I just don't want them to sag.

And while I'm on a roll here, God—what about this pouch around my belly? Is it possible to lose that pregnancy pouch with excessive working out? I don't think so, because I've been trying. You know how hard.

I've been good, God. And I swear I'll stop eating chocolate. Maybe I'll even enroll my kids in Sunday school. Whatever it takes, God. I'm only thirty-four. If my breasts are sagging now, I don't want to imagine what they'll be like when I'm fifty-four.

Or seventy-four.

And when Margaret ends her prayer, she is haunted by the vision of what her breasts could look like when she's seventy-four.

Sagging so far south, her nipples can touch her knees.

Her husband will be dating a thirty-year-old with implants.

Margaret is horrified by the thought.

So she heads downstairs to the kitchen and grabs the yellow pages. She looks up cosmetic surgeons. Maybe it's time to consider a tummy tuck and a breast lift.

Because Margaret knows that God helps those who help themselves.

Or maybe Margaret ultimately decides against cosmetic surgery. She tells herself, *Screw it.* She's going to love herself for who she is, not what she looks like naked in the mirror.

She's going to embrace all that it means to be a woman.

Even the sagging breasts.

———

Kayla has always been creative and can't remember a time when she wasn't scribbling a story somewhere or sketching a picture. After discovering that people actually earned money writing stories, at the proud bra-wearing age of thirteen she submitted her first fully illustrated children's book to Scholastic Publications and received a letter saying that they were "seriously considering" publishing her story. While she has worked at various jobs, Kayla is most happy when writing, which is why in four short years she has had thirteen original releases hit the shelves. Visit Kayla at www.kaylaperrin.com.

SUPERFUDGED

| *Cara Lockwood* |

My brother Matt (seven years younger in actual years, light-years younger in emotional years) was like most baby brothers: he spent his entire childhood trying to get me in trouble. I was his only sibling, and as he calls me now, "more infallible than the pope," when it came to my parents. I could do no wrong, and worse, didn't even try to do wrong and get away with it.

My brother, in fact, holds a grudge against me to do this day for not properly breaking in my parents with rebellion, sneaking out late, and, as my brother was prone to do, having parties where (drunk) high school varsity football players knocked down my dad's front door.

In fact, to this date, my very worst rebellion occurred at age ten when I "ran away." Technically, I wasn't the one doing the running. My bad-influence friend, Christi, had decided she was fed up with her parents and wanted to run away. I was only tagging along to convince her to go back home.

Christi got us both caught before I could convince her to go home, because she made the mistake of trying to lug an extra-large pink Samsonite suitcase out the front door of her parents' house. She made it no farther than a block. Back then, suitcases didn't have wheels. Her arms gave out along with her will to rebel.

"You didn't break in the parents for me, you know," Matt tells me even now. "I mean, you didn't do *anything*."

He says this as if not having a kegger party when I was a sophomore is a character failing.

"You were b-o-r-i-n-g. Boring." Matt likes to spell things out for effect and to prove he can.

In my defense, being the "good kid" wasn't entirely my fault. Not exactly.

I had the typical Eldest Child Syndrome. The very first thing Mom told me when she let me hold my baby brother was "Remember, you're the oldest now, and that means you've got a lot of new responsibilities."

At age seven, I didn't know what this meant exactly. My only responsibilities up until that time had been making sure I kept my Barbies out of the path of my dad, who would curse if he stepped on one. I soon found out that being the oldest meant I had to do more work. Namely, keep my brother out of trouble. This was a full-time job.

Matt, you see, had a nose for trouble. He, like Fudge—the infamous little brother of the Fudge books—was a trouble magnet. I like to imagine that if Peter Hatcher's younger brother made it to his teen years, he'd be just like Matt (police visit at age thirteen for joyriding in a girl's car, kegger party at age fifteen, brawl outside homecoming football game at age seventeen).

It was my responsibility to keep him from eating the things he found on the floor. He had a taste for dead crickets. He also liked to play with electrical sockets, sharp edges, and glass. I'm sure if there were cyanide capsules in the house, he would crawl right to them.

And then my brother started to walk, and my life was never the same again.

Like Fudge, Matt was a whirling dervish of trouble. Did he get into my stuff and destroy my toys? Check. Did he fall down and hurt himself, and did I get in trouble for it? Check. Did he blame me for things he ate/broke/destroyed? Double check.

And when I complained, what did my mother say? "Cara, you've got responsibilities now. You're the oldest, and you're supposed to look after your younger brother."

When pressed, Mom would gently remind me that I asked for a little brother.

It's true that I was one of those kids who bugged her parents all the time for a little brother or sister. That's because I had no idea what Play Doh could do to my hair.

I lived in a neighborhood of teenagers and retirees. I was lonely and wanted a playmate. You see, I had delusions of the ideal little sibling. He or she would naturally know that I knew best instinctively. He or she would always want to play the games I wanted to play, how I wanted to play them, because I'd be the wise, all-knowing older sister. In short, my younger brother or sister would be my indentured servant, waiting upon my every need, idolizing and worshipping me.

I had a vision of a little brother like Tattoo on *Fantasy Island*. He would wear a white tuxedo and do my bidding, and the only words he'd be allowed to speak would be, "The plane, boss! The plane!"

I asked for Tattoo. What I got was the Tasmanian Devil.

Worse, I was no longer the best, cutest, or most loved child of my parents. This is something Peter knew all too well. In the Fudge books, Peter's little brother is the "cute" one. Fudge is even picked to be in a television commercial.

Like Peter, I couldn't understand why everyone suddenly thought my little brother was so adorable and I wasn't. I was seven, but I felt like I should be doing a scene in *Sunset Boulevard*. Overnight, I wasn't cute anymore. Or adorable. I was over the hill.

Dad bought a brand-new video camera (the first we'd ever had) and set it up on a tripod in front of Matt's baby swing. I might as well have been Norma Desmond asking for her close-up, because Dad had no interest in filming me. All he wanted to do was focus the camera lens on Matt.

This, I could not understand. From my perspective, Matt was a talentless hack. The only thing he could manage at age six months was drooling. And pooping. Neither of which, I thought, was very film-worthy.

I, however, had talent. I could smile and pose for the camera. I could do cartwheels. I could sing *and* dance. I knew all the lyrics to "Rainbow Connection." But was Dad interested? No.

I was a washed-up studio actress. I was a has-been.

I knew then that things had changed, and not for the better.

And they would only get worse.

From the time my brother could crawl, his mission in life was to get me in trouble. Like Peter, I got blamed for things my little brother did, or didn't do. Mom had a soft spot for Matt, just like Peter's mom did for Fudge, and I was now the "big sister with responsibilities" and was always supposed to keep an eye out for my brother.

Unfortunately, Matt was more interested in keeping an eye on me than I was on him. Matt's favorite game was called "Get Cara in Trouble." He did this in a number of ways. Like Fudge, he'd get into snacks like cookies or animal crackers, devour them all, and then if caught, he'd blame me. He'd blame me when he threw one of his toys across the room or if one of his toys broke. But he didn't stop there.

He thought up elaborate schemes to get me on the wrong side of Mom, including one called the Tonka Truck Ploy.

His con was evil but simple.

He'd sneak up behind me while I lay on the carpet watching cartoons, then clunk me on the head with his giant metal Tonka dump truck. Naturally, in fair retaliation, I'd swipe at him, landing a blow (a lot less painful than a heavy metal truck, I might add) on the leg or arm.

Matt, a master flopper even then, would turn on the waterworks and start screaming as if I'd just removed one of his toes with a pair of pliers. He'd run to Mom, claim I'd beaten him within an inch of his life, and instantly Mom would start in on her "Cara, you've got responsibilities" speech.

This would have probably eventually led to a concussion, except that Mom caught him once whacking me on the head with his favorite Tonka, and that ended that charade. But my brother soon found new ways to torment me.

Like all younger siblings, he wanted to get into my stuff. I don't know if Mom watched him during the day or if she just patted him on the head and let him waddle into my room unattended, but every day when I got home, I found my room in shambles. My Barbies lay strewn across the carpet, decapitated and dismembered. My diary and coloring books would have pages ripped out or colored in. And my sticker collection? Forget it. The precious unicorn puffy stickers I'd been delicately saving would be plastered all over my wall, or worse, the toilet.

The toilet, in fact, was my brother's favorite toy. With his never-ending toilet fixation, I was convinced he'd grow up to be a plumber. He flushed entire rolls of toilet paper (including the roll bar). He flushed potpourri, Matchbox cars, my mom's mascara, the dog's collar, and an entire box of Legos. He kept flushing until he plugged up the toilet and it overflowed, and then he'd clap his hands, laugh manically, and run away, as if it was all part of his plan for world domination.

Ironically, while he loved flushing inanimate objects down the toilet, he took forever to potty train. (He wanted to use the toilet for every use, except for the one it was intended.)

I tried putting up "Do Not Enter" signs, along with "This means you, MATT!!!!" warnings, but they were useless, in part because Matt couldn't yet read.

Fudge also loved invading Peter's room. In *Tales of a Fourth Grade Nothing*, when Fudge sneaks into Peter's room and destroys his class project poster, Peter furiously cries to his mother, "You don't love me!"

I knew exactly how he felt. In fact, when he asked his mom for a lock on his door, she replied diplomatically, "We're a family, Peter. And families don't have locks on their doors."

Well, family or no, I wanted a lock on my door. In fact, Peter asking for one gave me an idea. I'd ask for one, too. Only I wouldn't give up as easily as Peter.

Like Peter's mom, my mom initially vetoed the idea of a lock. That's when I decided to appeal her decision to a higher power: Santa Claus.

That Christmas, the only thing on my list was a lock on my door.

At age ten, I had no idea how much locks cost. For all I knew, they were really expensive. But I wanted one. I wanted one worse than a bike or Barbie's Pink Corvette.

Mom kept asking me, "You're sure you don't want something else? A Cabbage Patch doll? Barbie's Swimming Pool?"

"No," I said resolutely. "All I want is a lock."

The way I figured it, without a lock, new toys would just be ruined in a matter of days. Matt would rip them apart and then flush the pieces down the toilet.

My mom finally took pity on me. She relented after Matt wrecked my Barbie dreamhouse. He stomped on it like a mini-Godzilla, then flushed pieces of the cardboard elevator along with Barbie's head down the toilet.

That Christmas, I got the lock I wanted. And a new Barbie.

Of course, like all things I asked for, the lock turned out to be a mixed blessing. My brother's next trick was locking me out of my own room. He did this by lying in wait outside my room when I left, then running into it and locking it from the inside.

I learned quickly how to pick my own room lock with a screwdriver, and so did my brother.

He and I were in an arms race, only instead of nuclear weapons at stake, it was my privacy. I wanted it, and so did he.

And every time I went to Mom, she said, "Work it out. This is your responsibility."

We didn't work it out. We were too busy fighting our own version of the Cold War. We couldn't openly declare war in front of our parents, but we both knew what was on the line. Total and complete household domination.

He ran over my favorite "My Little Pony" with his tricycle. I changed the channel during important parts of his favorite cartoon, "Thundercats." He flushed my Bonnie Bell collection down the toilet. I took all the batteries out of all his toys and hid them. He ran—naked—through the house, embarrassing me in front of a cute boy visiting his grandparents next door. I put him in a headlock and tickled him until he cried uncle. He stole my diary and ripped out all the pages, then told everyone my secret "crush." I sent him into a bush to get a Frisbee where I knew a couple of wasps lay in wait.

Our fights were so numerous and so bad that my grandmother told us we couldn't come to visit anymore. We spent two weeks with her one summer, and by that time, she'd had enough. This is the woman who is a born-again Christian, and who is, by all accounts, the sweetest woman on earth. And she uninvited us.

Sure, I could've been more patient. More inclusive. More caring of my Fudge. But come on. He played in the toilet and ran around without pants on. It's not exactly the sort of show you want your friends to see.

And worse, like Fudge, Matt got everything he ever asked for. He was spoiled—through and through.

Mom told me I couldn't have bunk beds in my room because I was only one person. Matt got a bunk bed. Mom told me I couldn't have small pets in my room. Matt got two guinea pigs, two lizards, and a hermit crab. Mom told me I couldn't have a television in my room. Matt got a TV with cable and Nintendo. And the list goes on. And on. And on.

But every so often, you're reminded that none of that really matters.

One afternoon, when Matt was four and I was eleven, everything changed.

Mom was getting ready for a party. She was having friends over, so she shooed us both out of the house so that she could clean. Cleaning was impossible if Matt was in the vicinity, with his sticky chocolate-covered hands and crayons, and besides, he'd probably just flush the sponges down the toilet.

Matt took his new motorized mini-three-wheeler (a plastic thing you could pedal or press a button to make it go—another injustice. I had only a Big Wheel and a bicycle—all manually powered. My brother, ever spoiled, had the option to buzz around on an electric-powered three-wheeler) and started taking laps around the kidney-shaped pool in our backyard. Mom admonished me just minutes before that I was to watch him and "make sure he didn't get dirty." This was a little like asking me to negotiate a peace treaty between Palestine and Israel, but I decided I'd do my best. My brother could find dirt from the inside of a hermetically sealed bubble, so it was an uphill battle trying to keep him clean for more than thirty seconds at a time.

It was spring but too cold to swim, even though the cover was off the pool. I saw him take a sharp turn, a little too close to the water's edge. And then, plop. He went in.

Now, my brother had taken his first swimming lessons the previous summer. He didn't learn much, though, in part because he had a habit of biting his instructor rather than letting himself be placed calmly in the water. While my brother loved toilet water, he didn't like pool water so much.

My mom was shocked that he was capable of such viciousness, but I'd been on the sharp end of those baby teeth a million times. I could've told her that Matt fought dirty. After the biting incident, he didn't get a lot of one-on-one time with the swimming instructor.

So I knew Matt wasn't a strong swimmer.

I ran over to him. The battery-operated tricycle had sunk to the bottom of the pool like a stone, tires still spinning in the water. Matt, bug-eyed and scared, was dog paddling in the middle of the pool. His mouth and nose bobbed just below the water, and everything about his face screamed panic.

Meanwhile, I was thinking *Mom is going to kill us.* Matt was wearing his "good" clothes, which were now soaked, and I was wearing a dress Mom bought especially for the party.

I leaned over and reached for Matt, holding my hand out, trying to grab him, but he was too far out. His head bobbed down under the water. He was sinking fast.

I glanced back at the house, thinking I should run to get Mom. But then I looked back at Matt and realized there was no time. His head bobbed up and then under again, and all I could think of was Mom's admonition to me: "You're responsible for your brother. Keep an eye on him."

So I did the only thing I could do.

I jumped in.

I grabbed Matt, pulled him to the side of the pool, and shoved him out. He was wailing at his dogs-and-the-entire-neighborhood-can-hear setting.

I took him by the hand and led him into the house, where Mom found us, dripping wet.

"What on earth have you done now? I told you two not to fight today," she shouted, angry that I'd ruined my new dress and that we were both soaked from head to toe, dripping pool water all over her newly polished floor.

"He fell into the pool," I told her, pointing outside. Mom glanced at Matt and his panicked face, and then she realized what happened.

Immediately, she consoled Matt, whipping him up in her arms, soaked and all.

"My poor baby!" she wailed. "Are you okay? You must be scared to death."

Naturally, Matt got all the attention, but that was okay. For once, I didn't mind. I was relieved.

Because the thing I realized that day was that I do love my brother. And I was glad to be there to look after him, because that's what an older sister is for.

Reading the Fudge books helped me understand that no matter how much of a pain they are, little brothers are worth having. Judy Blume helped me see that you can love someone, even if he or she can be annoying, because that's what family is all about. After coming close to losing him that day, I realized that no matter what Matt did, I'd never trade him for any other brother or sister in the world. Because he was *my* little brother. And although I saved Matt that day, maybe one day he'd be there when I needed him, and he'd save me back. Because that's what family does.

And I'm pretty sure Matt understood this, too. As a show of respect and gratitude for pulling him from the pool, Matt waited a solid hour before flushing one of my Strawberry Shortcake dolls down the toilet.

Cara Lockwood is the author of I Do (But I Don't), *which was made into a movie for Lifetime Television, as well as* I Did (But I Wouldn't Now), Dixieland Sushi, *and* Pink Slip Party. *She is currently at work on a book series for teens, which are being published by MTV Books. Cara lives in Chicago, nearly twelve hundred miles away from her younger brother. Bickering is kept strictly to Thanksgiving and Christmas.*

ARE YOU THERE, MARGARET?

| *Alison Pace* |

Growing up, I enjoyed the lucky safety of knowing I was surrounded by good people, good friends. Though never the most popular, and certainly never the best at academics or sports (definitely not sports), I can remember in my childhood the feeling of being liked and in the company of friends. There were seats saved at lunch tables, there were Ding Dongs shared. I often felt, for the most part I'd say, included and happy. The thing is, though, I didn't always feel the same. Which is where Margaret came in.

Margaret, of *Are You There God? It's Me, Margaret* fame, this character created on paper with such vividness and authenticity by Judy Blume, was the only person I knew, other than myself, who was almost in seventh grade and didn't yet need a bra. And, more than that, she was the only friend I had in the world who, like me, was half Jewish and half Christian. And, yes, I know it's not very often that bras and God are mentioned in corresponding sentences, but for Margaret, and for me, the two seemed to hold a very large significance.

Are You There God? It's Me, Margaret was one of the first books I ever loved, one of the first books that made me feel really, truly understood. And so it was Margaret who became one of my favorite and most understanding friends. Margaret knew what it felt like to be half one religion and half another, knew what it felt like to have to explain that it didn't *really* mean you were *technically* this or *technically* that, or worse than that, nothing. Margaret knew what it was like to have people ask you if you didn't believe in God, and also knew what it felt like to dread bras and bathing suits and anything even remotely up-the-shirt related.

Much in the manner of the brokenhearted, who are certain that every sad song about someone who's done somebody wrong has been written expressly for them (actually, I do that, too), when I first read *Are You There God? It's Me, Margaret,* right before seventh grade, I was pretty sure that every understanding and in-tune word had been written just for me. It's a rarity still for me to feel like a book "gets it," gets *me,* the way I felt at twelve, that *Margaret* got it.

Like Margaret, I, too, had a Philip Leroy, a crush to whom I remained somewhat unbeknownst. His name was Andy Cammaker, and he was good at sports and wore a green rope fisherman's bracelet—the kind that shrank to your wrist—for all of sixth grade, long after most other people's mothers would have made them take it off. I can still remember the looks of Andy Cammaker, who had beautiful black curly hair, who had milky white skin and freckles, and who was so far out of reach to me.

"Have a good summer, Pace," he'd said to me on the last day of sixth grade as he walked toward his mom's car. "You too, Cammaker," I'd said, wondering even as I said it, *did I sound cool?* And if I had managed, somehow, someway, to sound cool while speaking to him, did I sound cool *enough*? As I replayed our final words of the year in my mind, all over the entire summer, the only thing that I was sure of was that I wasn't cool. I wasn't quite sure I knew anyone would understand how hard it was to feel cool around certain people, certain boys, and how hard at other times it was to feel cool in general. And then, at the end of that summer, when I read *Are You There God? It's Me, Margaret* and at last met Margaret, I was sure that if I'd been invited to New Jersey to a sleepover at her house along with her slightly annoying (and bossy and untruthful) friend, Nancy Wheeler, and sat down and explained it to her, that she would have understood.

And the reason she would have understood? Because Margaret Simon, much more than anyone I'd come across, knew the deep, inextricable connection between "boobs, having them," and "cool." A thing I'd always felt was very much related to the lack of romantic attentions from Andy Cammaker was the fact that I, much like Margaret, was a bit lacking of bust. Unlike Margaret, though, I did not sit with my best friend practicing the "I Must, I Must, I Must Increase My Bust" exercises because my best friend was Jenny Layton, and Jenny was already a proud proprietor of a very nice-size chest. I did my chest-increasing exercises on my own, and my negotiations for the speedy and imminent arrival of breasts were admittedly more with the breasts themselves than they were, as in Margaret's case, with God. Though to be fair, my chest, in its absence, did attain such mythic proportions in my young mind that it became quite godlike in importance.

On that last day of sixth grade, I explained to my mother, "I'm giving my boobs until the end of the summer to grow." I believe she nodded, if not in comprehension, then at least in agreement. I wanted them, reasonably so, for the first day of seventh grade. I wanted them for the first-day-of-school pictures we had taken every year. I wanted them, most of all, for the next time I saw Andy Cammaker. Andy Cammaker would ask me, and my new boobs, to go out (which really just meant we would talk on the phone). And, of course, we'd all three say yes. He'd be smitten, he would need only in life to be with me. He wouldn't think I was skinny; he wouldn't call me a Carpenters Dream. If Mrs. Cammaker ever took a group of us again to Great Adventure like she had in fifth grade, he wouldn't say that since I was the smallest, I had to sit in the way-back of the station wagon. And he definitely wouldn't turn around constantly throughout the entire three-hour car ride to New Jersey to remind me that I couldn't talk because I was in the way-back where the dogs go. He'd never decide that for the duration of the trip I was a Basset Hound. "You are a Bass-et Hound," he wouldn't say, all elongated, *Bass* and *Et* like two separate words, *Hound* all stretched out, again and again the whole way there and the whole way back. "Bass-et Hooouuuund."

And when the first day of seventh grade arrived, devastatingly too soon with *nothing at all* to fill out my lime green T-shirt with the bright blue E-S-P written on the front and the R-I-T written on the back, leaving me to wish I'd worn the red Benetton sweater instead, because the geometric illusion might have tricked the eye and the material would have added so much more bulk, I felt I had no other choice but to renegotiate. I told the boobs they had until Christmas vacation. But that was it. And I was sure then that Margaret would have understood. I was sure she would have known that almost as bad as not needing a bra was waiting to need one.

But cleavage aside (if it's ever really possible in this world to put cleavage completely aside), what it was, what made me read the book two times in a row and refer to it numerous times throughout my middle school years, was that Margaret, like me, was half Jewish and half Christian. Margaret's circumstances were the reverse of mine: her dad was Jewish and her mom was Christian; it was her Christian grandparents who were not accepting. For me, my mom was Jewish and my dad was Christian (technically both Episcopalian and Catholic, though he will tell you that religion isn't a heritage, something my Jewish-But-Not-Practicing mother might be pretty quick to refute). It was my nana who was disapproving, who invited me over on Passover to search for money and a matzo cracker and to tell me that my father was from the wrong side of the tracks.

Both Margaret's parents and my parents made the same decision: to raise us without religion. "Spiritual but not religious" is the way that people might describe it today, but back then, in the early eighties, growing up on Long Island, a place where it seemed so many things were separated by religion, it became not so much a designation as a recipe for a walking identity crisis. Margaret, who also felt this identity crisis quite deeply, dealt with it rather constructively by trying to learn about as many different religions as she could. I had my own variation on the theme. I tried to *be* as many different religions as I could. I slyly tried to get Nana to sign me up for Bat Mitzvah training, just as I implored Grammy to take me with her to church, even though by that point she was no longer her religion, Episcopal, or even her late husband's religion, Catholic, but a later life convert to Ethical Culture.

I didn't get very far, due mostly to a parental reminder to the grandparents that I was being raised without religion. And so I

moved on to what I saw as being religious by omission. On Rosh
Hashanah and Yom Kippur, I was very Christian, sitting in the
lunchroom lamenting with all the other Catholics and Protestants
the fact that we had to be in school while all our Jewish friends
stayed home. There I was again, at school on Good Friday, at one
with all my Jewish friends. I had, of course, suggested to my parents that in order to more fully understand my heritage, I should
stay home on all religious holidays. They had not, as I believed was
so very often the case, seen my point. So, to school, I went. Em-
braced, I very much wanted to believe, by all religions; the one-girl
religious melting pot I thought maybe I could be.

Everyone was either Jewish or Catholic or some sort of Protes-
tant. And I wanted so much to be able to say something simple like,
"I'm Jewish," "I'm Catholic," "I'm Episcopalian," rather than the
complicated and ever-lengthy, "My mom is Jewish and my dad is
Catholic and Episcopalian, and my parents decided to raise me
without religion," or the somewhat self-esteem-challenging, "No,
I'm nothing." And because I didn't have a friend to my name who
wasn't fully Jewish or fully Catholic or fully something else, back
then I really did take a lot of comfort in the fact that there was
Margaret.

And I think then in high school I may have forgotten a bit about
her. Though far from the celebrated arrival I had for so long been
optimistically anticipating, I had secured boobs. I'd been long
enough in my role of half-this and half-that to be a bit more comfortable in my skin so as to not be bothered so much when people
would inquire, "What are you?" Or maybe it was just that I went to
a pretty small school, and by high school, people just knew me and
had already asked.

But after high school I remembered Margaret again. By the time I got to college, I'd been half Jewish for a while, for my entire life; I'd gotten used to it. But when I arrived at American University in Washington, D.C., a place where it seemed the entire student population was Jewish, I wasn't half Jewish anymore. Suddenly, I was *not* Jewish. At American, I was called for the first time—other than by Nana—a shiksa. I was shunned. *By my people.*

Later, once people discovered that I was half Jewish and that the Jewish half was actually the mother half, I was consoled that since it was my *mother* who was Jewish and not my father, technically, I was okay. On behalf of my father, I found this insulting. And then, with the whole "technically, you're Jewish" hurdle successfully leapt over once again, Adam Silverstein, proud member of the Zeta Beta Tau fraternity, became my first college boyfriend.

Adam, a junior, was short in stature and had fair skin and longish, wavyish hair. He majored in political science, smoked cigarettes and pot, and drove a black Mazda RX-7. He kept his seat reclined more so than what would generally be considered normal for driving; in order to reach the steering wheel, his arm, always just the left one, had to be fully extended. I always thought he looked like a racecar driver. A really laid-back, stoned racecar driver who wore basketball sneakers and a baseball hat on backward. I've always had a bit of a thing for racecar drivers.

Adam was very popular with American University women and supposedly had dated a senior when he was only a freshman. Supposedly, people said, he'd driven her crazy. But the thing was, the driven-crazy girl in question, she was in this sorority in which supposedly all the women were crazy, so really who's to say if it was Adam who did her in or not? And also, I like to think that if you're the type of person who's going to let someone drive you crazy, you, more often than not, already have a set of directions waiting in your glove compartment.

Adam and I started dating exclusively. Previously, I'd actually always thought dating implied exclusivity. Among the things I learned at American University: it doesn't. And only a few months later, Adam attained the title of the first man to ever break my heart, by breaking up with me the night before my sorority semi-formal. And the reason he gave me for said unceremonious end? I wasn't Jewish, and he just didn't see the sense in dating me. He'd promised his parents, he'd told me, a freshman in college, he would only date someone Jewish.

I didn't explain to him that *technically* I was Jewish. I remember having a sense of foreboding right then that felt very much the way it felt when Jessica Kleinman sat me at the dorky table at her Bat Mitzvah. Even though being Jewish and Catholic and Episcopalian (oh, my) could indeed mean I could date Jews and Catholics and any variety of WASPs without my parents so much as blinking an intruding eye, I sensed that perhaps it might not bode well for me. I can remember time traveling right then, in my mind, during that breakup. For a moment, I was in my pink 1980s bedroom with the Laura Ashley bedspread, and I was wondering how Margaret might have dealt with this same issue had she faced it at whatever college she went to. Make that at Penn, because now that I think of it, I'm quite sure that Margaret went to Penn.

Sure, there have been other issues in my life, and I imagine there will be more. For starters: I'm older than I'd like to be and still single. My friends tell me I have to go on Match.com. Deadlines freak me out, which isn't the best thing, considering I'm at

work in a pretty deadline-heavy field. My personality could be categorized with some degree of ease under the general umbrella of
neurotic. And I think there might be some other things, too.
Though for the sake of brevity and privacy, I'll resist the temptation
to digress.

But I can say with all certainty that having Margaret there for
the first things I ever saw as issues in my life made me feel at once
understood and not alone. Something I'd later understand as a uni-
versal thing that books can do and would make me want to read
them all, and eventually once I got my nerve up, write them, too.
The friendship I had with Margaret showed me that it was okay,
that it was perfectly fine, to be a late bloomer, to feel different, and
to have no religion but still believe in God. It told me that my feelings made sense and it told me that it was okay. It told me that
other people, even people with churches and temples and big
boobs to call their own, felt that way, too.

I wish that there had been an entire series of *Margaret*, that I'd
been able to see Margaret navigate her way through high school,
college, and early career choices; through the weddings and first
children of her friends, asking God if maybe he could hurry up with
her soul mate, since he had repeatedly ignored her requests for
anything other than an A cup. I'm quite sure I would have felt
some solace in seeing Margaret up on the fifth floor of Blooming-
dales, debating the merits of the Wonderbra. Or perhaps logging
onto Match.com and checking off "spiritual but not religious"
under religion and taking some solace of her own in the fact that so
many other Internet daters have checked off that unaffiliated box,
too. I think Margaret would have really liked that. And as much on
her behalf as on my own, I do, too.

———

Alison Pace's *writing career began in third grade with a short story about how God might have created the world with a bathtub faucet and a rubber band. She survived a late-blooming adolescence to become the author of the novels* If Andy Warhol Had a Girlfriend *and* Pug Hill *and a contributing editor at* The Bark *magazine. Her third novel,* Through Thick and Thin, *was published in 2007. She lives in New York City.*